ROUTLEDGE LIBRARY EDITIONS: MANAGEMENT

Volume 53

THRUSTERS AND SLEEPERS

THRUSTERS AND SLEEPERS

A Study of Attitudes in Industrial Management

A PEP REPORT

Routledge
Taylor & Francis Group

LONDON AND NEW YORK

First published in 1965 by George Allen & Unwin Ltd

This edition first published in 2018
by Routledge
4 Park Square, Milton Park, Abingdon, Oxon OX14 4RN

and by Routledge
605 Third Avenue, New York, NY 10017

Routledge is an imprint of the Taylor & Francis Group, an informa business

British Library Cataloguing in Publication Data
A catalogue record for this book is available from the British Library

ISBN: 978-1-138-55938-7 (Set)
ISBN: 978-1-351-05538-3 (Set) (ebk)
ISBN: 978-1-138-48024-7 (Volume 53) (hbk)
ISBN: 978-1-138-48029-2 (Volume 53) (pbk)
ISBN: 978-1-351-06330-2 (Volume 53) (ebk)

Publisher's Note
The publisher has gone to great lengths to ensure the quality of this reprint but points out that some imperfections in the original copies may be apparent.

Disclaimer
The publisher has made every effort to trace copyright holders and would welcome correspondence from those they have been unable to trace.

THRUSTERS AND SLEEPERS

A STUDY OF ATTITUDES
IN INDUSTRIAL MANAGEMENT

A PEP REPORT

London

POLITICAL AND ECONOMIC PLANNING
12 UPPER BELGRAVE STREET

GEORGE ALLEN AND UNWIN LTD
RUSKIN HOUSE   MUSEUM STREET

PRINTED IN GREAT BRITAIN
in 10 on 11 point Times Roman type
BY UNWIN BROTHERS LIMITED
WOKING AND LONDON

PREFACE

This report is the result of a two-year research project made possible by a generous grant from the Nuffield Foundation. It has been written by Anthony Gater, David Insull, Harold Lind and Peter Seglow, four members of the research staff of PEP. Professor J. R. Parkinson, Professor of Applied Economics at Queen's University, Belfast, has acted as consultant to the study and the work has been under the guidance of a Steering Group.

The report was completed in June 1964 and, while it was possible to make certain final alterations in November before going to press, some of the chapters, particularly in Part Three, must be read in the light of any subsequent changes of economic policy.

In acknowledging the help which it has received during the past two years PEP wishes to thank particularly the forty-seven firms who co-operated in the study and allowed their senior executives and shop-floor representative to be interviewed. All firms were assured that the results of interviews would be confidential and anything that was later published would omit any specific reference to people or firms. It is for this reason that it has not been possible to acknowledge firms by name and there is no reference in this report to any firm or individual. Each firm was sent a draft of Parts One and Two of the report and its comments were taken into account where possible.

PEP would also like to express its gratitude to the executives of many other firms and of the nationalised industries, members of the staff of research associations, of universities and of the British Institute of Management, members of professional institutes and of the Association of Management Teachers, senior civil servants and a number of management consultants who have contributed to the report by making themselves available for interviews and discussions. Special thanks are due to those who read the drafts and gave advice on sections of the report. The research team also wish to express their gratitude to their secretary, Mrs Brigitte Carter, for her cheerfulness, patience and hard work throughout the preparation of numerous drafts.

CONTENTS

PART ONE
THE SETTING

CHAPTER 1

INTRODUCTION

In the past few years there has been much criticism of Britain's economic performance, prompted mainly by the country's slow rate of economic growth and its failure to achieve an adequate increase in exports. An earlier PEP report, *Growth in the British Economy*, published in the autumn of 1960, had some influence in calling attention to Britain's economic shortcomings.

Much of the discussion about these problems has been based on 'league tables' comparing the performance of Western countries in respect of economic aggregates such as gross national product, total investment or exports. This has been a useful exercise and the value of such analysis, and the efficacy of policy measures to increase aggregates such as investment or exports, should not be underrated. But there has been a tendency to stress this global, macro-economic thinking at the expense of the study of decisions and actions in individual firms, which are the motive power of a decentralised economy such as Britain's.

In the last analysis, the growth of the economy as a whole depends on the efficiency and growth of the individual firms and these, in turn, are determined largely by the men who manage them. *Growth in the British Economy* had concluded that one major barrier to economic growth was that people are not sufficiently interested in it[1] —a conclusion that was particularly important in the case of managers in view of their special influence on economic activity. It appeared, therefore, that, before it would be possible to formulate a fully effective policy for a sustained increase in Britain's rate of economic growth, an examination should be made of the attitudes and practices of the men who manage industry. PEP accordingly decided to undertake a detailed study at the level of the individual firm.

---

[1] 'It is probably true that the chief impediment to a faster growth of the British economy is that we do not want it enough. Both management and labour and, more widely, people in general, do not attach such a priority to material progress as might lead them to great enough efforts to achieve the economic results for example of the United States, or Western Germany or the Soviet countries.' (*Growth in the British Economy* (PEP), 1960, p. xi.)

One difficulty of this approach is how to cover the vast number of individual firms making up the British economy. Altogether there are more than 20,000 enterprises with twenty-five or more employees in a multitude of different industries, the qualities and levels of attainment of whose managers are so varied as to evade any comprehensive review.

Previous investigators in this field have adopted a variety of approaches but most have concentrated on a very small sector of industry, confining themselves to firms within a restricted locality or to a particular, limited segment of an industry. Attempts are now being made, mainly by official agencies, to undertake studies of wider scope. The Ministry of Labour has established a research unit to investigate problems of manpower planning and this unit is now beginning to examine manpower requirements in one or two industries and to study certain other related problems.[1] Similarly, the National Economic Development Council (NEDC), which originally operated mainly at the macro-economic level, has now begun to establish councils for particular industries in order to examine them in much greater detail than could be done as part of a general economic plan for the nation as a whole. As yet, neither of these two major projects is far advanced, but it is likely that, pursued along constructive lines, they will lay the groundwork for a greater understanding of the workings of British industry.

The PEP study has approached the problem from a somewhat different angle. It has examined the attitudes and practices of managers in forty-seven firms in a number of industries. In this way it was hoped that the findings of the study would indicate which attitudes and practices are likely to be associated with a high and sustained growth in firms and thus in industry as a whole. It is important to be clear at this stage what is the connection between national growth and the growth of the individual firm. At the national level a growth rate in the gross national product which is higher than the increase in the total number of man hours worked must mean that productivity is rising. At the level of the individual firm, however, it does not necessarily follow that an increase in output entails higher productivity, since this could result merely from an increase in the labour force at the expense of some other firm. An individual firm may, therefore, increase its production without increasing its productivity, although in practice these two indicators very frequently go together. The major interest of this study is, however, in those firms which are in fact increasing their productivity and not merely their production, since it is only through

1 See Chapter 14.

such firms that the nation's productivity and thereby its output can steadily be raised.

It became apparent that many of the firms visited did not apply even comparatively simple techniques that should contribute to high productivity. This is demonstrated so frequently in the interviews that it seems likely that indifference to modern practices for improving productivity and efficiency is widespread within certain strata of British industry. It is probable that this criticism applies far less to the relatively small number of giant firms which can afford to run their own specialist departments. Such firms have problems, but they are not usually of this sort. The present study has, however, concentrated on rather smaller firms: few in the sample have more than 5,000 employees.

It is difficult to avoid the conclusion that the evidence given in Part Two points to weaknesses of management in some firms that are a serious barrier to higher productivity. It is hoped that this material will suggest means by which these firms can improve their performance. Part Three deals with the wider issue of how far policy-makers in Britain can produce an economic environment which is more conducive to growth and efficiency than the present one. In particular, it suggests how external help and incentives can be used in order to improve firms' efficiency in certain important areas of their activities. The suggestions made are by no means extensive; they represent a compromise between what appears desirable in theory and what is acceptable in practice to the average businessman and trade unionist. It is, however, important to stress that it is not necessary to adopt the particular proposals advanced in Part Three, nor to accept the lines along which a compromise has been drawn, in order to recognise the lesson of Part Two. The key conclusion is that management practices must be improved and modernised if industrial efficiency and the rate of growth are to be rapidly increased. Dissatisfaction with Britain's economic performance is certainly not enough. It becomes fruitful only if it leads to the right conclusions, either by individual firms or by the Government, so that an improvement can be effected. It is as a contribution to the discussion of what are the best policies for British industry that this book is offered.

CHAPTER 2

THE SELECTION OF INDUSTRIES
AND FIRMS

The last chapter explained that the purpose of this report was to describe attitudes and practices in British industry in order to examine how far managers are likely to achieve for their firms a high and sustained growth rate. In planning the research it was decided that the most expeditious procedure would be to select for study firms whose managers were likely to display attitudes and practices conducive to growth, and compare them with firms whose managers were thought not to possess such attitudes.

The first problem then was to decide how to select firms whose managers are likely to have adopted attitudes and practices that are conducive to growth, i.e. firms that are likely to be 'growth-orientated'. One method of selecting them would be to examine the records of a number of firms in an industry in order to pick out those that have increased their productivity most in recent years. In practice, however, this method was found to present serious difficulties. Figures of output and manpower which are needed to establish productivity are not usually available in respect of British firms. The figures that all public companies do publish, such as profits, capital employed or total assets, require considerable interpretation before their trend can be accepted as reflecting sustainable growth of production, still less of productivity. A further disadvantage of studying accounts is that a firm's financial results may have improved during past years for any of a number of reasons that may not be attributable to the current attitudes and practices of its management.

It was therefore decided to select firms instead by consulting experts on certain industries in order to find out if there was a consensus of opinion as to which firms had the best prospects. The experts were asked to compile two lists of firms. The first list was to feature firms which they expected to be prospering in ten years' time, either on their own or as subsidiaries of large companies which had bought them up because they were prospering. The second list was to include firms whose prospects they considered to be unpromising. One further condition was made: firms on the second list were to match, as far as possible, the size and operating conditions of firms on the first list.

In deciding how many firms to visit the determining factor was how long it would take to study them thoroughly without seriously inconveniencing them. In other field studies this problem has been approached by a variety of methods, which have involved either despatching questionnaires, analysing accounts or interviewing personnel, or some combination of all three of these. The questionnaire approach might have been appropriate if the aim had been to collect factual information on one particular aspect of a firm's activities, but to expect that it could effectively cover all a firm's managerial activities was clearly unrealistic. The alternative of intensively interviewing executives for several hours each would be intolerable for most firms, besides consuming a disproportionate amount of the research team's available resources and thereby restricting the scope of the research. From these possibilities the method chosen was the interviewing of executives in two-day visits to each of the firms supplemented by the analysis of accounts. A less important factor was the time needed by the two members of the research staff responsible for the interviewing programme to communicate with firms, to read published material about them, to travel to them and back, and to study the results of each visit. With these two considerations in mind a provisional target of fifty firms was set.

It was then decided that, in order to compare a spread of firms of different sizes and performance, approximately eight firms should be visited in each of the industries chosen. It therefore followed that it was possible to include six industries. In trying to make these industries representative of British industry the research team was guided by the need to include old and new industries, science-based and non-science-based industries, contracting and expanding industries, capital and consumer goods industries, craft and mass production industries, localised and non-localised industries, and American-influenced and wholly British industries. The industries finally selected were wool textiles, machine tools, shipbuilding, electronics, domestic appliances and earthmoving equipment.

In conversation with the experts on each of the six industries it became clear that certain firms enjoyed the reputation of being 'ahead' of others and it was these which formed the first list. Despite the fact that there was not always total agreement in their recommendations, there was sufficient concurrence among the experts for the research team to feel that it could identify certain firms as those most likely to be prospering in ten years' time. It was assumed that these firms were likely to be growth-orientated, and the interviews together with the analysis of financial results later confirmed that this was on the whole the case. The attempt to compile the second list met with less success. While reputations for backwardness certainly existed, it was found that those consulted were rarely willing to disclose the names of such firms. As the experts were trade association officials, stockbrokers, journalists and economists with a special interest in an industry, their reluctance was hardly surprising. To supplement the inadequate number of names put forward by the experts, the research team decided to choose additional firms as required. In addition to supplementing the second list, the research team added two firms from each of two additional industries in order to increase the number of large firms in the sample in which management practices were to be examined.

The approach to each firm took the form of a standard letter enclosing a brief summary of the background and aims of the research project. Each managing director was asked to allow a two-day visit from a member of the team, who would interview him and those of his senior colleagues whom he considered to form the firm's decision-making body responsible for production, research and development, finance, marketing, exports and personnel. In addition, he was asked to arrange for the convener of shop stewards or, if such a position did not exist, the nearest equivalent to be available for interview. The request to meet a representative of the firm's labour force was included on the grounds that labour relations within a firm could not be assessed without the views of at least one representative from the shop floor. The request to meet members of the executive team responsible for specific management functions was intended to provide the opportunity of questioning and discussing with the appropriate decision-makers all important matters under their control.

To make the best use of limited interviewing time lists of questions were prepared for each executive function which, taken together, were designed to cover the important aspects of each of the seven subjects under enquiry. Replies to questions on plant replacement would, for instance, tell the interviewer on what basis a firm decided to replace a piece of plant and what action was taken. It was planned that the same basic questions should be used for all fifty firms and that additional questions should be asked as necessary in view of an industry's special nature. All interviews would be ended by the respondent being invited to enlarge upon any of his replies if he felt that he had omitted anything relevant.

It was decided that all interviews would, with the consent of the respondent, be tape-recorded and later transcribed. The decision to use tape-recorders was made with a full appreciation of the arguments for and against their use. Against their employment was the possibility that the freedom with which any of the respondents conversed might be inhibited; in favour of their use was the undisputed fact that memory is both unreliable and selective. A summary written after each interview would lay all the material at the mercy of memory and therefore greatly increase the risk that any bias on the part of the interviewer would find its way into the final report.

The research staff were aware that, whether a tape-recorder is used or not, the interview method is open to the drawback that the interviewer depends to some extent on the accuracy of the respondent. While it was not expected that the research would encounter deliberate untruths, it was thought likely that limited time, the possibility of misunderstanding a question and the all too human propensity to rationalise or leave out disagreeable details would often prevent the whole truth from being revealed. Intelligent interviewing and an unwillingness to believe too readily all that was said would be the only antidote to this drawback during the interview. Later, some factual cross-checking could take place against the accounts of other executives, or against firms' financial results.[1] By the end of two days and eight interviews in each firm it was hoped that a broad picture of history, attitudes, policy and practices would have emerged, to which could be added later the impressions of the interviewer.

The actual programme of organising visits and interviewing firms lasted fifteen months. After the experts in the six chosen industries had been consulted and the lists drawn up, written approaches were started. By the time the last firm had agreed to participate in the study the approaches made numbered 128—eighteen in shipbuilding, twenty-three in machine tools, thirty-four in wool textiles, twelve in earthmoving equipment, eighteen in domestic appliances and twenty-three in electronics. The fact that more written approaches were made in each industry than the minimum figure of eight and that the number varied from industry to industry is explained by the unwillingness of some managing directors to participate in the study and the failure of others to reply. To take one industry, machine tools, it was necessary to write four letters to firms on the first list to be accepted by three of them and seventeen letters to firms on the second list to be accepted by four of them. It was consistently found that more approaches were required to firms on the second list than to firms on the first list in order to try to secure equal acceptances

---

[1] Before firms were visited Moodies Services Ltd processed their accounts in order to supply the research staff with a condensed record of their recent financial results. In the case of exempt private companies, accounts were, of course, not available.

from each group. In the end a balance between the two categories was not achieved: the research staff visited twenty-five firms on the first list and twenty on the second list, a result directly attributable to the extra difficulty of gaining access to firms on the second list.

By September 1962 the research staff had started interviewing firms and continued doing so until the following September, by which time forty-seven firms had been visited—nine in wool textiles, seven in machine tools, seven in shipbuilding, eight in electronics, six in domestic appliances, eight in earthmoving equipment and two in other industries. Out of a maximum possible number of 376 interviews slightly over 300 took place. This number was determined by the fact that certain firms did not have a separate executive for each of the areas of activity included in the study. In a small wool textile firm, for instance, the owner-manager undertook to answer questions on every single one of the topics covered. While many managing directors could presumably have answered all the questions, few of them had enough time to spare, nor did the research team wish to encourage any reduction in the number of informants. It was felt that the study of firms' characteristics would be made most effective by interviewing as many of the senior members of the executive team as possible.

To end the account of the field-work and to give the feel and flavour of the research it is worth including a generalised description of a typical two-day visit. In most cases the interviewer aimed at arriving at the firm between nine and ten o'clock in the morning, depending on the firm's distance from London and on travelling arrangements. At the airport or station he was generally met by a car which sometimes had been offered and sometimes requested. On arrival at the firm he was either ushered immediately into the presence of the managing director for explanatory discussions or a background briefing, or placed under the wing of the personnel or public relations executive. Initial discussions, therefore, were conducted in very different environments. Sometimes they were held under the gaze of the firm's revered ancestral founders, staring from their sombre portraits on the wall, or under the menace of a broadside of guns from a drawing of a nineteenth-century frigate. At a less exalted level, preliminaries began in a crowded office, with telephones ringing, foremen or apprentices knocking at the door, and the steady background hum or pounding of the machine shop. About half the firms involved had given some thought to the planning of the two-day visit and had circulated a memorandum around management giving a list of interviews with their times. The other half had left arrangements fluid.

An interesting point that arose during the initial discussions was the apparent absence in most firms of a management organisation chart. While a small minority of managing directors (which included all the American chief executives) were able to open a drawer of their desk and produce such a document, the rest were unable to do so, although one of them attempted to improvise by sketching a suitable chart on the back of an old envelope. Various reasons were given for the absence of charts. Some managing directors explained that their firms had too few executives to require a formal document showing management responsibilities, others had considered their use but had not taken the necessary steps to introduce them, and at least two thought that the best place for keeping the only copy of their firm's management organisation chart was the company safe, where it could remain securely locked up.

Once the day's programme was settled and misunderstandings corrected, work began in earnest. It always started by the research staff being shown round and this tour was undertaken by the works, mill or shipyard manager. In nearly every instance great care was taken to make the hour's circuit informative and detailed. When walking round, production executives drew attention to a variety of matters, which included the condition of their firm's machine tools, the way in which shop-floor operatives undertook their work, the difficulty of manufacturing in old and dilapidated buildings, the particular information campaign which their firm was running, the special safety precautions which were observed, and their plans for expansion. The cleanest, most spacious and best laid-out factories were those of American subsidiaries. In general, the older the firm the worse its manufacturing facilities. This was particularly notice-able in old wool textile mills, where different stages of wool pro-cessing were carried out on different floors of a three- or four-storey building. Many of the older firms had attempted to improve 'worker amenities' by building adequate lavatories, by installing washing facilities with hot and cold water and by providing individual lockers, but the gap between the best and the worst facilities still remained wide.

After the tour was over the interviews began. No order of prefer-ence was stipulated by the research staff, except that they wished to conclude with the managing director. Thus, the sequence of the interviews was either laid down by the managing director himself or was haphazard, depending on when personnel were available. Only the request to see the convener or his equivalent provoked occasional anxiety. In most firms he was inadequately informed about the purpose of the visit and in six firms the research staff were not allowed to see him. Either vital negotiations were in progress, which might possibly be disrupted by interviewing, or, in one memorable instance, the interviewer was told that asking the convener questions would be unrewarding as he was very ill-informed about the firm and his replies would therefore be misleading. At another firm, where the convener was seen, the managing director asked to hear the tape-recording, so that he could correct any mistaken impressions that might have been received; he was reminded that all the respondents were assured that their remarks were not going to be mentioned to anyone in the firm.

The place of interview with the convener, who frequently wished to be accompanied by another trade unionist, posed a problem for nearly all the firms. No convener had an office (nor did the research staff meet any who wanted one), and the locations were as varied as the works conference room, an interview room, the personnel manager's office (discreetly vacated) and the boardroom. It was clear from the comments of two conveners who were interviewed in the boardroom that they had not been there before and they did not expect to return.

After initial hesitation all respondents appeared undisturbed by the use of a tape-recorder and interviews flowed freely. Only two executives refused to permit the use of a tape-recorder; equally out of the ordinary the convener who insisted on bringing along his own and making his own recording. As might be expected, the more important the executive the less time he had to spare, but even the most hard-pressed, once under interview, gave generously of their time and the hour requested by the research staff was often exceeded.

With one exception, lunch was provided by the firm. Again, the location varied. In large firms alternatives included the directors', managers', heads' of departments and foremen's restaurant or hourly-paid employees' canteen. In firms with new premises the arrangements for lunch have often been a headache. Who should eat with whom, where and when, are problems that have received serious attention. Some firms acknowledged the American principle of management lining up with the men at the counter but it was found in practice only once. Lunch itself varied from the sumptuous to the frugal. Drinks were usually provided but consumption was in moderation. Lunch was seldom lingered over and interviewing re-started as soon as it was finished. In the evening the research staff stayed at the local hotel, generally arranged, but never paid for, by the firm. In only one case was there any evening entertainment suggested and this took the form of a visit to a famous Glasgow music-hall. On the following day the interviewing was completed, usually by lunch-time. The research staff left after lunch and on the return journey tape-recorded impressions of the firm. Whatever conclusions were reached about the firm's operations, it was always felt that the time spent had been informative and enjoyable.

The research data on each firm consisted of the transcription of its executives' and shop-floor representative's replies to the questions asked. The average length of this material was ninety pages. In studying the transcripts it was found, not surprisingly, that the various interviews revealed widely different attitudes and practices. In order to evaluate how these characteristics contributed to growth orientation the research staff had to form assumptions as to which attitudes and practices are conducive to the growth of productivity. Among management consultants, senior businessmen, authors of management textbooks and industrial economists there is some controversy as to the detail of such characteristics, but a wide consensus of principle does allow the building up of a specification of the attitudes and practices that are likely to lead to higher productivity and hence growth. In the course of the interviews the research staff were able to elaborate the detail of this specification. For brevity those attitudes and practices reported in the present study which corresponded best with the features of the specification are described as 'thrusting', while those which corresponded least well with them are described as 'sleepy'.

After establishing broadly the extent to which the attitudes and practices found in the firms appeared to be conducive to growth, the research staff re-analysed the interview data in order to arrange the thrusting and sleepy characteristics under the following subject categories: management development, management techniques, plant replacement, purchasing, industrial training, management consultants, personnel, research and development, marketing and exporting. These categories then became the material on which the chapters in Part Two are based.

Each chapter covers a certain area of management's responsibilities and within that area the thrusting and sleepy characteristics of firms are demonstrated by means of quotations from the transcribed interviews. A number of quotations have also been used which do not fall into either group as they are explanatory of an industry's or a firm's particular situation. The first concern in presenting the quotations has been that each one should be unidentifiable to a third party. Subject to that precaution, information about the industry and the job of the respondent has been given where it is relevant. The size of firms has been indicated by describing them as either 'small' (0–500 employees), 'medium-sized' (500–1,000 employees), 'large' (1,000–2,000 employees), or 'very large' (over 2,000 employees). The number of firms visited by the research staff in these four categories were ten, thirteen, thirteen and eleven respectively.

Great care has been taken in choosing quotations so as not to tear them from context or misuse them.

It is realised that the circumstances of those who made the quotations differ radically and that there will be many reasons why some managements hold some attitudes and follow certain practices while others do the opposite. But the concern here is with describing, wherever possible by quotations, the thrusting and sleepy characteristics encountered in the field-work and not with attempting to explain why certain policies and not others are adopted.

The emphasis of Chapters 4 to 9 is on individual attitudes and practices found in the research and how far they are conducive to growth. From these chapters two questions naturally arise. First, are thrusting and sleepy characteristics randomly distributed among firms or do thrusting attitudes and practices in different fields of management tend to be associated with each other with the result that it is legitimate to describe certain firms as thrusting and other firms as sleepy? Secondly, if thrusting and sleepy firms can be said to exist, do their financial results tend to show above and below average profitability and growth? Both these questions are explored in Chapter 10 and the evidence leads to the conclusion that some firms can be described as thrusting and that where thrusting attitudes are found in a firm they are likely to pay.

CHAPTER 3

THE SIX INDUSTRIES

Some background information is essential to an understanding of the six industries selected by the research team. To provide it the present chapter gives a short account of their histories and salient features. Much of the data has been summarised in the table on pages 39–40. It is based on the most up-to-date and comprehensive national statistical sources but the accuracy of the information contained in columns 1 and 2, based as they are on the 1958 *Census of Production*, will be subject to more recent changes.

Wool Textiles

The wool textile industry is one of the oldest industries in Britain. In the fifteenth century the main areas of production were in Somerset, Gloucestershire, Suffolk and Yorkshire. Towards the end of the eighteenth century the industry became centred on Bradford, where labour, coal and water were in ample supply and the climate was suitable for wool processing. During the nineteenth century the industry developed a pattern of numerous competitive private firms each specialising in one aspect of wool production. In recent years there has been some rationalisation of its structure. The industry, however, remains predominantly one of small firms, the large majority of which are private companies. Today there are 1,400 enterprises only eleven of which employ more than 1,000 people. The typical firm specialises in one, or at the most two, of the processes by which raw wool must be treated to produce either tops,[1] yarn or cloth. The integrated mill on the other hand combines the operations of scouring, carding or combing, spinning, weaving, dyeing and finishing, which together produce either woollen or worsted cloth.[2] It is almost unknown for new firms to establish themselves in the industry.

[1] 'Top: The sliver which forms starting material for the worsted and certain other drawing systems which is usually obtained by the process of combing.' The Textile Institute, *Textile Terms and Definitions*, 5th Edition, 1963, p. 157.

[2] The difference between woollen and worsted yarn is that in the production of woollen yarn the fibres of wool are not arranged in any particular position; in worsted yarn production they are laid as nearly parallel to each other as possible—an effect achieved partly by combing.

Machinery for each manufacturing process has remained relatively unchanged during the last fifty or sixty years with the result that many mills are using very old plant. A recent survey[1] showed that 41 per cent of British textile machinery was over ten years old and 34 per cent over twenty years old. Since the war there have been some developments in the spinning of yarn with the introduction of the Raper Autoleveler and the Ambler Superdrafter, and in the weaving of cloth the advent of the automatic loom has been of great benefit to firms producing long runs of cheap and medium-priced cloth.

The labour force of the industry is about 190,000 strong and includes a high proportion of unskilled women. Just under 8 per cent of the total labour force is composed of foreign workers. Altogether there are 9,250 Indians and Pakistanis, 1,100 Austrians and Italians, 3,750 Poles and 1,350 others.[2] Judged by the criterion of days lost in industrial disputes the industry's labour relations are good. Many factors combine to account for this situation, but the small size of individual manufacturing units and the paternalistic attitude of owners provide the kind of setting in which disputes tend to be rare. The wages of both men and women are lower than the average for manufacturing industry and the unions have made limited headway.

From the twelfth to the nineteenth century wool was Britain's most valuable export and in overseas markets its products enjoyed wide fame. Overseas sales of wool textiles have averaged £160 million per year during the last ten years, although their share of total world wool textile exports has been declining since the beginning of the century. Exports have traditionally been handled by merchants, but some firms do have their own export organisations. The industry sells abroad 28 per cent of its output and is the sixth largest exporting industry in terms of value. It is one of the few industries to operate a compulsory levy, which works out at 10½d. per operative week, of which 4½d. is spent on the promotion of exports. The balance is mainly used to support the Wool Industry Research Association (WIRA), which was founded in 1918 and is one of the oldest research associations in Britain. In the home market wool textile firms have had the benefit of higher import duties on all foreign wool products than those of most other industrialised countries. Recently manufacturers' security in the home market has been broached by the arrival of cheap Italian woollens and the first shipments of Japanese wool goods under the Anglo-Japanese commercial treaty concluded in November 1962. As yet these latter

[1] See *Machine Tool Directory* (Milln and Robinson), 1964, p. 16.
[2] The situation at 31 December 1963. Communication from Wool and Allied Textile Employers Council.

imports cannot be described as damaging in view of the fact that in 1963 Britain exported £4,874,000 worth of woollen goods to Japan, while it imported from that country only £38,719 of woollen goods. Total imports from all countries in recent years have amounted to an average of £12 million per annum.

In terms of the value of output and exports wool textiles was the most important industry included in the study. It is none the less a declining industry, whose output fell by 1·4 per cent between 1957 and 1962 and whose consumption of raw wool declined by 0·6 per cent. In commenting on the industry's prospects in its first report, *Growth of the United Kingdom Economy to 1966*,[1] NEDC forecast a period of slow growth in home demand and increasing competition in export markets. The outlook for the industry is not therefore expansionary.

Machine Tools

As a class of machinery, machine tools have three definitive features. First, they work on metal either by cutting it or forming it; secondly, their source of power is external and not manual; and, thirdly, they can 'reproduce themselves' in the sense that they themselves produce the parts from which further machine tools can be assembled. Ever since the invention of the first tools between 1770 and 1830 the industry has been of crucial importance to the economy and can claim to be the foundation of the country's engineering industries. By the middle of the nineteenth century Britain had established a world reputation and a major lead in the production of machine tools, but as other countries became industrialised it was inevitable that Britain's predominance in this field could not be maintained. By 1962 Britain had dropped to the fourth largest producer of machine tools with 8·7 per cent of the total of world production and 8·2 per cent of world exports.[2]

The industry's decline in world status in the late 1950s and early 1960s has led to intermittent criticism of its performance. While this criticism was often uninformed and exaggerated, it did prompt the industry to set up, in conjunction with the Board of Trade, a committee to consider some of the points being voiced and in particular those published in the Melman Report.[3] These comments were critical primarily of the industry's lack of research and development,

---

[1] NEDC, *Growth of the United Kingdom Economy to 1966* (HMSO), 1963, p. 122.

[2] Communication from the Machine Tool Trades Association.

[3] Seymour Melman, *Report on the Productivity of Operations in the Machine Tool Industry in Western Europe* (privately circulated by the European Productivity Agency), [1959].

as demonstrated by the amount said to be spent on it, and the paucity of qualified research personnel. Critics claimed that the industry had been content to produce an output mainly composed of general purpose machines and that it had paid insufficient attention to the new developments of electronically controlled machines and transfer lines. The industry, on the other hand, contended that much of the blame for not developing new techniques should be attributed to the conservatism of its customers.

In its answer in 1960 to the Melman report, the Mitchell Committee confirmed the validity of some earlier criticisms and suggested various ways in which the industry could improve itself.[1] Between 1959 and 1962 the industry took several steps to raise its general level of performance. Among them were the establishment of ten post-graduate scholarships at Manchester College of Science and Technology, the creation of a research association, the commissioning of two surveys to be undertaken by *Metal Working Production*— one on the age structure of machine tools in use in British firms and the other on the future prospects of the industry—and, finally, the setting up of a Careers Advisory Service to assist in graduate recruitment. It is too soon to determine how effective these moves have been, but it is possible that more drastic changes will have to be made in the industry before any major gains in effectiveness are realised.

The industry consists of about 330 firms many of which are old-established and family controlled. Nearly all the principal firms belong to the Machine Tool Trades Association, which claims a membership responsible for 95 per cent of production in metal cutting and 65 per cent in metal forming—percentages which together represent about 200 firms. The industry is primarily concentrated in the midlands where 30 per cent of its workers are employed and the second largest concentration is in London and the south-east with 18 per cent of the labour force. A hundred and fifty firms produce 92 per cent of the industry's turnover and twenty-five firms contribute 70 per cent. In recent years there has been some tendency towards rationalisation and concentration, some of the larger firms buying up a number of smaller firms each of which manufactures a different type of machine tool. About 98,000 people are employed in the industry of whom an unusually high proportion (48 per cent) are skilled—the category of labour the scarcity of which in the 1950s and 1960s has been one of the limiting factors to expansion.

On the selling side some firms have combined to form groups,

[1] Board of Trade, *The Machine Tool Industry, A Report by the Sub-Committee of the Machine Tool Advisory Council appointed to consider Professor Melman's Report to the European Productivity Agency* (HMSO), 1960.

while others have given their agency to one of the large manufacturers (called factors) thus avoiding the necessity of maintaining an individual sales force. Most of the industry's overseas selling is also carried out in this fashion although some firms do have their own organisations. This marketing structure has the advantage of enabling the factor to build up his agencies and offer a complete range of machine tools, but it does concentrate the selling effort of the industry in a few hands and places the small producer at one remove from his customer, thereby making him less responsive in meeting the customer's requirements.

More than in any other industry, machine tool firms feel that they are vulnerable to the cyclical fluctuations of demand which stem from the capital programmes of other engineering industries. For example the home order-book for machine tools in 1959 was worth £5·2 million, in 1960 £9·3 million and in 1963 £5 million again. This feeling of vulnerability has led to a hesitant attitude on the part of managements who are often reluctant to expand to meet demand. When demand has been high, order-books have lengthened and managements have striven to meet requirements, often to the neglect of their other functions, like research and development. When the order-book has fallen, managements have not felt justified in incurring extra expenditure.

The long-term future of the industry is promising. The survey conducted in December 1961 by *Metalworking Production* showed that 59 per cent of machine tools in British firms are over ten years old and, by this criterion at least, obsolescent.[1] Potential demand at home is therefore high and so also is demand from overseas.

Shipbuilding

British shipbuilding is another industry which gained world predominance between 1850 and 1914 when the British merchant fleet carried a large proportion of the world's deep-sea cargoes and British builders produced as much as 80 per cent of world tonnage. Such a position could not be maintained indefinitely and some relative decline was inevitable. By 1947 British yards accounted for 55 per cent of world output; sixteen years later the figure had fallen to 12 per cent. Since the war many countries which did not previously possess a shipbuilding industry have developed one, frequently with the assistance of government subsidies to both builders and owners. Other countries, like Germany and Japan, have completely rebuilt their industries since the war. The progress of Japan in particular has been impressive. In 1954 it built 0·5 million tons of

---

[1] *Metalworking Production* Research Department, *The First Census of Machine Tools in Britain*, 1961, p. 9.

shipping, in 1958 2·5 million tons, and in 1963 2·4 million tons, despite the general shipbuilding recession. The full impact of foreign competition was not felt, however, until the 1961 shipbuilding recession when British yards had their smallest order-book at any time since 1940.

The location of the industry was set by about 1920, with most of the main yards sited on either the Clyde, Mersey, Wear, Tyne or Tees. The industry is most heavily concentrated in Scotland, where 24 per cent of its workers are employed. During the last thirty years only one new shipbuilding firm has been established but within the industry there have been alterations in structure. In the slump of the 1930s capacity was reduced by one-third and in the recent recession twelve yards have gone out of business. Extensive modernisation and expansion have also been undertaken by most yards in the post-war years. Between 1946 and 1959 £110 million was invested, and during the last few years an additional £90 million has been spent. There has also been some tendency for shipowners to acquire an interest in certain yards. Today there are 1,025 listed shipbuilding enterprises, the vast majority of which are small boat builders. The main firms in the industry are only fifty in number and are members of the Shipbuilding Conference. Ninety per cent of the industry's production is accounted for by thirty yards and 50 per cent by only six. Many of these yards have gained world-wide reputations and can build practically any kind of ship for any owner—a versatility which may have become a disadvantage as some owners have begun recently to concentrate on specialised ships.

As with the machine tool industry, the decline of shipbuilding has been accompanied by stringent criticism. The industry is said to have been backward in adopting the latest advances in technology like welding and prefabrication. On behalf of the industry it has been pointed out that the first all-welded ship was British, built in 1920, and that prefabrication was introduced as early as 1930. The survey referred to earlier reported that 87 per cent of the machine tools used in shipbuilding and marine engineering were over ten years old[1]—a figure which must be interpreted with some caution as no allowance was made for the differing values of individual machines. Shipyards have also been criticised for employing proportionately fewer university graduates of all disciplines than any other industry— a criticism which did not acknowledge the number of graduates working in the British Shipbuilding Research Association and in other research institutions used by the industry.

In response to these criticisms the industry established the Patton

[1] *Metalworking Production*, Research Department, *The First Census of Machine Tools in Britain*, 1961, p. 15.

Committee in 1960 to examine productivity and research in British shipbuilding. The Patton Report[1] published in 1962 drew on an assessment of practices in twenty-seven British yards and nineteen foreign yards and listed a number of features which it regarded as the chief weaknesses of the industry. They included lack of sales consciousness in individual yards, absence of detailed preparatory planning as compared with continental yards, lack of flexibility and interchangeability of labour, the fact that those parts and services which together constitute two-thirds of a ship's final cost are cheaper abroad, and insufficient training of supervisors and management.

The industry has had many difficulties with which to contend. Among them has been the conservatism of British shipowners, who since the first world war have been slow to accept many of the main advances in world shipping, such as the adoption of large tankers and bulk carriers, the full use of diesel engines, and new methods of financing ship construction, or to recognise the importance of speed for larger ships and the value of standardisation.[2] Besides delaying technical change in shipyards by their conservatism, British shipowners, to whom builders expect to sell over three-quarters of their output, have drastically reduced their orders during recent years. This is best illustrated by comparing the shipbuilding industry's total order-book in 1957 and 1963. In 1957 there were 879 ships on order representing a tonnage of 6,952,000. In each succeeding year the number of orders outstanding has declined until in June 1963 it equalled 228 ships representing 1,822,000 tons. Not only have owners reduced their orders but they have also begun to turn to certain foreign yards where cheaper ships have been available for many years. New shipbuilding capacity in other countries and higher prices than those of many overseas builders have contributed to the steady decline in exports of British vessels during recent years. In 1962, admittedly a poor year for shipbuilding, ships worth only £36 million were exported—about 8 per cent of total output. With world shipbuilding capacity held to be double expected world demand and with some British owners tending to purchase abroad, the competition for orders is expected to become still keener. British yards are still undercut in price by certain foreign yards, mainly in Japan and Sweden, and will have to concentrate on offering the right type of ship and on raising productivity.

The industry is noted for its difficult labour relations and their ill

[1] *Productivity and Research in Shipbuilding, Report of the Main Committee under the Chairmanship of Mr James Patton, O.B.E., to the Joint Industry Committee,* 1962.

[2] See S. G. Sturmey, *British Shipping and World Competition* (The Athlone Press), 1962, Chapter 15.

effect on productivity. Most yards have as many as twelve different unions among their labour force. Uppermost in the minds of men is the memory of the slump and the desire for job security is ever pressing. The fact that yards do not give permanent employment to all their workers heightens the insecurity of shipyard employment. The fear of redundancy has affected productivity in shipbuilding in two ways: first, it has been largely instrumental in maintaining demarcation, which has in turn led to a measure of overmanning and, secondly, it has prevented the introduction of work study. Against the background of a labour force which has shrunk from 100,000 in 1960 to 76,000 in 1963,[1] efforts to solve these difficulties have met with only limited success.

Electronics

While the origins of the three industries already described go back two hundred years or more, the electronics industry dates from the invention of the thermionic valve in 1904. Over the last sixty years, and more particularly during the last twenty, the industry has expanded rapidly until today it employs slightly over a quarter of a million people and its annual output is valued at £350 million. Involved in this industry are just under 500 firms ranging from some of the largest electrical firms to some of the smallest. They are represented by nine different trade associations, the principal ones being: the Electronic Engineering Association (EEA), with forty-four firms manufacturing capital equipment, such as broadcasting and television transmitters, control and data processing equipment, radar and radio communications and aircraft electronics; the British Radio Equipment Manufacturers' Association (BREMA), with forty firms making radio and television receivers and other audio equipment; the British Radio Valve Manufacturers' Association (BVA/VASCA), with nine firms producing all types of valves; the Radio and Electronic Component Manufacturers' Federation (RECMF), with 120 firms making all kinds of components such as capacitors, resistors and inductors; and the Scientific Instrument Makers' Association (SIMA) with 130 firms assembling electronic measuring equipment. These trade associations together have spoken for the industry in its dealings with NEDC. Firms may more simply be divided into two categories, assemblers of electronic equipment and makers of components, but some of the larger firms do both. New firms are entering the industry every year.

The expansion of the industry has rested on a number of discoveries involving the exploitation of electronic principles and has been regulated by the speed with which these principles have been

[1] Communication from Shipbuilding Employers' Federation.

translated into commercial possibilities. The early growth of the industry was largely in the development of radio and television while more recently it has been in navigational equipment, scientific instruments and the application of electronics to industry and commerce. The industry is most heavily concentrated in London and the south-east, where 45 per cent of its labour force is employed. In 1960, 1961 and 1962 the industry exported goods worth about £210 million, which together represented 23 per cent of total output.

Three other features of the industry are worth pointing out. The first is the heavy reliance of the industry on female workers. Of its 250,000 workers 44 per cent are women. The second is the size of the industry's research and development expenditure, which amounts to £50 million a year, including Government money. This figure represents 17 per cent of net output and involves about 8,500 qualified engineers and scientists or 3 per cent of total manpower. In an effort to rationalise some of the research now being done and to disseminate information on applied research to firms, the industry's trade associations have been negotiating to establish a central research association which will probably be known as the National Electronics Research Council.[1] The third characteristic is the dependence of the industry on Government contracts, mainly of a military nature. Of the £50 million spent on research and development £30 million is provided by the Government. In military contracts the industry has in the Government at once a financier and a customer but in commercial contracts a financier only. Recently some of the emphasis of Government expenditure has been switched from military to civil contracts and leaders of the industry argue that many important developments cannot go forward without Government support.

The future of the industry is very bright. While it may not be able to maintain its past rate of expansion, it is firmly established as a growth industry and has told NEDC that it expects to expand by 59 per cent between 1961 and 1966. Exports are expected to rise at 10 per cent a year.[2]

Domestic Appliances

Domestic electrical appliance products form part of the output of the electrical and allied engineering industry. Manufacture of electrical goods began at the turn of the century, since when it has become one of the country's biggest and most dynamic industries, whose growth rate between 1948 and 1960 exceeded that of any

[1] The National Electronics Research Council has been established since the time of writing.

[2] NEDC, *The Growth of the Economy* (HMSO), 1964, pp. 90 and 93.

other industry. This expansion is reflected in the fact that demand for electricity has more than doubled every ten years. As a percentage of the value of the electrical industry's output domestic appliances (excluding refrigerators) have fluctuated little since 1935, the first year in which statistics were collected. In that year domestic appliances worth £10–11 million were produced, representing approximately 10 per cent of the electrical industry's gross output. Almost thirty years later domestic appliances worth £150–170 million were manufactured, again representing about 10 per cent of total output and slightly over 2 per cent of total consumer spending. The growth rate of domestic appliances averaged, however, 9·3 per cent a year in real terms in the seven years between 1954 and 1961, while in the same period the whole electrical industry grew at a rate of only 6·4 per cent.

Today the domestic appliance industry employs about 64,000 people, only 15·9 per cent being craftsmen or their equivalent. Compared with certain continental countries there is a surprisingly large number of firms in the industry, the majority of which belong to the British Electrical and Allied Manufacturers' Association. Altogether there are 142 enterprises manufacturing domestic appliances, the biggest concentration falling in London and the southeast. Included in the industry are some of the largest electrical manufacturing firms in the country, producing a range of equipment from turbines to toasters, as well as some of the smallest, which concentrate exclusively on one appliance. This multiplicity of makers is one of the chief characteristics of the industry and one of its biggest headaches. Thus, there are 162 manufacturers and importers of all heaters and 1,021 different models, twenty-six foodmixer suppliers and seventy-five models, twenty-two electric iron makers and eighty-one models, and twenty-three kettle manufacturers and ninety-four different models.[1]

Despite the likelihood of occasional alterations in hire-purchase restrictions and purchase tax, the industry can look forward with confidence to the future, although, unlike the 1950s when virtually any manufacturer could make a profit, the coming years will be severely competitive. One reason for confidence is that, compared with certain countries, notably the United States, the extent of domestic appliance penetration in British homes is still low. Despite the phenomenal growth rate in the 1950s, refrigerators can only be found in 34 per cent of British homes and washing machines in 49 per cent (1964 figures). In the United States the figures are 98 per cent and 74 per cent (1964 figures) and in Switzerland 45 per cent

[1] See Nicholas Stacey, 'Domestic Appliance Mergers Ahead', *Statist*, 15 May, 1964.

and 66 per cent (1961 figures). Many manufacturers, some of whom were newcomers to the industry, showed themselves keenly alive to this potential when there was a stampede to extend capacity at the end of the 1950s—an increase which was over-optimistic and left many firms with excess capacity on their hands. One characteristic of the industry which may have contributed towards such enthusiasm was its belief in the effect of advertising. In 1961 the industry spent £6·5 million on advertising or 4·9 per cent of the value of total home deliveries (compared with 1·3 per cent of the motor industry).

One way in which some firms have snatched a lead over their rivals has been by dissolving the traditional wholesaler/retailer method of selling. In the early 1960s it was normal 'for the whole-saler to take 12½ per cent of the final wholesale price, and the retailer 25 per cent of the retail price. This means that, if purchase tax is left out of account, conventional distribution adds anything up to 50 per cent to the factory price.'[1] The method of direct selling has been exploited particularly in the last two years but its nature restricts it to certain domestic appliance products which are suitable for home demonstration.

Earthmoving Equipment

Of the six industries covered by the study the earthmoving equipment industry is the youngest and that with the greatest proportion of American firms. In 1935 its output was less than £5 million but since then it has increased rapidly to its present output of approximately £90 million per year. Its products include dump trucks, excavators, graders and tractors, besides a mass of other equipment the purpose of which is to assist construction work whether of buildings or roads. Most of the firms in the industry belong to the Federation of Manufacturers of Construction Equipment, which has a total membership of sixty-six firms that together manufacture a broader range of products than that included in the Standard Industrial Classification under 'earthmoving'. Of the eight firms visited by the research staff six belonged to the earthmoving industry and two fell outside it but were members of the trade association.

During the war most of the firms in the industry were engaged in some branch of armament work, so that after the war the industry had largely to start from scratch. In contrast, the experience of the American construction equipment industry was very different. During the 1930s it received tremendous impetus from the New Deal programme and in the war it supplied most of the equipment required to build aerodromes and roads for the Allies. By 1946,

---

[1] 'Challenge to the Durable Goods Shops', *Financial Times*, 22 September 1962.

therefore, it had gained a wealth of valuable experience, was producing plant of up-to-date design and was in an overwhelmingly
strong position.

In the post-war years the prolonged demand for earthmoving
equipment has provided an opportunity which the British industry
has seized. New equipment was developed and produced so that by
1948 the total value of output had risen to £19 million. During the
late 1940s and early 1950s a number of American firms set up subsidiaries in Britain to manufacture earthmoving equipment and the
influence of American technology and management was further
extended by mergers and licensing agreements. In 1962 American
subsidiaries and American dominated mergers accounted for a large
proportion of total earthmoving output.

Not only is the earthmoving equipment industry the youngest and
the most American-influenced of the industries covered, but it has
also had the most striking export performance, both in terms of the
percentage of output exported (approximately 42 per cent) and of
the growth of exports during the last ten years. It is also worth
drawing attention to the fact that of the industries included in the
study the earthmoving equipment industry has much the highest
record of exports per man employed, with a manpower force of
26,000 exporting in 1962 goods worth £43 million. Much of the
industry's export success must be attributed to the presence of
American firms. Several of the subsidiaries were started in Britain
because, first, advantage could be taken of Commonwealth trade
agreements and, secondly, markets which had previously been
supplied with expensive United States products could be taken over
by cheaper British-made equipment.

During the last five years, the output of the industry has increased
in value by 42·7 per cent. With demand for the building industry at
the highest peak ever and orders from abroad pressing, the industry
should enjoy a further period of dramatic growth.

TABLE 3.1

Salient Features of the Six Industries

1	2	3	4	5	6	7	8	9
Industry and number of enterprises	The 3 areas of largest concentration of each industry as a % of total manpower employed for the whole industry	Manpower 1962	% of men and women in each industry's work-force	Craftsmen or their equivalent as a % of the total work-force	Serving apprentices as a % of total employees	Machinists and semi-skilled as % of total work-force	Research and development employees as % of total work-force	Scientists and technologists as % of manpower
Wool textiles	1,440	74·8 (E. and W. Riding) 9·5 (Scotland) 4·5 (North-West)	193,000	men: 48·0 women: 52·0	17·1	0·7	52·0	0·03	0·3
Metal-working machine tools	334	30·0 (Midlands) 18·1 (London and S. East) 14·6 (Eastern and West Riding)	98,000	men: 86·5 women: 13·5	48·8	8·3	10·8	0·37	1·5a
Ship-building and marine engineering	1,025	24·4 (Scotland) 22·0 (Northern) 13·6 (North-West)	264,000	men: 96·0 women: 4·0	52·6	10·8	24·0	0·19	2·0
Electronics	491	45·3 (London and S. East) 18·0 (Eastern) 6·4 (North-West)	266,000	men: 55·7 women: 44·3	17·3	3·1	25·2	n.a.	3·05
Domestic appliances	142	41·3 (London and S. East) 18·0 (Midlands) 7·5 (Wales)	64,000 (excludes refrigerators)	men: 62·3 women: 37·7	15·9	1·8	31·0	n.a.	n.a.
Earthmoving equipment	129	25·8 (North Midlands) 14·8 (Eastern) 12·9 (London and S. East)	26,000	men: 88·5 women: 11·5	37·1	5·0	9·3	n.a.	n.a.

Source: Columns 1 and 2—*Census of Production*, 1958; Column 3—*Annual Abstract of Statistics*, 1963; Columns 4–7—*Ministry of Labour Gazette*, December 1963 (only apply to firms with eleven or more employees), figures for Shipbuilding and Marine Engineering and Wool Textile Industries—*Ministry of Labour Gazette*, April 1964; Column 8—FBI, *Survey of Industrial Research in Manufacturing Industry*, 1961; Column 9—DSIR, *Scientific and Technological Manpower in Great Britain* (HMSO), 1962.
a *Source:* Machine Tool Trades Association.

TABLE 3.1—continued

Industry	10 Value of total output. Average of '60, '61, '62 in £ million	11 Value of output in 1962 in £ million	12 Output as % of total manufacturing output in 1962	13 % increase in value of output in the last 5 years with average of '56, '57, '58 as base year to 1962	14 Value of exports Average of '60, '61, '62, in £ million	15 Value of exports in 1962 in £ million	16 Exports as % of manufacturing exports in 1962
Wool textiles	554 b	535 b	2·11 b	1·4 b (Decline)	155 c	147 c	4·6 c
Metal-working machine tools	113	127	0·44	44·2	35	42	1·3
Ship-building and marine engineering	440	415	1·63	15·9 (Decline)	60 c	36 c	1·1
Electronics	310 d	344	1·36	34·9 e	72 d	85 d	2·7
Domestic appliances	167 f	166 f	0·65	55·1 g	34 f	35 f	1·1
Earthmoving equipment	86	89	0·35	42·7	36	43	1·4

Source: Except where specified, *Annual Abstract of Statistics.*
b Wool, waste and rags, noils, tops, yarns, cloth, blankets, felts, others.
c *Source: Trade and Navigation Accounts.*
d *Source:* NEDC.
e Based on Ministry of Aviation figures which are lower than NEDC's.
f *Source:* British Electrical and Allied Manufacturers' Association.
g 1957 figures not available. The 1956 figure was low because of hire-purchase restrictions.

PART TWO

THE MANAGEMENT OF GROWTH

CHAPTER 4

MANAGERS

Part One has stated that the purpose of this report is to find out how far the attitudes and practices of managers in industry are conducive to economic growth. It was explained that the main interest of the study was in the rapid growth of productivity in firms, rather than in the growth of production as such. Before examining attitudes and practices in detail, therefore, it is as well to define productivity clearly.

Productivity is the ratio of outputs to inputs in an analysis of any productive unit, whether it is a nation, an industry or a firm. Frequently, in such analyses, productivity indices are prepared which compare for similar periods the ratio of output to the input of one factor of production. Thus, the index of labour productivity for the whole country will express the trend of national output against the number of man years put into it and for an industry or a firm it will show the quantity or value of output against the operative hours worked. It will be noted that in each of these three cases productivity is defined as the ratio of the output to the number of man years or man hours worked.

The word 'productivity' is so often used as shorthand for 'labour productivity' that the two concepts may be taken by many people as synonymous. This fallacy may appear to place the onus of economic growth entirely on labour and, within the firm, on that section of labour which is most readily analysed: the shop-floor workers. But productivity is the ratio of all outputs to all inputs and the responsibility for increasing it rests squarely on managements. Improvements are seldom due to workers expending more physical effort. Higher productivity usually follows changes in, for example, production techniques, the setting of standards and measuring of performance, organisation of the work or incentive payment schemes: all changes that must be implemented by management.

Thus the performance of managers is crucial to economic growth and it is appropriate that this part of the book should begin with the managers themselves.

Objectives

In describing the objectives of their companies, some managing directors made no reference at all to productivity or growth. A retired service officer who had recently become the managing director of a large firm placed the emphasis on providing both a service and employment.

'I'm not quite sure myself, being a new boy in the industry, what is the object of running a company. Some people tell me that all you do is to make money for the shareholders. I don't think that's the object at all. I think you provide a service and you employ and give a livelihood to a number of people. I mean the whole country runs on industry. If there wasn't any industry in the country, it wouldn't exist and a firm has to do its best in keeping the country going, providing the livelihood for the citizens.'

The managing director of a medium-sized firm which went public shortly after the war stressed, in addition to employment, reasonable profits, a happy atmosphere and hard work:

'I've always been brought up to the fact that the first responsibility is to provide work for these chaps—to keep the shop occupied—that, you see, used to be the main one when it was a family business. Now I've got a responsibility to the shareholders as well—to see that they get a reasonable return on their money if possible. There are three partners in the business—there are the work-people who are engaged on an hourly basis and the staff and the shareholders—and my main job is to create an atmosphere in which the staff and the work-people work happily and get something out of life in the process, and to keep putting across to them the facts of life that we've got to work hard and use our time effectively.'

The managing directors of two firms in the electronics industry, on the other hand, were more concerned with the yardsticks of finance and turnover. The managing director of one of them discussed his job:

'I suppose looking after the objectives of the company—maintaining the profit objective and the return on investment objective—that's the most important aspect of my job. As a subsidiary aim, keeping people happy in their jobs is extremely important. But the thing that occupies my life mainly is keeping the profit and the return on investment constantly before us and making sure of meeting them.'

It was, however, in the other firm—a foreign subsidiary—that the emphasis on formulating objectives was most discernible. The firm was the only one visited which told the research team that it handed to each employee a statement of company objectives. These aims included: making an important contribution in their field of electronics; earning a specified profit on all current operations; recognising the personal worth of employees and creating a spirit of opportunity; and directing growth towards strength for the future. In discussing the company's growth the managing director said:

'We feel that we can be one of the big three and split the market roughly three ways in ten years. This is one of our objectives in fact. Our particular type of business in the UK is currently worth X million pounds per year—growing at the rate of 15 per cent per annum—and we feel that by the end of 1970 we can be taking Y per cent of the market.'

The percentage named was based on market research, which had been undertaken to determine the size of the firm's market, the present share of the market held by each of the firm's main products, the rate at which it was expanding and each line's future prospects. Indeed, both these electronics firms had plans and numerical targets for their operations over the next five or ten years.

The first two quotations express human values that cannot be gainsaid. Without them, the targets of profitability and growth that were objectives of the latter two managing directors would be worth little. Yet without profitability and growth, as measures of efficiency and dynamism, the other values can hardly be upheld. For in the modern world, and especially in an economy which is as open to the world as the British, employment will be threatened and living standards fall far behind those of other countries unless firms are efficient and dynamic. It is, therefore, no criticism of the values expressed by the first two managing directors if they themselves are criticised for failing to give enough weight to profitability and growth. Those values will, on the contrary, be in serious danger unless high standards of efficiency and dynamism are attained, which is not likely to be the case unless the rapid growth of productivity is at the centre of companies' objectives.

Criteria of Good Management

A statement of long-term and short-term objectives raises the question of the attainment, and focuses attention on the effectiveness of management in directing a company. Some chief executives gave as the criterion the production of an article that satisfies the customer:

'If you ask me in modern terms what is good management, then I would have to ask you to introduce [a firm of management consultants] or bodies like industrial consultants to analyse us. I am not competent to judge. I can only say that the end product is a function of good, indifferent or bad management. We have been from our inception a very prosperous company. We have built a reputation in the industry. . . . Eventually you're either in the market or you're out. If your product isn't good they won't come back but they come back time and again to us. The only answer I can give you as to whether our management is good, bad or indifferent is that our designs compare favourably. Similarly a ship is a wonderful testing ground for good, bad or indifferent. It has to face the ocean and you would soon hear if anything went wrong.'

A fuller definition of effective management was given by the managing director of a medium-sized wool textile firm:

'Good management, I think, can have only one objective criterion and that is efficiency in the particular direction in which you are talking. If it is personnel management, for instance, efficient personnel management means, among other things, that you would have good human relations within the factory, in addition to having a small labour turnover and so on. All these things are efficient aspects of personnel management. Likewise if you take financial management, efficient financial management, it means that you have the right amount of money at the right time and not too much eating its head off in the bank when it ought to be earning money outside and so on—proper control of your finances. All of this is part of efficient financial management. So, each aspect of management is obviously entirely different. The only common factor one can find really is this word "efficient", that you are utilising your resources, whether they be human or money or what have you, as effectively as you can.'

Managing directors were asked what they regarded as the most important aspect of their job. Some of them were inclined to discuss their role in terms of leadership. This attitude was most cogently expressed by the managing director of a small private firm in the wool textile industry:

'My first concern is towards the troops, like an officer's. If you've got a contented work-people, then I think you're well on the way to success.'

In contrast, the chief executive of an electronics firm with about

3,000 employees saw his main role as assessing and fitting together his management team:

'I think the most important aspect is to study the people that work directly under me and to try and truthfully assess what are their strong points and what are their weak points, and as far as possible, to try and balance these things up. Because I do think that, in a company such as ours, it's quite impossible for one man to have a tremendous effect on it. He can have some effect, but basically the company runs according to the effort of a team at the first and second levels and so the careful watch and assessment and the fitting together of these people is really the most important job I think I have to do.'

Direction of this sort is basic to good management, and it depends more on ability to understand people and on judgement and experience in dealing with them than on any formula or system. The interviewers found hardly any evidence that managers in British industry are lacking in judgement of this sort. But in many of the firms there was little or no awareness of the importance of systematic management development. It is, certainly, no coincidence that the chief executive last quoted was able to give his full attention to understanding the characters of his managers and getting the best out of them, and that he had at the same time instituted a highly organised system of management development, the running of which was in the hands of a first-class personnel executive.

Management Development Schemes

Rapid growth of productivity is not likely to be achieved without continuous improvement in the performance of managers. Several of the firms visited had, accordingly, introduced management development schemes. The director of one very large firm said:

'I think it would be fair to say that up to five or six years ago this company had no scientific management. It was a haphazard business. People were promoted from off the shop floor or came from here, there and everywhere. They took all decisions as they appeared best at the moment without looking forward. Now we are in the middle, I think, of a change-over to a more scientific approach . . . trying to get continuity, get proper training and look to the future and see your replacement programme of individuals and new people coming up.'

This quotation brings out the two main objects of a management development scheme: improving the calibre of management and providing for future succession. The managing director of a very large electronics firm described how his company had recently started such a programme:

'In the last two years we have had this rapid acceleration. We've had to go in for a lot more outside recruitment than normally we would. We've now got established in this company—and we are, I think, one of the few that are doing it, certainly of our size—a programme of what we call management succession and development. We've got consultants in to help us on this and they've set it up. We're now in the early stages of developing it. From this we expect to get very good guides as to what we have for future promotion material in the place, and what we hope to do, of course, is never to get to the stage where we have to go outside to get top people.'

Many of the chief executives interviewed, while not appreciating the full significance of management development, mentioned important aspects of it. A typical comment came from the managing director of a medium-sized firm in answer to a question on the selection and promotion of management:

'In a small organisation like this you do it [selection and promotion] rather on an *ad hoc* basis. The total number of people in this organisation is slightly less than a thousand. One of the things I have been insistent upon since I came in is to see a line of succession and I am always trying to make sure that, if someone gets run over by a bus, someone down below can step into his shoes. That hadn't been done in this firm before—otherwise I wouldn't be here!'

Recruitment

Management development schemes begin with an assessment of present and future management requirements. On the basis of this, the planning of all the other aspects of management development can proceed. A starting point is the formation of a satisfactory recruitment policy. It is a sleepy practice to ignore important sources of supply.

An extreme example was provided by a small wool textile firm controlled by one family. The managing director explained that it was company policy that any member of the family should try to obtain a qualification in textile technology and continued:

'I would say that the firm's got to continue on a family basis but we are very largely an ageing management and we're going to have to look to the future. That is one of the difficulties that we have at the moment. The arrangement we have now is that the eldest sons of the eldest brother can come into the business. At the moment there's no one qualified because they're all well below the age of eighteen.'

Throughout the history of British business, there have been examples of family firms thriving and expanding with each new generation. But they are the exceptions rather than the rule. It is unlikely that a recruitment policy depending on the eldest sons of the eldest brother will steadily ensure management of good quality.

Another way of blocking recruitment from many important sources is by placing too great a reliance on executives who have 'come off the shop floor'. A director of a large firm told the interviewer that his company did not employ any graduates because:

'We have better value in the man with practical experience and the knowledge of our method of working. Selection of top management is a subject which quite careful consideration is given to. In general, as far as it is possible, this is achieved by upgrading people with long service and knowledge of the business.'

In contrast, some firms search widely for their seed-corn. The managing director of a large earthmoving equipment firm explained company policy:

'We run three schemes for young men. Firstly, we've management trainees—chaps taken from the shop floor to train. Secondly, we've got this university graduate scheme. And, thirdly, we've also got these boys who are doing "thick sandwich" courses. And out of all those we hope that eventually we shall get managers.'

Training

Once a firm has settled its recruitment policy it has to decide how to ensure the best use of its young managers so that the future requirements of the company are met. They are developed by a combination of formal training and training on the job. In the former managers either attend outside training courses or, if the firm is large enough, join a course run by the firm. For junior management, courses are designed to inculcate recognised business techniques, like work study or budgetary control, and for senior executives education is given in management strategy. Training on the job consists of planning a young manager's early career so that he carries out a number of different and responsible jobs and thus gains experience of several sides of a firm's business. During this job rotation he comes under the special supervision of individual senior managers part of whose task is to write regular assessments of his performance and discuss them with him.

Nearly all the firms interviewed acknowledged the importance of management training, though some were inclined to comment that they were either too busy to let anyone go on an outside course or too poor to afford it. One large shipbuilding firm which did not make provision for formal internal training provided an excellent example of how a firm can ensure that it is not infiltrated with new ideas. The managing director explained that he had not done very much about sending executives on management courses:

'At the moment I think I'm more successful in training my own managers. Getting intelligent people in the first place and then after that training them in policies which this firm wants carried out, I think that is the most successful way.'

In a second shipbuilding firm one of the senior executives appreciated the need for exposing management to new ideas but seemed to be making only limited headway:

'I think I've managed to convince the managing director that we need a higher calibre of management. We have the people with the potential but they're not getting any experience. They're not being exposed to the kind of thinking which we would like them to be contaminated with. We haven't been successful because of the inertia and resistance to anything which is non-traditional.'

The managing director of a very large manufacturing firm which had enjoyed steady growth during the post-war years described how it had skimped on formal training:

'I must say that we've probably been rather backward compared to other big firms in this respect [outside training], because we felt, rightly or wrongly, that we ought to be able to train most decent people up within our own organisation by shunting them around and carefully selecting the material, then starting to give the chap a chance to develop within the company, so that we have not used outside courses to any great extent.'

Three examples of firms which have made use of outside training courses make an interesting contrast. The first is given by the only

managing director interviewed who had attended an American
business course after the age of thirty-five:

'We had two or three managers at Churchill College on the long
course there. I mentioned before the American Management Association Centre in Brussels, which we use. We've used the technical
college here. The technical college near here has put on a special
course for us. One course they conducted on our premises for top
managers. They have a management development course which we
helped them build up and we have sent people to about the first
four or five courses on that. I think we've done a very great deal.
Conferences run by the Ministry of Labour in combination with the
Institute of Personnel Management—I've been there at those things
and occasionally give a lecture. I think we've done a very great deal
of it. I'm tempted to say almost too much.'

A very large manufacturing company sent a lot of its senior managers
'to a great variety of courses', which were not confined to this
country:

'We use Harvard Business School to teach the senior management.
And then we've got the senior managers to run training courses
within the company once they've been on the Harvard Business
School courses themselves. We try to squeeze as much out of it as
possible.'

The managing director of a medium-sized domestic appliance firm
recounted how his firm had changed its practices as a result of such
a course:

'They [research and development, forward planning, organisation
and methods] changed four or five years ago when I attended again
another of these management training courses, where I went to
study forward product planning. I was very impressed. I immediately
came back and reported to the board—I was X manager in those
days—that I thought this was exactly what we wanted. I thought
that up to then the introduction of new products had been a bit
slap-happy. Ever since that day we've had regular meetings. We
have a regular agenda. We have a regular programme for research
and development.'

The other part of management training is on-the-job training or
development within the company. Sleepiness in this respect lies in
keeping junior and middle managers for long periods in the same job.

The positive approach to this subject was voiced by the personnel manager of a very large domestic appliance firm. After he had talked about company training policy he went on:

'We have then to develop him [the young manager] rather than to train him. We have to see that the man who for a start is blossoming well in his particular sphere is given the opportunity to move into another sphere. We then develop him further and we get him away to courses. We expose him to different problems—put him under different managers for development rather than fixed training.'

While several of the firms visited said that they were operating a management development scheme, the practice of regular assessment of management was rare. The managing director of a small American subsidiary was almost alone in asserting the value of assessment and practising it:

'We do twice yearly assessments by questionnaire and by interviews on all management candidates and all people who we consider are growth potential in management—that's supervisors upwards within the company. This is a thing that's done seriously. We assess the person. We get several people to assess them—the people who work with them, anybody who feels capable of comment on a person's performance—the American idea. And that is the basic assessment which is held on record, and we feed that back to the person himself, of course. We tell him what we think about him. We point out any weakness, if we feel he can take that kind of criticism, in the hope that he can improve. We give him a pat on the head where necessary and review again in six months' time—keep on reviewing and watch for the growth pattern.'

Promotion and Responsibility

One of the aspects of a fully operating management development scheme is that promotion will be made more according to talent and ability and less according to luck, longevity or influence. The kind of situation which the chief designer of one medium-sized domestic appliance firm complained of will be avoided:

'I cannot say to young people, "Come into the design office and stay here, and there is every possibility you will go right the way to the board in future." I cannot say that to them. I should be able to. I have to say, "I'm sorry—I can take you on, but you won't get any further than you are doing here. Maybe you'll get a salary adjustment from time to time." '

In another firm, the impression was fostered that promotion was possible for everybody. The chief executive made a practice of regular management meetings:

'We've got the smaller management committee, which is a few of the foremen, the people that we feel are the really best people, who have a rather wider outlook, and it's been done for two reasons: (a) we think it is extremely useful to them, and also to us, for them to know how things are going on, to be able to make suggestions and feel they are taking part; and (b) also it does let the people on the floor realise that promotion is possible and they are really being given a chance to come right though the firm. We find that this builds morale.'

Another important aspect of management development, which is at the same time a vital feature of a well-organised management structure, is the delegation of responsibility. Unless they are given real responsibility, junior managers can hardly grow to the stature required when they are promoted to senior positions. In interviews with managing directors it was clear that not all of them appreciated the importance of delegating. Several reasons were volunteered why it would not be in the best interests of the firm. One of them was put forward by the managing director of a small wool textile firm, who explained:

'We're at the moment reckoned to be super-efficient because the plant is watched every hour it runs by the managing directors, whereas, if it ran twenty-four hours a day, I'm not prepared to get out of bed in the middle of the night and come down here.'
Interviewer: 'You would have to appoint a deputy?'
'Yes, and nobody—human nature being what it is—looks after plant like you look after your own. This is brought out by foster mothers. They try very hard but they don't watch a child as if it were their own.'

A second reason which was given for not delegating responsibility was that middle management was incapable of handling additional responsibility. This point was heard in a large machine tool firm where little effort was made either to send managers on outside training courses or to train them within the firm.

In all the 326 interviews held, the word 'risk' was mentioned barely half a dozen times. One time when it did occur was during the reply of a divisional managing director to a question on management.

He explained that his company believed in decentralisation and added:

'It's founded on a belief in people. This may sound stupid but we give people amazing latitude, and we very seldom give them direct instructions. They're youngish people. We take a risk on them because inevitably they are not universal geniuses.'

This firm has grown steadily during the last five years and its executives argue that one cause is the policy of creating divisions, even quite small ones, for different product lines and letting young men manage them. One executive went so far as to say that one of the company's problems was how to slow down its growth rate.

Besides giving young executives responsibility, delegation allows senior management time to think about the major problems of the company and concentrate on future policy. Several senior executives complained to the interviewers that they were immersed in routine detail and did not have sufficient time to think about broader issues. Yet only one chief executive stressed the implication of this for management structure:

'I think it is very important for the managing director to try and keep his fingers out of the day-to-day pies so that he can sit back and see things a little clearly and not get mixed up between the trees and the forest.'

Safeguarding Succession

It has been pointed out that the object of a management development scheme is both to strengthen present management and to provide for its succession by high-calibre executives in the future. The managing director of a large machine tool firm mentioned the consequences of failing to provide for this:

'This company has recently lost three of its senior executives and consequently there has been a gap in management—in adequate follow-up facilities.'

To prevent the recurrence of insufficient staffing, the managing director intended to institute a different organisational structure for the company which would allow for more training of individual executives but:

'In the meantime, we've got to rely upon the momentum of the company as a whole to carry us along.'

Yet the option of outside recruitment is always available. Not even the most thorough forecasts and comprehensive plans can guarantee that a firm will be adequately staffed in the longer-term future. A firm may expand faster than planned; it may wish to undertake a new product line; or it may need rapidly to raise the calibre of management. In all these instances additional executives may have to be appointed from outside the firm. On the subject of outside recruitment, however, several managing directors showed considerable reluctance to seek top quality managers. A director of a small machine tool firm spoke for many executives when he explained that he would regard it as unethical for his firm to make the first approach to an outside manager:

'If he approached us, we should have no difficulty at all in fitting him into our organisation, but it would certainly not be by any approach made by us directly while he was fully employed by the other company. We shouldn't like them to do it to us, and therefore we shouldn't do it to them.'

The compromise between no outside recruitment and direct bidding which was followed by a number of firms was to engage a firm of consultants and ask them to find a suitable candidate. A director of a medium-sized domestic appliance company said the firm favoured internal promotion but failing that their chosen method was:

'. . . getting the best possible person from outside, employing outside specialists in the field to do so, but not losing sight of the fact that that person has got to work with your existing staff and therefore you may have to lose something in the way of technical ability to give you the ability to knit the new and the old staff together.'

If succession from within the firm does not result from a policy of long-term management development, outside appointments may become necessary at the highest level. The most drastic example of this was found in a subsidiary company of a large group where a new managing director had been appointed some years ago to combat what was described 'as a million pound loss situation'. By bringing in a new management team the company was in the managing director's words 'cleaned and refurbished' and its commercial situation greatly improved.

Many firms, however, dilute their efficiency because they are not prepared to move out of positions of authority executives who have not fulfilled their early promise or who were wrongly appointed in the first place. The research team heard several cases of change being retarded because a chief executive did not wish to hurt the feelings of a senior colleague. An executive who had recently joined a light-engineering firm explained why a research and development department could not be quickly established:

'We shall have one I think, but old ideas die very slowly and very hard. Relationships in this firm have always been very personal. Attempts have always been made to avoid hurting people and in any way cutting across them and therefore, if you've got that sort of atmosphere, it is obviously not very wise to adopt sweeping changes.'

He went on to add that if a company 'has got time at its disposal' then the gradual approach was best. But the pace of technical change is such that, for most companies, gradualism of this sort is a luxury they can ill afford.

It was the managing director of a large shipyard who made the most forceful and comprehensive statement on management development, emphasising not only the need to ensure succession but also the importance of educating managers within the company and outside it, and of giving them a broad understanding of management by making them work on different jobs:

'We make managers say, "Right, who's going to replace you?" and every now and then we pick somebody out of management and use them for some other purpose. We might send them on a course. We might use them for some things other people would employ a consultant for—in other words to do a study. They might do a study for me. I might take one of the managers and put him on a study of material handling costs. Managers turn round and say, "Here, you can't take away so-and-so, he's the only man I've got." Our attitude is, "Well, get somebody else bloody quick", and they don't get caught twice. They've got some idea of where to get people. I think this is one of the great mistakes of industry in the past that we have had no proper management promotion scheme or management development training scheme. I personally believe very strongly in continuity of education. Most of our education goes on within the firms but people should be chucked out. They should be made to work in other firms—in other industries—sent on courses, given all sorts of assignments to broaden and widen them.'

The Urge to Grow

It may be concluded that a well-organised scheme of management development is not only valuable but, for a firm that has grown beyond a certain point, a necessary condition of efficiency. But it is not, of course, a sufficient condition of successful and expansionary management. Several of the chief executives made this point to the research team when they mentioned the word 'entrepreneurship'. One director drew on the history of his own very large company:

'Mr X who started the company was a great entrepreneur. He was always prepared to take gambles. He was always prepared to expand if he could, and therefore there was a natural tendency for the business to expand while he was in control of it. Later Y Z took us over after the war and were always willing to support expansion schemes with the necessary finance provided they were soundly based, but whether a scheme is put up or not is dependent on the man you've got in control here. Now there have been at times conservative spirits and at times adventurous spirits but on the whole adventurous spirits, particularly the present managing director. I think if one had somebody in control of this business whose attitude of mind was, "Well, we're doing very nicely, thank you. I don't know why I've got to worry my guts about all these ventures. Why should I try and increase my sales by spending a lot of money overseas?", then we wouldn't have grown. I think basically growth lies in the men.'

Amongst the firms visited were several in which this vitality, or adventurousness, as it is described in the above quotation, was reflected in a high rate of expansion. There were likewise firms that lacked such adventurousness and were not interested in physical expansion. A managing director of a small wool textile firm explained:

'I am not personally ambitious. I am quite prepared not to drift through life, but I would rather run a small efficient unit than try and run a large efficient unit.'

In contrast the managing director of one medium-sized firm in the domestic appliance industry described how his firm reacted to a lengthening order-book:

'You've sweated your guts out to expand and you've advertised and there's nothing more gruelling than to find somebody writing in and saying, "I ordered your product six, eight, ten weeks ago and I'm still waiting. Why haven't I got it. Why do you advertise? We'll go to one of your competitors." Of course that's such a red rag to a bull to us—as it should be to any progressive company—that, if needs

be, we'd all come in here on Sunday and work the machines ourselves.'

The chief executive added later that reference to Sunday working
was a slight exaggeration. It had been done in the early days of the
company but was no longer practised.

A further example of vitality in management is evident in the
recent history of a large engineering company. Started as a private
company in the middle of the last century the firm until recently
manufactured its products in its original works which over the years
had become surrounded by a large town. Shortly after the war the
managing director decided to move his factory:

'We could have continued in our own works with a very comfortable
profit and money in the bank—we should have gone on until we
gradually fell out of the market because we couldn't increase our
turnover substantially there [in the old works] and we certainly
couldn't build the range of machines we must have. It was a challenge
to a firm which was then in its second generation and might have
died.'

One of the executives interviewed, who had recently joined the firm,
thought that:

'. . . a pretty courageous decision was made that this company is
going to go places.'

The Growth of Professionalism

While vitality or entrepreneurship alone may be enough to expand
the small firm, however, it will not be enough to maintain the
momentum of expansion once the firm has grown beyond a certain
point. As a firm grows, the danger of depending on one man and the
necessity of introducing professionally qualified management increase. Executives in several of the medium-sized firms referred to
the growth of professionalism. One managing director of a small
wool textile firm explained the absence of professional managers in
the Scottish tweed industry as being due to:

'. . . the fact that we're suffering from the end of a large family era,
when it was a question of son succeeding father, whether he was
particularly good at the job or not. But my feeling is we've got to
bring new people in and pay them.'

Another chief executive, in a medium-sized machine tool firm, referred to the existence of operating manuals and described recent changes in his firm:

'As far as we are concerned, we are going through a transition period, where there has been considerable change of management, of ideas, of continuity. We're moving from the traditional family-controlled firm with rather old-fashioned ideas on payments and methods and so on into a professionally controlled engineering company.'

The change-over to modern professional management is a crucial phase in the development of a firm. Without it further growth is unlikely. With it and with the spirit of adventurousness, the chances of expansion are at their best. Thus it may be doubted whether there was much prospect for the sustained growth of a large shipyard unless its managing director were to alter his belief that success in shipbuilding depended on the avoidance of modern management practices:

'In particular you've got to be right on labour, and you've got to be right in knowing what you can leave out. In most businesses you make your money out of what you can leave out or don't have or don't do. Any fool can have an enormous top-heavy staff, complicated planning department, personnel department, progress chasing and all the rest of it. But only a clever man can achieve the same results without the need for these departments. It is our constant problem in shipbuilding that we've got to keep our overheads very low to survive, and at the same time we have got to have a really efficient labour force—a labour force which can do its own work simplification and is interested in progressing and programming the work.'

Yet some chief executives who were running companies with less than 500 employees had already introduced the majority of recognised management techniques. The managing director of a small wool textile firm told the research team that his firm had decided to adopt 'modern management practices' after it had been exhaustively surveyed by management consultants. Their report was handed to the firm in the early 1950s and it had taken the firm several years to introduce their recommendations. Now the situation could be summarised as:

'You know this phrase, "modern management practice", which people put in inverted commas. Well, we attempt to put a great deal of it into practice here. We have fairly elaborate management procedures, and managerial organisation generally, to try and cope with every aspect of management, and not do some things well and neglect others. The aim here is to have an organisation, a management organisation, which does enable every aspect of the business to be catered for properly—financially, personnel-wise, technically, development-and-research-wise and so on. Let's face it. In many industries some of these aspects are neglected. Some are looked after and some are neglected. We try to cover them all.'

Use of Management Consultants

Improving the quality of management by training and development schemes is essential for the long-term health of the British economy. But it is necessarily a process that takes a considerable time, and the use of management consultants, while in no way removing the need for long-term development and training, can introduce modern management techniques that will bring important increases in productivity in a comparatively short time. In the great majority of firms visited, management consultants had played a big part in introducing such techniques. Forty out of the forty-seven firms visited had at some recent period employed consultants. Often their visits had prompted the firm to start its own work study department and sometimes one of the consultants had stayed with a firm and become one of its senior executives. The impact which consultants can have on a firm and particularly on an old-established firm is considerable. The next three quotations from different firms tell their own story.

The chief accountant of one medium-sized domestic appliance firm credited consultants with his firm's dramatic rise in productivity:

'We were attempting in various ways to put in bonus schemes or piece-work schemes, and they were just not satisfactory. And we knew, going back to the profit and loss account, that something had to be done about it. So we decided to get hold of X. We got them to do the whole factory. They certainly increased our productivity by a vast amount—as I told you earlier, 33·3 per cent or 40 per cent. Before we got X, we were basically on ordinary time work—day work with no really effective bonuses.'

The works director of a wool textile mill put the impact of consultants into historical perspective when he commented:

'Most of this improvement in productivity is attributable to the management consultants. If you have old-fashioned firms that have been rolling along for a century and a bit and you fetch management consultants in, they can make one hell of an impression. But the problem comes when you then try and bring them back for a second go, because they've done most of the easy and obvious things and then you fetch them back for individual problems . . . but the result of having them in obviously made us much more work study conscious. We've now set up a proper work study section of our own.'

The managing director of a machine tool firm was briefer in his comments but no less emphatic:

'Consultants' terms of reference were to review and improve on our costing system, our incentive system and our production control system, which is very all-embracing, and all of which they did. We're now at least up to modern standards, I think, having continually improved on what they did. I think it would be true to say that management techniques advanced ten years, maybe twenty years.'

To have ignored consultants or to have used them too narrowly can be regarded as a sleepy characteristic. Most frequently the firms visited which had not employed consultants were largely dominated by one executive. One managing director had very strong feelings about consultants:

'No, we never have employed them. We abhor them. I think they are rather the parasite type of individual who feeds on particular ideas which are in the organisation and which possibly haven't been vented to higher levels. I think one should encourage one's own organisation to vent its problems and to put forward ideas and suggestions rather than put outsiders in.'

Although this was the view of a small minority, many firms had limited consultants' terms of reference to a specific purpose, such as introducing work study and/or working out an incentive payment scheme based on it. The managing director of an engineering firm said:

'We brought consultants in for two things—first of all to organise the transfer of production from X to Y and to lay out the shops here for us, which they did most efficiently. Then I employed them to reorganise the spares department but not actually to organise the management, shall we say, because I reckon that I know a little bit about it. I mean I've done thirty-five years in the army.'

In only two of the firms visited were management consultants given a completely free hand to look at all parts of the firm's business. The managing director (the only one) who had been appointed as a result of consultants' recommendations was naturally enough not unenthusiastic about their efforts:

'When the consultants came in, in 1957, they had a completely free hand. They produced a report first of all on the whole company. Then they broke it down into various categories of management, covering all kinds of things—costing, production control, design, and development, and the like.'

Most of the firms quoted from had not invited consultants to investigate them before 1950. Some of them were evidently satisfied that a further visit was unnecessary but others, like one firm in the electronics industry, saw work for consultants stretching many years ahead:

'You've probably heard that we're just bringing into use a new punch-card installation, which will deal not only with accountancy but, more importantly, with our planning and production control, stores and so on. I have sought the advice of various specialised consultants on this—I've got in mind that probably for the next five years, maybe for the next fifty years, we'll always have in this place somewhere a consultant looking at one particular part and trying to improve it.'

Another service which firms can use to help improve their management is provided by the Centre for Interfirm Comparison (CIFC). The Centre is an offshoot of the British Institute of Management (BIM) employing a small body of accountants who specialise in preparing operating ratios for firms in the same industry. All firms which wish to have their results subjected to comparisons are requested to supply figures based on up-to-date valuations, and sales and cost figures broken down in far more detail than any company has to publish. After this information has been processed by the Centre the firm will receive back its results and those of all the other participating firms, about ten to fifteen generally, expressed anonymously in operating ratios. The key ratio chosen by Interfirm Comparison is return on capital, which expresses the relationship between 'true' profit and the total assets of the company. In addition the Centre supplies secondary and tertiary ratios which show operating results of other parts of the company. So far about 1,100 companies from forty industries and trades have used the Centre[1] and the most significant aspect of the results has been the extraordinarily wide discrepancies revealed in the primary ratio. In footwear firms using the service the range has been from $0 \cdot 2$ per cent to $38 \cdot 6$ per cent, in food firms from 6 per cent to 29 per cent, and in engineering firms from $2 \cdot 5$ per cent to $17 \cdot 3$ per cent.

Examination of operating ratios can show up the weaknesses in a firm's operations as compared with its competitors, and the use of Interfirm Comparison may be regarded as a thrusting characteristic. All firms were asked what their attitude was towards Interfirm Comparison, and the research team found a much keener appreciation of its potential value in the electronics industry than in other industries.

Conclusion

Improvement of the quality of management is fundamental to the growth of productivity. In this process two of the major factors, discussed in this chapter, are the systematic development of junior and middle managers and the introduction of modern management techniques, often undertaken with the help of management consultants. The following chapters consider in some detail the application of such techniques in various sectors of management.

[1] Communication from CIFC. Position as at 11 June 1964.

CHAPTER 5

MANAGERS AND MEN

The efficiency of a firm is a function of the people employed in it and their performance must therefore be a prime concern of management. This chapter accordingly considers, first, labour relations in general and, secondly, the recruitment and training of workers in particular.

The Quality of Labour Relations

The quality of labour relations is a crucial factor in determining the profitability of a firm's operations and the part which it can play in helping to increase the growth rate of the economy. This is not simply a question of the number of strikes: contrary to the picture given by the press, the time lost through strikes in British industry is not very substantial. Far more important are the brake on progress caused by labour resistance to changes in the accustomed production methods and the wastage caused by absenteeism, high labour turnover and shoddy workmanship. These factors rarely make news but they have an incalculable effect in inhibiting productivity. Overcoming the workers' fears of the effect of improved methods of production is, therefore, a basic condition of good management directed towards efficiency and growth.

It is clear that the change in the industrial environment since the 1930s has brought a completely new dimension to labour relations to which some people on both sides of industry have never become accustomed:

'Occasionally one thinks that it might be a quite good idea after all if there was some more unemployment so that people would realise that jobs are at a premium and hence work harder, and there would not be so many demarcation problems, restrictive practices, go-slows, stoppages.'

This is matched by the convener of a shipyard who said:

'The good old British working-men as usual stand by each other.

Whether they are right or wrong, they always seem to take sides against management.'

A better appreciation of the situation as it now is came from the managing director of a medium-sized mill:

'I think one of the first essentials of a good manager today is his ability to get on with people. Before the war I think you would have taken on a man as manager purely on his technical credentials. These are still most essential, but I think coming well up on the list now is the ability to get on with people and to have an approach to employees quite different to what it used to be. After all, you used to manage by the big stick. The threat of sacking, unemployment, what have you—this has not been so since the war and you have had to have an absolutely new approach.'

Full employment is one of the political facts of post-war life, and no firm can realistically base its labour relations on any other assumption. But the labour problems which firms encounter do not depend solely on the national employment situation. Firms with a largely female labour force or comparatively few trade union members will, for instance, rarely suffer a strike, but they may find that labour turnover proves a serious problem.[1] On the other hand, firms in areas with a long history of bad labour relations, facing militant trade unions, may find that industrial conflict frequently leads to strikes or threats of strikes. It is this wide difference which makes it difficult to take any one particular definition of good labour relations and apply it generally. This in part explains the variety of definitions that were given in answer to the question of what was understood by good labour relations.

In a large shipyard:

'Strikes are probably the easiest way of measuring labour relations.'

In a very large electronics firm:

Interviewer: 'How do you convince me that you have good labour relations?'
'We have never had a stoppage.'

[1] The effect of this on costs can be gauged from the fact that one large woollen firm has to train its operatives for five weeks and has an annual turnover of 47 per cent.

C

In a large machine tool firm:

'As far as we are concerned, good labour relations means no trouble.'

In a very large firm which had a small craft union membership:

'I think the measure of labour relations is labour turnover.'

In a medium-sized machine tool firm:

'Good labour relations means having more initiative than the local Communist Party.'

These descriptions of good labour relations are extremely partial. Many managers, like the personnel manager of a large earthmoving equipment firm, went much further in explaining their own conception of good labour relations:

'I think that in good labour relations inside the company the major thing is access, approach to settle shop-floor problems. If a man has got a problem on the shop floor, you have got to have some machinery to settle that problem. By and large, I think the main thing is the question of consultation and that the man should know that, if he doesn't get satisfaction to suit him at a certain level, he has a right to appeal somewhere else.'

The same point was made by a trade unionist in a small electronics firm:

'It's a tricky phrase—"good labour relations". I think it's trust, just trust . . . a manager trusting the workers and the worker just trusting the management to know that they are not out to catch you and to get every ounce they can out of you. I think that's the biggest thing, just mutual trust in each other.'

Clearly the above answers attempt to deal with the question of labour relations at a rather deeper level than the earlier ones, but even here the tone tends to be superficial compared, for instance, with the description given by the personnel manager of a very large electronics firm who said:

'Basically, the whole of our personnel policy is aimed at making the conditions under which individuals will give their best.'

A textbook definition of labour relations, with emphasis on the objective of maximising productivity and hence of growth, was given by the personnel manager of an electronics firm:

'Good labour relations are a set of employment circumstances where the maximum productivity is achieved with a maximum profitability, and in the course of achieving both these targets, a friendly cordial relationship exists in the day-to-day working conditions of all levels throughout the organisation.'

It was significant that a knowledge of the textbooks was accompanied in this firm by a most constructive labour policy.

In spite of the fact that certain firms may have greater, or at least more obvious, difficulties in improving their labour relations, it is clear that, whatever the situation, there are more and less effective ways of approaching it. In dealing with a trade union noted for its militancy, for instance, the following two quotations from large firms in one industry present an interesting contrast. This is especially so, as the first comes from a region of traditionally less militant unionism than the second:

'I feel sure that, however good a management may be, they will have an uphill struggle for many years to get reasonable agreements with the X Union—which is probably one of the worst unions.'

'We would like to understand the X Union, what makes them tick, what's their history, what has been their approach on demarcation and so on. The X Union are very militant and active here. The things that they are asking for are reasonable. They want more money. They want more work. They want their group to have more duties so that their union can become larger. But those things are not particularly unique.'

It seems reasonable to assume that it is possible for management to act constructively in any set of historical circumstances in order to limit the degree to which bad labour relations can be a barrier to improving productive efficiency. To do this, however, the causes of conflict in industrial relations have to be examined.

Wages and Other Incentives

The most obvious sphere of conflict between the two sides of industry is that of wages. The workers' wages are costs to management, and clearly there is every incentive for workers to try to increase their earnings, while at the same time managements are trying to cut their costs. There is a widespread feeling among managers that the question of wages and financial incentives is the only really important one in industrial relations.

Asked what he thought made men work, the works director of a small machine tool firm said:

'Hunger, of course! That's the only reason a bloke went out with a club and hit a rabbit and put it in a pot. He's got to eat.'

The personnel manager of a medium-sized domestic appliance firm said:

'The pay-packet, of course! There's no question about that. The men only work for what they can get. I am being sincere when I say this—they work for the pay-packet. . . . My experience of shop-floor workers is that there is too large a percentage who don't give their best unless they are being entreated to do so.'

And the managing director of a very large shipyard replied:

'A man is only interested in his pay-packet. He will tell you that without any hesitation. He tells me that over the conference table.'

The managing director of another shipyard said:

'I think that the reason why men no longer work hard is that they have no incentive. Until that is returned I don't think that the country will be put right. There is no argument about it in my view, that some incentive scheme is going to be the saving grace in this industry. But exactly how to apply it is very difficult to say. Piecework as we knew it thirty or forty years ago seems to be impossible nowadays, but I feel certain that there has got to be some equivalent established so that a man has got to produce something for what he earns.'

Wages are, of course, very important, but they are not the whole story. A very different view of their relative importance was put by other managers, especially by those working in the newer industries, such as electronics. This was shown by the works manager of a large electronics firm:

'I think that most of these financial incentives are just utter nonsense. Of course finance affects people. It affects all of us, because we would like to have more money. But, undoubtedly, beyond a certain level, what makes these people tick is a feeling that they are wanted, that they are creating something and that if they were not here you would miss them. Now this is the basis of my policy and I achieve some fantastic gains in productivity. . . . We cut out piece-work—we cut out all forms of these alleged incentives—because I wanted a situation here where I could say to people, "Right, lads, we've improved by 5 per cent! What can we do to improve by 10 per cent?" Under any sort of system that is tied to directly measured financial reward of the piece-work class, the moment you start saying, "How can we improve?", you get this fear of rate cutting. I want to be free of this. I want to be able to say without any chance of being misunderstood, "All right, Jean, you have done this thing in thirty minutes. Let's see if you can do it in twenty-five." I can only do this if Jean is pretty happy with the job she's got.'

The managing director of another, smaller, electronics firm said:

'You find in mass-production factories where there is an incentive payment system that, if the men make a mistake, they will try and cover it up and pass it through. They don't really feel conscience-stricken, because there is an inspector at the end of the line who may or may not get it. Usually he does get it. The customer does not see the problem—the chap's made his rate on the line but the factory's got a piece of dud gear. We don't have that here.'

A trade unionist of another firm whose management was against incentive payment systems explained how their absence affected his attitude:

'You don't get a bonus here as an incentive for working hard. But at the same time there is a feeling that, "I wouldn't like to let the foreman down", that probably makes you work harder and more accurately.'

A works manager, in making a detailed and intelligent analysis of workers' motivation, did not mention financial incentives at all:

'I'm very interested in what makes people tick. . . . Why is it that when a person pursues his hobbies, he throws everything he's got into it and, when he does his work, he tells you he's working very hard and tries to give that impression—but he's so far away from fatigue that it's just not true? The man is going at about one-tenth of the pace he could go at. . . . I started experimenting. I personally directed an experimental line over a period of two years. I learned to live with the people and to try and understand them. In the first six weeks of running the line I got all the conventional answers. They referred to draughts in the corridor and smells in the lavatory, but they're not really the things that affect these people at all. When they get to know you better and they know you're an ordinary sort of guy who has much the same weaknesses and emotions as they have and makes just about as many mistakes, they start to be much more frank about the things that go wrong, the things they like and don't like—and it's surprising how many of them you can do something about. Some you can't, but a lot you can. The environmental conditions in which they work, the attitude of people who serve them, the storekeepers who supply them, the people who buy materials and tools for them, the colour on the walls—all these things have much more effect than people think. No girl in a factory will ever tell you that she'll work better if you paint the wall green—because she doesn't know—but she's affected by her environment to a far greater degree than she realises, or most managements realise.'

Staff and Workers

The interviews showed that one of the non-wage factors that looms large in workers' minds is the difference in treatment between staff and shop floor. Although the earnings differential between the two has narrowed since the war, the same is not generally true for fringe benefits. This was shown clearly for one small firm in the machine tool industry by the works director:

'We have no pension scheme for the men on the shop floor, at least no official one. We do supply our old servants with a little pension. This is not in any terms of employment or anything like that. We don't do anything about sickness pay, except we have helped our old faithful servants. Like the lord of the manor used to look after his household. That has been the principle. . . . For the staff we have a proper pension scheme.'

This distinction between staff and shop-floor workers was found in the majority of the firms visited but the reasons given were never very convincing. The works manager of a small earthmoving equipment firm believed 'that people working more with their eyes and their head probably want a little bit of differentiation', while the managing director of a very large shipyard based his reasoning on the 'fact' that 'everyone in the Civil Service takes eleven weeks holiday and puts it down to sickness' and so 'you can't rely on human nature'. The present bargaining system by which many firms negotiate with trade unions through their employers' organisation was also given as a reason why these differentials persisted in their firms. As the works manager of a machine tool firm said:

'Holiday pay is negotiated at district level and we have no individual authority to do anything else but follow that.'

The welfare officer of a woollen mill said:

'I don't know why girls on the shop floor are not paid if they're sick. It's one of those things.'

The assistant managing director of a heavy-engineering firm said:

'I think there ought to be more equal treatment all round, but I think it will take a hell of a long time to do it. I must admit I haven't thought about it particularly.'

It was even suggested, occasionally, that the existing differentials between staff and workers on the shop floor were not large enough. The works manager of an earthmoving equipment firm said:

'Before the war the staff had two weeks holiday a year. The other fellow had a week that he couldn't afford to do anything with. He now gets a fortnight that he can probably afford to do something with. I think this is one of the things in engineering that's got to be looked at. We've got to try and bring back the differentials.'

This distinction was frequently resented by the men on the shop floor, as the following quotations from conveners of firms in three different industries show:

'Differentials are one of the big faults with this firm in my opinion and I'm speaking now on behalf of the general opinion on the shop floor. There's no need for them. We're all employees of the same man and therefore we should all be classed the same.'

'You always get that undercurrent that the staff man is treated better than the man on the shop floor. Take the case of a junior coming into the office and after about six or eight months he'll probably fall sick. He gets his full pay. Yet a man in the shop with twelve or thirteen years' service gets no sick pay whatsoever.'

'You've got a magnificent suite of offices just put up over there and you've got the most prehistoric lavatories you've ever seen in your life here in the factory. There isn't a roof on top of part of them. When it rains you've got to tuck your sleeves into your overall pockets otherwise you're going to get them wet. That's something that's very important to me from the point of view of hygiene and comfort, but it's also important from the point of view of labour relations. People say, "Look at this lot", and then they look at what they've put up across the road. The same could apply to the washing facilities. In their day they were very good—you know, a long trough with a pedal that operated hot water. Now it's so dilapidated that if you put your foot on the pedal you get water squirting up your trouser leg.'

Not all managements wished to perpetuate these differentials, which clearly cause much resentment and reduce the prospects of co-operation between the two sides of industry. The personnel manager of one large machine tool firm explained his firm's policy:

'We want to have more equality. That's why we bring in half-pay for sickness. We have all sorts of schemes—a trust fund, the pension schemes, and so forth. As far as possible we try and treat the works and the staff on a very similar basis.'

A distinction between staff and shop floor over redundancy was a particularly sore point for many shop-floor representatives, like the convener of a very large machine tool firm:

'You always hear, "We're all in this together", but I have a loaded question to ask our management on this. They say we are all in it together, but in times of redundancy when our work-people have to go down the drive, how many supervisors, how many junior executives go with them? None!'

Redundancy and Demarcation

The interviews confirmed that one of the most important aspects of labour relations, other than wages, was the question of job security. Thus, the convener of a large Scottish shipyard said that security 'was the one thing the working man wants' and went on to explain that in its absence he 'can only plan from week to week because he doesn't know how long he's going to be kept on in his job'. This problem is felt especially in depressed areas and is perhaps most severe in the shipbuilding industry, where management accepts it as a perfectly reasonable and normal thing to sack a proportion of its labour force at very short notice, when work declines, in the full expectation of being able to take more men on when work picks up. The idea of planned, phased redundancy seems foreign to firms in the industry. This was illustrated by the general manager of one of the shipyards visited:

'In this region there tends to be a floating labour force. Every yard has a nucleus of regulars who stay with it for years and years, but, being such a confined area, with shipyards a few miles from each other, there is a floating group who travel from yard to yard, depending on the availability of work.'

None of the shipyards visited gave more than two or three days' notice to their men.[1] Many gave less than this:

'We only give a man a few hours' notice. On the other hand if we did give a man more notice—if we gave him a week's notice as they do in engineering—it is generally accepted that you wouldn't get production from that man during that week of warning. But I must admit that it gives them a sense of insecurity when they are in that position.'

Only a day's notice was given in one of the yards visited:

'We do warn the work-people that there will be some redundancy in this department or that department. Obviously we don't name the people two or three days ahead. They are normally named only twenty-four hours ahead, but we give as much warning as we possibly can—two or three days.'

The casual attitude held towards shipyard labour is shown clearly in one yard where a manager treated workers much as though they were an expendable raw material:

'As work gets slack and we don't need men, they're paid up and, as work comes again, we take them on. It's as simple as that. But there's no bad blood. We pay a lot off and start a lot.'

The same management attitude towards redundancy is often the expression of an industrial philosophy. Some managers, like a director of a Scottish shipyard, believed that the threat of redundancy is an aid to efficiency:

'I don't think it would help production one iota if we guaranteed a man employment for six months. In fact, I'm old-fashioned enough

---

[1] The interviews were conducted before the Contracts of Employment Act, 1963, came into force. However, since this applies only to workers with more than six months' service, it is unlikely to make any great difference to an industry like shipbuilding with a considerable floating labour force. In any case, the attitudes formed before 1964 will take many years to disappear.

to say that it would probably be the reverse. I think it's been proved over the years that when things become a little tight and men can see that certain people are going to lose their jobs, there is a tendency to increase production generally.'

This view was, hardly surprisingly, not shared by the workers in many shipyards. An interesting sidelight on the above quotations comes from the convener of a shipyard where this kind of redundancy policy had been carried out:

'Naturally, if there's no orders in hand, a man says to himself, "If I work hard what's going to be the result? I'm going to work myself on to the Labour Exchange two months, maybe four months, sooner than I would if I could just carry on and work at the speed I'm doing." '

The state of mind created by insecurity among workers in shipyards is also well illustrated by the following quotation from another convener:

'You don't get any notice. There's a rumour going about the yard now that there's a pay-off tonight. So far nobody knows, but there's a very strong rumour that there's a pay-off tonight in the yard. It may only be a rumour. These things happen.'

The interviews with conveners showed that short periods of notice are harmful to productivity and make any sort of co-operation between management and labour extremely difficult. A further consequence of fear of redundancy that is most damaging to the growth of productivity is the way in which it encourages demarcation.

The convener of one shipyard explained why he believed there were no demarcation disputes in naval dockyards:

'. . . because they're all established workers. It doesn't make any difference whether you are working a caulking machine or a riveting machine—you'll get your wages. There'll not be any redundancy.'

Where workers were not established, however, the situation was very different:

'The carpenters, for instance, say, "Well, we'll shove up bulkheads." Then the platers say, "If we allow this, this is the thin edge of the wedge, and the next thing is that they'll be able to sack off so many platers and employ more carpenters." '

For management, on the other hand, as one shipyard manager explained, demarcation leads to an uneconomic use of labour and therefore higher costs:

'One thing that we feel could be much more economic to the company, and with no harm to the labour force, is the trade or workpeople doing jobs like tack welding . . . a tack welder at the moment is only allowed to do tack welding and many minutes of every hour he is doing nothing. We'd like him to have more freedom within that job.'

Demarcation can not only lead to an inflexible use of labour but can absorb, as one director explained, a great deal of managerial time and lead to strikes:

'We've spent hours, days, weeks of my time seeing my managers and sorting out demarcation problems within the Boilermakers themselves. . . . We've had strikes here because caulkers and platers, who are both in the Boilermakers' Society, don't agree and one side walks out. Now, it doesn't matter whose side I agree with I'm bound to be wrong. I offend somebody. This hasn't happened once—it's happened quite a few times. How management can get on and build ships under these conditions, I really don't know!'

Lack of security not only helps to explain the presence of demarcation but goes some way towards accounting for the resistance of workers to change. Attempts to establish work measurement meet with strong union opposition even when it is unlikely to lead to redundancy. The works manager of an earthmoving equipment firm remarked that, if he sent a man into the shops with a stop-watch to check on times, 'the place would shut down', and, as might be expected, many of the shipyards experienced the same sort of union pressure.

It is clear that the conservatism of many workers presents a major obstacle to growth. Nevertheless, it is a sleepy attitude for management to do nothing positive, but merely to blame the unions, like the managing director of one shipyard who restricted his answer to a statement of the problem:

'I take the view quite strongly that the trade unions instead of helping are generally hindering production. Whilst they're not openly causing strikes, they're forcing their members to introduce all kinds of restrictive practices. . . . Now that is clearly affecting the rate of growth.'

On the other hand, the interviews give numerous examples of better results being achieved by managements that take their responsibilities seriously in respect of matters such as demarcation and redundancy. That such an attitude is effective, even under unfavourable conditions, is shown by the following quotation taken from the shipbuilding industry in the north-east, where the unions are militant and there is a history of poor labour relations. One managing director explained:

'For weeks and weeks before we went into production on the new system, we held meetings with the unions. Not just the men in the yard but with their district delegates. The breakdown in the system of building a ship was put on to the table. There was a complete schedule drawn up with proposals of what we thought would be the right way to do it to keep the men employed. It was fully discussed between the men, the delegates and management. There was a little bit of argument here and there, but eventually a complete demarcation schedule was drawn up and agreed by the unions for the first two ships to see how it worked—on the understanding that there would be no stoppage, no matter what it was, on these first two ships. At the end of the first two ships we held a further meeting and said, "Right, now then, are there any points to raise on this demarcation?" There were two points raised. . . . It was settled within about an hour. There was no further argument about it. The unions agreed to sign this as the demarcation agreement for this yard. The unions were given every chance to have their say before the job was tackled.'

In some firms, managers have accepted the principle that their responsibilities to their workers do not apply merely to wages and conditions of work, but also include the provision of a secure job. Further, they agree that where economic conditions make such a provision impossible or undesirable, the worker concerned deserves compensation from his employer as of right. This comes through clearly in the following quotation from the personnel manager of a small woollen mill:

'The last man we had to declare redundant had three years' service and we gave him £70. He left here on Friday and started a new job on the Monday, but we were quite happy about this. In fact if we had taken the man back the following week, he would still have had his £70, but this would be bad management and would be the price we would have to pay.'

Such attitudes are found most frequently in new and heavily capitalised industries. The following quotation comes from the personnel manager of a very large industrial firm:

'It's not quite the same thing in handling one or two individuals as it is in shutting a factory. Shutting a factory is a bigger operation. Then, we aim to tell all concerned about six or eight months beforehand. It's a highly thought-out operation, hour by hour. Every man gets a letter telling him just what his treatment will be. We have a fairly generous scale of redundancy payments and they're told what they'll get, providing they'll stay as long as is needed. We aim to allow them to leave and get a job within the last two or three months. . . . When we shut the factory the top man, aged fifty-seven, got £850 and went straight to another job. I don't think the money is really wasted. Everything went off very smoothly and happily and it left a good impression, and really the global total of money wasn't big. In the case of individual redundancies, we give a minimum of two months' notice to anyone. Payment is based on salary, length of service and age.'

Joint Consultation

A third source of conflict other than wages is the feeling of workers that they do not know what is going on. The greater the extent of communication between management and labour the less likely it is that the latter will resist changes in techniques. The personnel manager of a small woollen mill explained how poor communications can lead to mistrust:

'When the management of a company plan to do something which is a change from the normal routine—if they do not explain to people carefully and in terms they can understand what they are going to do and why they are going to do it and what the effect will be, then people will arrive at their own conclusions, which are likely to be the wrong ones.'

If there is to be an organised attempt by management to keep labour informed of the progress of the firm, some machinery has to be devised for this purpose. The usual form which this takes is the creation of a works council. This is a committee where representatives of management and labour discuss matters of interest and concern. In this way, communications can be improved so that any factor likely to embitter relations between labour and management can be brought out into the open and examined. It cannot be expected that such councils will overcome immediately suspicion which may have been breeding for generations. A convener of an engineering firm in Scotland showed his basic scepticism:

'We know what's going on. Whether they're telling us the full story or not, I can't say. Whether they're telling the truth—you don't know.'

The attitude of a shipyard convener was similar:

'If they want to take us into their confidence and give us the whole picture, we say that they've got to give it to us in black and white. It's no good a gentleman sitting there and telling us that everything is bad and gloomy, that men are being paid off, and then a week later, as happened on one occasion, a 25 per cent dividend is announced. It doesn't lead to good feeling between management and men. I would say yes, if they want us wholly in the picture, and that's a thing they're always talking about, putting us in the picture. Management only shows half the lantern slide, they don't show us the other half.'

Pressure for joint consultation does, however, exist in many firms. The convener of one machine tool firm said:

'I would like to have more information on the future plans of the firm. For instance, they have just bought a factory and we believe that some of our ideas could have been used. . . . But the management made their plans and didn't brook any interference.'

The effect of such frustrations on labour/management relations is vividly illustrated by the convener of a small engineering factory who said:

'You can talk [to management] till you're blue in the face. Higher management just don't care. We've reached a stage where the members [of the union] are virtually on the point of giving up. . . . We haven't got a social club as such. There's an annual fraternisation at a bowling club dance. It's known as the "creepers' ball".'

Management sometimes appears to be deliberately obstructive in order to ensure that joint consultation does not take place. The convener of a shipyard described what happened after his last meeting with the managing director of the yard:

'Prior to the New Year we had a meeting with the managing director and we asked about the future of this yard. He could give us no hope whatever. He just said that he was living in hopes. He was estimating for orders all over the world, but he promised us faithfully that at the end of February he would call us all together again to give us a further insight into what was happening. Months later we're still waiting for that meeting. When I asked the shipyard manager what progress had been made in getting the men together, he gives them some sort of answer. He says, "I'm sorry, but I have nothing to do with it." When I told him there was demand from my members for me to see the managing director he says, "You're not going to see him." There's nobody sees the managing director at the men's request. The only time you see him is at his request. Why does the managing director promise us that he would give us a report on progress and still not carry out that promise? Every month I get this thrown at me by my members and what answer can I give them? I can't tell them anything.'

There are other reasons why management reject the idea of joint consultative committees. The personnel manager of a large wool textile firm observed:

'The company has always been, I think, a very benevolent one. There has always been a benevolent, if not paternalistic, attitude towards labour. The family atmosphere has shown up in labour relations generally. We've outgrown that stage now and I don't quite know that we've settled down in the new era and brought ourselves really up to date in our labour relations. We don't believe in works committees or works councils. . . . The attitude is that such works councils can be a sheer waste of time. They tend to deal with trivialities and small things that should be dealt with in the ordinary course of management. But I think we lack a system that makes for a free flow of information both ways.'

Twenty-one firms visited did not have a system of joint consultation. Eight of these had operated one but had now abolished it. The main reason for this appears to have been that managers had started off with an exaggerated view of the immediate use it would be to them. The mill director of a wool textile firm, explaining why the works council had been abolished, said:

'We had got one or two hotheads nominated on to the committee. It was getting a little bit out of hand—they were telling us what to do. They were getting beyond their powers as a works council. We looked on it more as a friendly body. A joint council's all right if it can be kept in its place. It can be very embarrassing for, after all, we're there to listen and some of the questions that are asked are a wee bit embarrassing.'

Sometimes, as in the case of a domestic appliance firm, joint consultation just petered out:

'We did originally have joint consultation after the war. It started off full of enthusiasm and ideas but, gradually, as we met, probably once a fortnight or once a month, the ideas that were brought forward gradually petered out and simply came down in the end to the quality of the tea in the canteen or something of that trivial nature.'

A joint consultative council, as the following quotation from a shipyard manager shows, does not have to be wound up officially in order to be practically dead:

'We have a joint consultative council, which doesn't meet at regular intervals, but we try to get a meeting in every six months or so. We had one about three weeks ago. It must have been somewhere about nine months since the last one. We've been going through a bit of a slump here, you see, nothing very much to discuss, but now that we've got a bit more work coming through, we've called another meeting. . . . The committee has no decision-making powers. I must say, as far as the management are concerned, the questions which are brought up by the workmen's side of the committee are things that would normally be dealt with outside of any joint consultative committee.'

The failure of a council is sometimes clearly attributable to lack of imagination on the part of management. The joint production committee described by the convener of a shipyard is now virtually moribund:

'We finished work at 5.30 at night and the joint production committee was to meet at 5.30. Well, you can imagine the likes of me working out in the winter-time—maybe soaking wet all day. It comes to 5.30 and the rest of the yard are away home to a comfortable fire and I'm here till 7.30 or 8 discussing how I'm going to increase production for the shipyard director and the firm, and not for my benefit.'

In many of the firms visited joint consultation worked effectively. The scope which such committees can have is illustrated by the following quotation from the personnel manager of an electronics firm who, asked what the joint consultative committee discussed, replied:

'It would be much easier to suggest what it doesn't discuss. We discuss everything from productivity to the employment of disabled persons, from forward programme planning of the company's financial interests to social activities within the sports and social club.'

The personnel manager of another electronics firm explained how management gained from its joint consultation procedure:

'The works council is used for explaining the plans to the people on the shop floor through their representatives. Now, this includes day-to-day things, not only complaints coming up but future plans of the management in terms of production and development of the factory generally. All are discussed here, well before the plans are brought into operation. And the plans can be amended through these discussions. We try to anticipate problems rather than wait until they're on top of us.'

This view was supported by the personnel manager of a medium-sized machine tool firm:

'The amount of time lost now through stoppages is practically nil. It did occur a few years ago, but now we have developed a form of consultation and we go deeply into any point or subject before we take any serious action. We have been very successful in getting full co-operation from the shop stewards these last two years. We lose very little time now.'

The most detailed description of the useful work of a works council was given by the personnel manager of a small woollen firm:

'The works council started seven or eight years ago. . . . There are ten representatives from the shop floor, including one foreman. This foreman is also a member of the management committee. We have four management representatives. One of these is the foreman, one the managing director, one the production manager and one the personnel officer. Now these people are representatives. They're not delegated, so they can make decisions if called upon to do so. The committee meets once a month. A prominent item on the agenda is information. Now this information is given first of all by the managing director. He gives his opinion on the state of trade. Then the production manager gives the actual details of the state of trade, in other words what the position is in the various departments, what we have on the order book. We also discuss future projects, how things are going, new developments. . . . Then queries raised by the representatives themselves. Management raises questions and we try and discuss problems. For instance, we are doing white pieces now. These are very difficult to keep clean because they are toted from one department to another. We explain to people why we're doing these white pieces. We've asked for their co-operation in keeping them clean. It's not just a question of saying these pieces are white and must be kept clean. We go into the reason, into the background and the results of not keeping them clean. We point out to people that if pieces are not up to standard we lose orders. They accept it as such, and it has in fact improved this particular problem. We get the usual items at the works council—people saying there's no hot water and the toilet doors are broken and this sort of thing, which we expect—but this is certainly not considered to be the main item of business of the council.'

The type of attitude engendered among the work-people by effective joint consultation was illustrated by an operative who was, in fact, chairman of the council:

'I don't say we've reached utopia by any means. We've a long way to go, but I think, in the time we've been working as a council with top management, we've done remarkably well. In my opinion to run a works council properly you must have the full confidence of your top management. They must lay all their cards on the table, otherwise the whole scheme breaks down. I think our management are trying to do that, and have done from the very start.'

Thus, joint consultation can, if thoroughly and wholeheartedly undertaken, create understanding between the two sides of industry and hence help to overcome a major barrier to change and efficiency.

Other Aspects of Communication

The managing director of a small electronics firm described how he influenced workers' performance by effective communication about the financial implications of their work:

'The shop floor are given the job of making, say, eight amplifiers a week as a production target, but we insist they also know what these eight amplifiers are worth. . . . They're worth £8,000. We also like them to know that the £8,000 output means so much profit. If we set a target of, say, twenty in a month, we usually find they try and make twenty-two in that month. And we put up charts which show them week by week what they have achieved.'

Another item of information which management can usefully give workers is the company results. Some firms do their best to ensure that everybody on the shop floor is fully informed:

'Everybody has a knowledge of the financial results of the year, because the accounts in their published forms are put up on the notice-boards throughout the organisation, in every works and sales office throughout the country.'

The convener of a similar firm explained how his company's financial results were presented:

'They usually show a big cheese, and they divide it up in what they've got for profit, what they pay in tax, and you get your quota of what the profits are. Last year they didn't pay out so much—they didn't pay us so much—but we got our share, I will say that.'

Many managements, on the other hand, find the idea of informing their workers about their profits anathema. The most succinct comment on this came from the managing director of a shipyard:

'I think it is an academic pipe dream.'

Others, like the director of an earthmoving equipment firm, were equally against the idea:

'I think you've got to be careful to whom you give detailed information so that you can be sure that they'll put it to the right use. If we show profit figures to the man on the shop floor, he'll say, "That's a hell of a lot of money!" He doesn't relate it to sales or capital investment. I think it would be dangerous to give them too much detail.'

To some managements, like that of a domestic appliance firm, the idea appeared to be new and surprising:

'Well, I suppose the reason that company accounts are not shown to workers is that there has been no direct request for it up to the present time. We don't feel profits are a great concern to the man on the shop floor.'

Many firms who were opposed to showing their results to their employees were, in fact, public companies. Frequently their conveners kept a very alert watch on their results, as the following two quotations from conveners show:

'Last year and the year before the firm paid out 25 per cent, which is reasonable by industrial standards. Whether or not they'll pay out 25 per cent this year, of course, I don't know.'
    Interviewer: 'How do you know that they paid out 25 per cent?'
    'I'm a regular reader of the *Guardian* actually, and I watch their City part.'

—and:

'In the past, when we've been doing well, the shareholders have always had a good pay out.'
    Interviewer: 'Does management tell you what happens to the profits?'
    'No, but I'm in a position to find out through the trade union you see.'

Here again an opportunity of communication is missed and the possibility of making workers feel that they are an integral part of the firm is ignored. It is little wonder that the 'us/them' attitude tends to flourish in some firms.
    Another field in which the co-operation of the labour force can be either encouraged or discouraged is that of suggestion schemes. Significant increases in productivity can be achieved by their proper use. The convener of an earthmoving equipment firm explained how they were organised in his firm:

'The suggestion goes to management and, if it is successful and your idea applied, they work out the savings over twelve months— and you get that.'

This contrasts with a firm in the machine tool industry where the convener said:

'They haven't got a suggestion scheme. It's virtually impossible for a person with ideas on any job in the shop to transmit them to management in the hopes of having some notice taken of them. Possibly some of the older members of management are resentful at what they might consider to be the workers coming into their own private reserve.'

Mistrust between management and workers can also be caused by the operation of suggestion schemes when the workers believe that management has used suggestions from the shop floor to cut piece-work rates. The convener of a machine tool firm was convinced, when pressed by the interviewer, that this had happened in his factory. In fact, this rarely happens,[1] but the convener said:

'In certain cases we've said to the company, "We can do it quicker this way or the other way", and before very long we find that the piece-work prices are being cut. So, for obvious reasons, we don't go running to management and say, "We can do this job quicker", because sooner or later the job will be replanned and, of course, there'll be a drop in earnings as a result.'

The Role of Shop Stewards

Another important factor in determining the quality of labour relations is the way in which management treats the shop stewards. In conditions of labour shortage nationally agreed wage rates are widely exceeded, so that the earnings of very many workers are negotiated by representatives from within their own firm. It follows that shop stewards have gained greater power to influence the views of workers and hence their reactions to management policies.

Managements generally seem to recognise the importance of workers' representatives when there is trouble, but their treatment at other times varies. The trade union organiser of a very large firm described the treatment he received from his management:

'They'll fall over themselves to give me any facility when there's trouble. Oh yes, you can have the moon! You can have the whole section! You can have anybody when there's trouble! But not otherwise. . . . I should like facilities for going around the factory instead of having to go through an iron-curtain routine. It used to be that when I walked through a section the phones were being picked up and people were being told exactly where I was going.'

But when there was trouble:

<hr>

[1] See Shirley W. Lerner and Judith Marquand, 'Workshop Bargaining, Wage Drift and Productivity in the British Engineering Industry', *Manchester School*, January 1962.

'. . . the entire section stopped. On the Saturday morning they called me up to the boardroom—the first time I'd ever been up to the boardroom like. The last time as well! They called me and they said, "Well, we don't know whether they're your members or not." I said, "They're not for a start." They said, "Would you intervene? Would you talk to the girls and try to get this sorted out?" '

Some managers, like the labour relations manager of a very large firm, however, do not wait for trouble to develop before they try to establish good relations between themselves and their shop stewards:

'I regard the unions as a necessity, but a desirable necessity. You can't pretend to negotiate separately with thousands of people. You've got to have a centre or focus for complaints and negotiations. I think the unions are growing up. They all started the same way— they had to—with a certain militancy, but now they're growing up and becoming very statesmanlike.'

Shop stewards are also used by some managements as a channel of communication to discover the feelings of their members. The convener of a medium-sized electronics firm remarked:

'We had a strike in the district a little while ago. The tool rooms in the other firms were on strike and I was tapped and asked whether I thought our tool room would come out in sympathy.'

The more responsible shop stewards certainly see their roles as preventers rather than instigators of trouble, as quotations from conveners of two firms show:

'My job in here is to create harmony and stop trouble. Management thinks that when I am not complaining everything is going all right. But maybe I'm away putting out a bush fire.'

and:

'My chief responsibility, having clocked in here of a morning, is to see that at all times 400 members remain at work. That's my chief concern, to see that they stop at their machines and stop at their benches for forty-two hours of the week.'

It was doubtful whether line managers and conveners always had the knowledge and training to deal with the very complex set of

situations which often face them. One convener in a large firm
criticised middle management:

'Top management is very, very good on the whole . . . but inter-
mediate management is very, very lax at times. Where we think
middle management falls down, is they don't know national agreements as they should and they don't know about union/management
relationships as they should. A top manager did say to me at the
last managers' conference that the standard of negotiating—shall we
say knowledge?—of their middle management was sadly lacking and
that most people at shop steward level were more conversant with
the way to carry on than their middle management. They did say
this off their own bat.'

Another convener admitted frankly:

'I haven't enough knowledge for my job. But unfortunately I had to
take it as no one else would.'

With such situations in mind, several of the firms visited believed in
encouraging their shop stewards to attend courses of one kind or
another. In some cases the management offer was rejected. In a
large shipyard the yard manager recounted:

'About five years ago we tried to get the shop stewards interested
and they just didn't trust us. They wouldn't have anything to do with
it. We tried to send them away on courses but they wouldn't have it.'

Another yard thought they had had more success:

'The maximum we have done at the moment is sending shop stewards
on courses. We have sent them off in pairs and they've attended up
to date five or six courses run by the Economic League. That is the
extent of the adult education that we've applied here.'

Another firm sent shop stewards to courses run by the Industrial
Welfare Society. Two very large firms, one of them in earthmoving
equipment and the other in general manufacturing, ran their own
educational departments and in both cases shop stewards received
direct instruction in matters concerning production. A personnel
manager commented:

'If we're going to introduce work study into a department the shop stewards and some representative work-people get a week's appreciation course in work study.'

Where managers take trouble over their relations with shop stewards the increase in plant bargaining and the resultant improvement in the role and status of the shop steward may (paradoxically as it may seem to some managements and the popular press) have served to improve labour relations, as it makes ordinary workers feel less remote from the centre of wage bargaining and therefore more ready to accept agreements when they are reached.

Recruitment
Apart from the quality of labour relations, with its incalculable effect on industrial change and hence productivity, the shortage of labour, and in particular of skilled labour, was cited by many firms as a major impediment to growth.

The managing director of a large machine tool firm identified the availability of skilled labour as one of the two factors governing the growth of his firm:

'Growth has been restricted immediately post-war by shortage of labour, and it has been restricted really substantially by that all along. The rate of growth has been dependent largely upon the rate of availability of skilled manpower and the improvement in productive methods.'

The same theme was reiterated by a senior executive of a small machine tool firm:

'Another problem which is always with us, and we can only deal with on a very long-term basis, is the shortage of skilled labour. In a very small way we've managed to achieve some growth in the labour force over a number of years, but we've a permanent order with the labour exchange.'

Some attempt had been made by this company to overcome its shortage of skilled labour. A member of management had been sent to certain of the depressed areas, like Belfast or Merseyside, where he had recruited a few people, half of whom later left the firm and returned home.

Three other firms from which quotations have been taken made more determined efforts to overcome the problem. One very large earthmoving equipment firm, faced with increased demand for its products and situated in a small town of 25,000 people with no surplus labour, explained how it met this problem:

'We brought some people down here. We took them round the district with their wives just to show them exactly what they were coming to—after all, that has a big bearing when changing their town—and we built them houses.'

Another thrusting response to a shortage of labour is manifest in this comment by the personnel manager of a medium-sized wool textile firm:

'There's been an acute shortage of women in textiles. So we made an agreement with the union to recruit labour from two continental countries where labour is abundant. We took Austria first and Italy second. When there came to be more employment in Austria, we brought them in from southern Italy.'

Yet another way of finding labour was described by the managing director of another wool textile firm:

'I can't expand here. I've had to expand in other ways. In small units where the labour is available. I've had to find these places where the labour is available.'

Similarly, several firms mentioned that they had already constructed factories in depressed areas or that their future plans included expansion in such places. One of them, a very large electronics firm, told the research team that to meet the immediate labour shortage wireless components had been delivered to workers' homes for assembly.

The most thrusting response to a shortage of skilled labour was found in three firms, one in electronics, one in earthmoving equipment and one in machine tools. In each case unskilled men had been recruited and the pattern of production then changed so that with some training they could do the work which had formerly needed skilled apprenticed labour. Management's ability to adopt such measures depends on the existence of amicable relations with the craft trade unions as the latter often object to dilutees (non-apprenticed) doing skilled work. The works director of a large machine tool firm described what happened to his firm in 1961:

'We had this upsurge in 1961, where the sales went from 100 units a month to 300 and 400 units a month. What did we do? Well, firstly, we're setting up more and more apprentices, but that's a long-term policy and will pay off in ten years. What we had to do—we had to try and rationalise the programme—that is, to make fewer models so that in theory the degree of skill needed was diluted—and, furthermore, we went out and brought in a couple of hundred trainees, people who'd never been into an engineering shop at all. And by the use of our skilled men in supervising these trainees, and by various means, we endeavoured to get them on to production, which is not very satisfactory but you've got to try and do it.'

Training

The general labour shortage is only one reason why firms need to pay special attention to planning their labour requirements and training their workers. Other reasons are fairly obvious. It is only through intelligent and forward-looking training that firms can enable their employees to develop their skills fully and thus attain their maximum productivity. Attention of this quality given to workers will also be a positive factor in the creation of good labour relations. The retraining of workers within their firms, perhaps several times in a lifetime, will at once make the workers and the firm more adaptable and versatile and consequently more able to meet shifts in demand and improvements in productive techniques.

In nearly all firms emphasis was placed on the importance of training. Only three firms took no apprentices. Two of them explained that their own particular kind of light engineering did not offer scope for a full apprenticeship training, while the production manager of the third reported:

'The matter of our not taking apprentices has been put to me before, but we have put boys through here, and before they have been with us about three years, before being indentured, they've gone and left us—because in the midlands they can command much more money in the motor trade without being apprenticed to a firm of this type. The people that do have a large apprenticeship scheme are the larger companies, such as Lucas and one or two more, ICI, GEC.'

But the general picture was that firms were developing and broadening the old apprenticeship structure. A few still recruited boys and let them spend four or five years learning their skill from one tradesman, but many had written examinations by which apprentices were chosen, a training school within the firm and arrangements by which boys were released for a day a week besides being encouraged to attend night school. In several firms boys were also released to go on sandwich courses at local technical colleges lasting three to six months. Alongside their expansion of the traditional craft apprenticeship scheme some firms were recruiting other kinds of apprentices—technical apprentices and graduate apprentices. The length of apprenticeship did not appear to be a burning issue with management though several executives tartly recalled that women welders were trained in six weeks during the war. Only in shipyards were the number of apprentices that a firm could recruit limited by union practices. The personnel manager of one Clydeside shipyard referred to what he called the unofficial bargain between management and unions:

'Apprentice policy is very clear. It is restricted by the fact that the trade unions will determine how many apprentices we have. At some places we are rated at one apprentice to five tradesmen, in other cases one to three tradesmen, in other cases . . . Oh, there is not a strong battle one way or another. Now, we would prefer to put more apprentices on the job but the unions restrict us strongly.'

While managements were restricted in their freedom to engage apprentices, there appeared to be no such restriction anywhere on the content of the apprenticeship course. None the less, little had been done to enlarge the traditional pattern of apprenticeship in a large shipyard—the shipyard manager explained:

'We don't operate any special scheme in the yard otherwise than what has been the traditional method of working in the shipyard. Apprentices practise alongside the journeymen, are put with the journeymen.'

The convener of a Clydeside shipyard had this to say about the suitability of shipbuilding apprenticeships:

'I think there will require to be a change in the apprenticeship structure. It will come, of course—again years after this—when it is accepted that the apprentice will become an apprentice shipbuilder instead of an apprentice welder or an apprentice plater. I think that will come but it will be a long time before that will be accepted. At the moment I don't agree that the boys are getting a fair chance, particularly boys who are serving their time as riveters. We still have apprentice riveters and the riveting trade is going out—I should say completely.'

A contrast to the narrow craft-based nature of shipyard apprenticeships was provided by the personnel manager of a medium-sized wool textile firm:

'We have a definite, laid-down programme of training for apprentices. This is a five-year textile apprenticeship. The first three years are spent gaining a wee bit more than an appreciation of the work in all the departments of the mill. They stay in some departments for quite a long time and they learn to do almost every job in the mill. Some of them learn to do them pretty skilfully. In fact they're competent on a lot of the jobs that are covered by their training. After three years the apprentice is interviewed by myself and perhaps one or two of the departmental managers, and he is asked what particular job he wants to specialise on, so generally the job that he's going to specialise on is worked out on the basis of what he thinks he's suitable for and what is available. We work out something that is agreeable to all parties and then he will specialise for the last two years of his apprenticeship. This is done in conjunction with technical college studies. They generally take the City and Guilds Certificate, the Ordinary National Certificate and the Higher National Certificate if they're good enough.'

The importance of giving an apprentice an all-round training was stressed by the personnel manager of a very large electronics firm. The practice of moving apprentices around a firm's departments indicates that both unions and management tacitly recognise that a five years' apprenticeship to learn one craft is often unnecessarily long:

'Apprentices are given a period of time in each department—three months, six months—to give them a thorough grounding and to make them appreciate the activity and problems that arise in these areas. So that, when a boy even gets to be just a sheet-metal worker or a wireman, at least he knows what goes on in the drawing office, the planning department, the material control and the store department, so that he can be a better operator for it. Too often we get trouble from the older people complaining about inefficiencies or shortcomings on the part of staff in the stores area or the drawing office, simply because they don't appreciate the problems those people have in those areas.'

Despite the amount of attention which thrusting firms gave to their apprentices, the research team did not find any insistence on apprentices in England taking any sort of final examination. Only in a Scottish textile mill did they hear:

'We [management] don't force them [apprentices] to attend these classes, but they all do. We also have an agreement with the trade unions that before an apprentice can be reckoned as a tradesman he must sit a proficiency examination. He must go through a test at a technical college to get his proficiency certificate.'

Besides trying to develop the scope of apprenticeship, thrusting firms will also be planning their manpower requirements, so that each year in addition to apprentices a number of other boys are taken on and prepared by careful training to fill certain posts in the future. The personnel manager of a midlands machine tool firm talked about the technician apprentices whom his firm engaged:

'Apart from the craft apprentices that are dealt with, we also take technician apprentices, who are boys with "O" level GCE, who are probably going eventually to end up in the drawing office or planning department. And also we take a number of boys, probably one or two each year, who have got "A" level subjects or who are graduate apprentices, who will either go to the College of Advanced Technology or university to take Dip. Techs. or degrees.'

A whole range of training from apprentice upwards was mentioned by the personnel manager of a very large electronics firm:

'We have every type of recognised apprentice training. We have the craft apprentice, engineering student, post-graduates. Then we have business and administration trainees, commercial trainees, and female trainees. The business administration trainees are in training from twenty-one years of age with a six-year training course to become junior assistant heads of departments. In the commercial field, the marketing field, the sales divisions—personnel, if you like— all the second-line management team is being welded together for 1975 to the 1980s.'

A wider difference between sleepy and thrusting attitudes lies in the emphasis which management places on non-apprentice training and retraining. As changes in technology increase, the attention which firms give to training and retraining all older adult workers will become steadily more important. The techniques of shipbuilding have changed in this country quite rapidly during the last five years. At one of the shipyards visited the yard manager, when asked about operative training, said:

'I regret to say there is none but it is a thing which we are very concerned about and are trying to do something about. In fact at the moment we are trying to evolve some scheme of training adult employees of certain classes.'

In a small wool textile firm the mill manager was similarly apologetic, when he said:

'I'm afraid we still work on the age-old principle of new workers standing with their tutor. In other words, nobody is taken out of production to do it and they simply spend about six weeks, if they are weavers, with an experienced weaver.'

But another wool textile firm had a special introductory training course for its employees, made necessary no doubt by their thrusting practice of importing every year workers from southern Italy:

'We have the training scheme for foreign workers, or for any workers who come. They have a month's training on a basis of wage for age. Roughly this amounts, for a girl of eighteen, to earning just above the £5 a week mark. Normally, they can learn the process in a month and get on to piece-work, which immediately sends them up. If they've taken full advantage of that month, it sends them up to about £10 a week, if they work hard.'

And in a large shipyard it was found that management had been more successful than the yard previously quoted from:

'Then there is the tradesman. I have run classes for tradesmen. I have had as many as thirty-three coming here to take the course of lessons and in that group we've had fourth-year apprentices right up to men who've been forty years in the place. The reason for this was that we were going to have a new system of building ships. We wanted to put it over to the men that there is a new system and they came very willingly.'

In a firm in the electronics industry, where techniques of production might be expected to alter rapidly, the research team heard how the personnel manager was anticipating change:

'Beyond two-and-a-half years I feel that certain new basic methods of manufacturing equipment are about to hit me. This will require a new approach on the part of the operatives. They'll probably find themselves using microscopes to do their jobs. Things are becoming more miniaturised. There'll be a higher grade of reliability required. There'll be different techniques of soldering without junctions and things like that. I think it will require a higher mentality of operatives, too, so that preparatory to this there'll be an intensive training programme.'

The convener of a firm making scientific instruments gave a grudging acknowledgement of his firm's training schemes for operatives:

'They have training schemes to suit their own purposes of course. If they want a woman who is only doing assembly work to be more useful, so that she can be switched more quickly, they will send her out to school for a week or two so that she can become competent at wiring and things like that.'

The training of foremen is also a vital factor in bringing about maximum productivity. They form the first rung of management and have a powerful influence on the efficiency of production and on the quality of labour relations. The personnel manager of one very large textile mill discussed some of the firm's growing pains:

'We have about fifty foremen in what we call our Section 1, our spinning mill. This is rather a large number for an individual manager to control. The result is that his finger is not quite on the pulse as it is always in the smaller mills. This is where I think we are lacking at the moment in successful management. We've grown very quickly, and in addition it's very difficult indeed in this area to get skilled foremen. We're in the process of training up our own youngsters. This will probably not come to fruition for three to five years, at which time I think we will be better off. At the moment we have what we regard as relatively unskilled foremen and this makes for difficulty in management. I couldn't say at this stage that we're very successful in that respect.'

Several firms saw some of their problems as being caused by inadequate foremen. In the case of those firms which did not take any trouble to prepare workers for promotion the fact that senior management has detected weaknesses in that area of supervision should be no surprise. One mill manager considered training for overlookers to be quite unnecessary:

'I don't think it is necessary myself. It isn't in our firm as it is at the moment anyhow. I mean, we train them as we're going on.'

In one shipyard where some attempt was made to train foremen after they had been promoted, the results, according to one executive, were not very encouraging:

'I send foremen on weekend courses. The supervisors, they go down to Troon for a weekend, or they go to Stirling or somewhere for a weekend on work study, budgeting, communications, or any of these courses that are run. When they get back they give me a report and it's good to get them to sit down and put their thoughts in words. I must honestly say that the quality of foremen and their ability to communicate on paper is not good. Their general attitude to any lecture or courses that they go to is, "Well, it's all common sense. There's nothing to it. It's all right but you can't apply it to shipbuilding." '

One of the more thrusting practices was to start selecting likely candidates for promotion to foremen some time before any vacancies would occur. These men received special training and when they were promoted they received even more intensive instruction. The process of early selection and education was described by a personnel manager of a very large firm:

'We attempt to train them from the time we take them on as fairly young men, through pretty well every job in the department, and, if they are good enough, they tend to emerge at the top as charge-hands and then perhaps as foremen. We consider that in this sort of process our foremen and indeed our departmental managers— sometimes we go even higher than that—ought to know a considerable amount of the technical detail of how to do the job. When they do come out at the top as potential foremen we don't believe they necessarily know very much about foremanship or managership and at that stage we try and train them in the arts of management. We think they are already adequately briefed technically. Then we try and train them by internal courses here, run by our own educational department and supplemented by outside courses.'

The greatest importance given to training foremen and other junior supervision was found in an American earthmoving equipment subsidiary. The emphasis was acknowledged by the convener when he said, dryly, that the management tried to fill the foremen's heads with yellow paint.

One of the advantages which very large firms enjoyed was their ability to operate their own training and education departments. In most of the eleven firms employing over 2,000 workers such arrangements for internal training were made. Firms which are not large

enough to run their own courses had to rely on outside establishments. Some managements would also argue that training is less
important in smaller units of production. Many firms of all sizes,
however, had the thrusting attitude that workers at all levels should
be trained so as to develop their abilities and their productivity to
the fullest extent.

The Role of Personnel Managers

In anticipating the possible manifestations of conflict and in training
workers so as to maximise their productivity, the value of a good
personnel manager can scarcely be overrated. To perform his function adequately, however, he must make his voice heard at a high
enough level of management. The importance of the work of
personnel managers is frequently not clear to higher management.
The personnel manager of a shipyard gave one reason why:

'One of the difficulties of personnel work, as I see it, is that any good
that I personally do—or the department does—can never be measured, because, if production goes up shall we say by 1, 2 or 10 per
cent, then the people who are going to take the credit for that are
the production managers. And they would be very foolish if they
didn't. Obviously they are the people who should—must take the
credit—but—who knows?—the fact that I have done something for
a particular person may stimulate him to work harder and produce
$0 \cdot 05$ per cent or $0 \cdot 005$ per cent more of the whole yard's output,
but that can never be traced back here.'

The status and responsibility of personnel managers vary enormously. The following quotation from the personnel manager of a
small woollen firm shows what scope he has when he is a senior
manager:

'I'm responsible to the managing director and to no one else. I'm
responsible for advising the managing director on all aspects of
personnel policy. This includes recruitment at all levels, management,
supervisory and operative, and also training at all levels. I also cover
the usual welfare functions.'

In contrast, the next quotation from the personnel manager of a
medium-sized domestic appliance firm illustrates a very much lower
level of responsibility:

'I cover selection of labour. Apart from that, I do all the welfare
work. Anybody on the shop floor can see me at any time. We get

D

all their little problems in the works, and I try to sort them out for them.'

The works manager of a machine tool firm put his personnel manager firmly in his place when he remarked:

'Of course, as I have said, I have an assistant who is the personnel officer. But all major decisions are taken by me.'

The qualifications required of personnel managers also vary considerably. The following is an extreme example of how one personnel manager of a shipyard came to hold his position:

'I was a foreman riveter and they asked me to have a go at this job.'

Other personnel managers, like one in a very large firm in the electronics industry, have a high degree of professional competence:

'I think they [the work-people] are alive to this constant endeavour to see that their employment conditions are at least as favourable as anywhere else. To put it in a cliché: "We are never knowingly undersold". We are sure of this because we are constantly appraising the situation. As I speak to you now, seven surveys are taking place. We are analysing our sick pay schemes for hourly paid workers. We are analysing the holiday entitlement within the industry for hourly paid employees. We are analysing the staff pension entitlements within grades of length of service—five, ten or fifteen years. We are analysing our pension rights entitlement for female staff. At the moment we have no pension scheme for them, although we have an annuity and endowment scheme. We are analysing starting and finishing times in other companies to see whether our present starting times are the right ones or if any area of adjustment is necessary there. We're analysing the benefits of additional sick pay coverage, through independent insurance companies, with the facilities for convalescence. This is the type of survey that's going on at the moment. In addition to that, we're analysing and breaking down into areas of responsibility engineering wage rates for engineers up to a salary of £1,800 a year and defining them within the terms of their responsibility, educational backgrounds and technical attainments and requirements, to see that our engineers are correctly paid.'

The Responsibility of Management

It is clear that there are wide differences in the way in which firms improve their efficiency. In the most thrusting firms, management has contrived to make its labour force a positive asset by encouraging workers to recognise when their interests and the interests of management are the same and by effective training schemes. In other firms, relations between management and the workers are allowed to deteriorate and little can be achieved without having to overcome the bitterest resistance from trade unions, where they exist, or, in the case of firms with a high proportion of female labour, the silent protest of a high absentee rate, a high labour turnover, and a general apathy towards work.

The ideal situation in industrial relations is for management and labour to be able to settle areas of natural conflict, such as wages, without giving rise to damaging stoppages or hardening the even more damaging resistance to change, and to be able to deal to the advantage of both sides with those areas where there is no inescapable reason for conflict. A necessary condition for this was expressed by the personnel manager of a woollen firm who, like the trade unionist quoted on page 66, put the emphasis on trust:

'It is that the men on the shop floor and the supervisors trust management. Now that's it shortly and simply. If you get this situation it implies also that the management trust the people on the shop floor, of course. I don't think you can have one without the other. If you get this trust, then you will get good industrial relations.'

On the other hand, an example of the effects of mistrust came from the works manager of a machine tool firm in an area which has had full employment since the war:

'The unions show anti-modern thinking, stemming, I think, from the older days of high national unemployment. We really have got to put modern techniques in very, very gently, very, very slowly. You can't have a meeting with a shop steward and explain carefully what you intend to do and prove the economics round the table and then go out and demonstrate that nobody is going to lose anything by it. It just wouldn't work that way. The tendency is to say no—"no" because it's a change, not "no" because it's going to harm them.'

The existence of this suspicion was confirmed from the other side of industry:

'Automatically, if the management says, "I'm going to give you a scheme that would make you another £5 a week", I couldn't help it but I would start immediately looking underneath it, round about it, to see where the snag is. I would take it back to the men and they would do the same thing. Rightly or wrongly, this subconscious mistrust is there.'

One explanation of how such bad relations arise was given by the personnel manager of a woollen firm:

'If the company in the past has pulled a few fast ones, as companies have been known to do, then I think that, even if you stop pulling fast ones, it will take a generation of people to forget that. Or, indeed, you may have a new management in a company where the old management were not trusted. The new management will not be trusted until they've earned this trust.'

In the absence of good industrial relations, the temptation to divide the world into 'them' and 'us' becomes overwhelming, and this gives latent class antagonisms a chance to make themselves felt:

'They [top management] have got on not because of what they know but because they've been to public schools. They have financial backing from their parents or legacies, call it what you like. They buy themselves a directorship on the board. They've never been on the shop floor to appreciate the problems the ordinary working-man has to face. They make their decisions without any thought of the repercussions on the man on the floor, how it's going to affect his working life and what effect it's going to have on his family. These thoughts, I'm convinced, never enter their heads.'

Nothing in the interviews went to contradict the saying that in the long run management gets the shop stewards it deserves. It would be unjust to lay all the blame for an existing bad situation on one side or the other of industry. There are usually considerable faults on both sides. Nevertheless, the great responsibility for improving the situation lies with management. A thrusting management can take action to ensure that none of the three major causes of conflict—wage disputes, fear of redundancy, and lack of trust and understanding—is allowed to fester without anything being done to improve the situation. To a large extent, the existence of full employment has forced managers to adopt acceptable procedures to deal with wage grievances, although even here piece-work rates which men seem to find difficult to understand can help to breed mistrust. As far as the other two are concerned, a great deal still remains to be done. The gap between the best firms and the rest in both respects is glaring. Perhaps better education of managers offers the only radical solution in the long run. But in the short run both individual firms and the country as a whole lose a great deal both materially and spiritually by the continuance of these conflicts. However, to alleviate the situation, managements must act positively. It is too easy merely to blame the other side as the managing director of a domestic appliance firm did:

'There seems to be an awful lack of drive today. I think it's one of the appalling features of modern industry—it staggers me. I think the only remedy is changing conditions so that there is a bit more competition for these jobs.'

As a complete contrast, and a demonstration of a positive attitude towards labour relations, the following quotation can serve to conclude this chapter. One of the outstanding problems which faces British industry today in achieving a high growth rate is how to get more managers acting on the sort of sentiments expressed by the personnel manager of a woollen mill:

'One thing we do believe very strongly here is that management is responsible. This covers a lot of ground, but nevertheless we believe it very firmly. If there are bad relationships, we are responsible. If there's a dispute, we are responsible. Management has to foresee the cause of disputes and, if they fail to foresee this, then it's the fault of management and management is responsible. We believe this very strongly, and I'm quite sure that if management in other companies really believed this—and I mean not just say it, but believe it—then I'm sure that we could do a lot towards improving relationships and efficiency in industry.'

CHAPTER 6

BUDGETARY CONTROL AND
COST REDUCTION

The term 'productivity' has been defined in Chapter 4 as the ratio of the outputs of a productive process to its inputs. Cost reduction per unit of output is, therefore, another way of describing the growth of productivity, which is central to the theme of this book. This chapter considers certain aspects of budgetary control and cost reduction: budgeting, cost control and work study; plant appraisal and replacement; and efficient purchasing of raw materials and components.

During the interviews, many executives acknowledged the need for improving efficiency and explained that past trading conditions had encouraged a lax attitude towards the management of their firms. The managing director of a medium-sized machine tool company reflected:

'There was no selling. There was no need to sell machine tools up to a few years ago. You took orders. The customer did more selling to you to take an order than you did to sell to him. There was no spur. Anyone could manufacture. Even the industries which were most inefficient could keep a top-class order-book.'

It was during the lotus-eating years of the 1950s that one large engineering firm:

'. . . developed a wider and wider range of products. We were, I maintain, industrial spivs in those days in the sense that we made all kinds of things that were completely uneconomic. Here we were, a small company [with about 1,200 employees] making some machines in half-dozens against people turning them out in hundreds with huge factories equipped solely for making them. That was in the days when the waiting list was two years. There was no incentive to improve efficiency, lower costs, buy new equipment or anything of that sort.'

In conditions such as these, which started for most of British industry in the early years of the war, most firms produced without enough regard for cost. The turning point for many firms came at the end of the 1950s when the spur of competition began to be felt and the possibility of joining the Common Market prompted senior management to take a searching look at the way companies were run. A third cause for examining efficiency was the increased importance being given to growth as a national objective, which was matched in many firms by the realisation that, if they were to expand efficiently, then they must undertake better planning of their human and physical resources. As a result of these considerations, attention was shifted from production at any cost to the subtler and more difficult concept of productivity and it became more widely understood that under intensifying competition the firms which will prosper will be those that can steadily raise their productivity. At the same time many more firms began to believe that the most expeditious way of raising productivity was by the systematic use of a number of management techniques. How the firms visited viewed three such techniques, budgeting, cost control and work study, will now be considered.

Budgeting, Cost Control and Work Study

The process of budgeting within a firm ensures that 'all members of management have a financial and/or quantitative statement published prior to a defined period of time of the policy to be pursued during that period for the purpose of attaining a given objective'.[1] The compilation of a firm's annual budget starts with the preparation of output budgets covering sales and production in quantities and value. Production executives are able to estimate their department's costs if their firm operates a system of cost control, which can take the form of either standard costing or marginal costing. Both systems in turn depend on work study which is the systematic assessment in terms of time of individual operatives' jobs, and the consequent setting of standard times for all operations.

During their interviews managing directors and executives with responsibility for financial management and production were asked to discuss their planning and control techniques with special reference to productivity. Of the forty-seven firms visited thirty told the research team that they operated budgetary control. Of these thirty, ten had introduced it within the last five years, often with the assistance of management consultants. One example was found in a medium-sized machine tool firm where the company secretary

---

[1] This definition of budgeting is taken from E. F. L. Brech (ed.), *The Principles and Practices of Management* (Longmans), 2nd Edition, 1962, p. 643.

explained how four systems had been implemented and described their advantages:

'Budgetary control was established by management consultants in 1958, together with a standard costing system, work study techniques and production control.'

It was three years before the systems were operating properly and:

'Statements are now being produced which bring every item of expenditure to light by incidence of expenditure and also against products so that we now have a complete analysis of our products, which are accurately costed.[1] Management are now in a position to know where losses and where profits are being made both in respect of finished products, spare parts and job contract work.'

Among the seventeen firms visited which did not operate budgetary control several reasons were volunteered why it was considered inapplicable or undesirable. One large machine tool firm prided itself on keeping a low proportion of staff to total employees and it was for this reason according to the company secretary that the firm:

'. . . didn't work on any system of budgeting of costs, or cost control. Obviously we have our yearly and half-yearly accounts, which are audited, and from that we have a system of control of costs in departments which virtually lies with the heads of departments, and I have the overall picture of what's going on in the company.'

An additional reason why this company felt it was unable to introduce budgetary control was its inability to forecast future demand—an inability that stood out oddly against the works manager's report that overtime had been worked for twenty-five years. The commercial manager lamented:

'I wouldn't like to "forecast" what orders we're going to have for machines next year. We're in the lap of the gods or the Government, whatever it may be, or the Treasury. At the present moment orders on the home market are declining because there's no capital investment but who can honestly forecast what is going to be the position next year?'

[1] It is interesting to note that a survey undertaken by the Institution of Works Managers among its 4,500 members in April 1962, and subsequently published as a leaflet entitled *Spanner in the Works*, listed insufficient cost information as one of the most important factors adversely affecting the improvement of productivity,

In small firms the fact that budgetary control had not been introduced was frequently due to the size of the company—management feeling that it was able 'to keep an eye on things'. (A firm in the electronics industry employing only 120 people was, however, firmly in favour of it and used it.) In other firms a variety of reasons were heard. Some of them were that high plant efficiency enabled management to ignore financial control, that budgetary control was a system which accountants discussed in the classroom but ignored as soon as they entered the real world of industry, that the special nature of the shipbuilding industry made realistic forecasting impossible—as one shipyard accountant put it, 'who can forecast the weather?'—that, when a business was 'growing in one direction or another', management did not want to be hindered by systems and that the experience and knowledge of senior foremen rendered any control system redundant.

On the subject of work study, practically all firms except those in the shipbuilding industry had introduced it and in most cases had operated it for many years. How a shipyard plans its operations without work study was explained by a production executive:

'We are at the tail-end of a change-over from a traditional craft industry run by the craftsmen themselves, the senior craftsmen in the shipyard, to an industry using modern methods. We've still got a long way to go. Work study as such is unknown in most yards. Certainly in this shipyard we haven't used it. We have to derive our programming basis from a statistical analysis of past achievements.'

One or two companies which had recently started budgetary and cost control were introducing them very gradually. This was necessary, one executive commented, 'out of respect for some of the older people who've been with the company over forty years'. Sometimes management operated budgetary control but did not use it effectively. A shipyard company secretary was almost apologetic in his reply:

'We do each year produce a budget of what we think should be spent in the following year on these charges, the variable and the fixed. I would confess that budgetary control on these establishment charges is not as tight as one might see in other companies. We produce a budget but we do not, as it were, find out how that budget is comparing with actual results from week to week or even from month to month.'

The failure of some companies to use budgeting, cost control or work study or to use them effectively stands in marked contrast to the thrusting practices of certain other companies. First, the emphasis placed on long-term planning which was present in a handful of companies is noteworthy. The best example of this occurred in a medium-sized machine tool firm. The general manager observed pithily:

'But in this company we plan long-term. And by planning long-term we can then plan short-term much better. We make our yearly budget and forecast against the long-term programme. This is for capital expenditure, staff and labour build-up. So we plan on a five-year period showing general company development.'

Within the envelope of long-term plans short-period budgets are easier to formulate. In one very large firm where budgets are prepared for the following three years as well as the following year the financial controller explained how the entire management of the company was involved in preparing the budget—a process which generally lasted three months. In some companies (and the research team visited two of them) he had heard that the budget was dreamt up by accountants but:

'Of course it is not so at all. In the last analysis all the accountant has done is to add together a pyramid of estimates made by an enormous number of people right through the organisation. In our budget compilation someone quite junior is making an estimate somewhere of what is going to happen in that section for which he is responsible. All these estimates are added up until they finally come to the complete budget which I present to the board.'

Mention of the board leads to the point that, just as senior management exercises ultimate control of the company through budgetary control, so similarly does the holding company of a group exercise control over its subsidiaries. The managing director of one subsidiary had his plans passed annually and:

'The main board are very good. They give us a great deal of freedom and autonomy. We set the goals which they have to approve at a board meeting. In about October of this year they want to see my next five-year plan in terms of growth and profitability.'

Once a budget has been passed by the board it becomes the firm's policy for the ensuing year and thus can act as a yardstick against which performance can regularly be checked. How regular and how detailed checking is depends on the thoroughness of the firm's costing system and the speed with which pertinent facts are revealed, generally through the medium of budgetary control statements. A general picture of how a company works to budget was given by the works manager of a very large electronics firm:

'We work here to budgets and targets. We set a budget at the beginning of the year from a sales point of view and a production point of view for every aspect of the company's activity. If we can achieve the target, then we achieve the end result, the profit, which is more or less budgeted to be made weekly or monthly, and if we keep going, we get it at the end of the year. Obviously we're trying to improve on that all the time. We're trying to beat the target.'

The process of regular checking against budget was explained by the company secretary of a large machine tool firm:

'We prepare accounts every month and compare them with the budget. We then submit a comparison with the budget to the board with explanations. Major variances are reported on, the reasons found for them and action taken to correct them.'

Most of the companies which operated budgetary control held their inquisitions on progress every month. One small firm in the electronics industry, however, checked performance weekly:

'We produce weekly operational statements. They [other executives] plot several basic figures, things like shipments against target, order rates against target, productivity, revenue per man per day against target. Every Monday afternoon we have a management group meeting and we discuss these figures. We consider what can be done, if we are behind target, to bring ourselves up to target, or, if the target looks as if it can be exceeded, then we set a new target and so on.'

Such a rapid production of operational statements is difficult in all but the smallest companies. Another electronics firm employing more than 2,000 people intended to solve this problem by installing a computer. The finance director explained that the multiplicity of products made their standard costing system awkward to operate— for the time being:

'Our manual system is of great help. We do get out cost figures but not the amount of detailed costs we would like to do. This is where a firm of computer manufacturers is going to help us. We are hiring their complete system. Of course, you cannot get out more than you put in, and here we have got to be very careful that we ask the right questions, but we have seen sufficient now to know that we can get out all sorts of information and data which at the present moment we cannot get.'

It has been mentioned that systematic costing is impossible without work study, which analyses jobs and sets times for their completion. Transmitted to the accounts department this information becomes the standard costs for a firm's products. A mill manager told the interviewer how his company had initiated work study:

'Inside here we have done a work study on practically every department. We have a work study engineer who is more or less my assistant. John and I have been to an eight-week course and have an appreciation of work study, and we set our standards for work load and things like that, and efficiency for certain machines throughout the factory. We create standards which we've got to try to attain. We know in every department, nearly on every machine, whether we've attained them or not.'

Once a firm knows the capacity of its plant and the time it takes to manufacture certain parts or complete products, it can load its factory efficiently. If capacity is not sufficient to meet the production schedule the firm will know exactly how much work to subcontract. Alternatively, if the production schedule does not require full utilisation of plant, the works manager will know how much subcontract work he can undertake. In a large company the calculations required to load machine tools to capacity are often lengthy and laborious. One works director described how his company had overcome the problem:

'We put in a computer in 1960 for production control. It increased our productivity by ensuring that our machine tools and equipment were fully utilised all the time.' [He explained how the computer assisted him.] 'The company lays down a quarterly production schedule of the number of each size of machine that we have got to produce. Information on that is then charted and we know the man-hours on each group of machine tools which are required to produce that machine. That's information which is already available on records. What you have then got to do with your computer is to marry that programme into a shop-loading programme. Now, the computer throws up every week the work you need to get through your department so as to meet your production schedule and ensure that all your components will be ready for assembly at the same time.'

One of the benefits accruing to companies which produce regular operational data is that foremen and charge-hands are in a position to know exactly how their section stands. The lack of cost consciousness among supervisors was one of the most commonly heard complaints of senior management. The finance controller of a medium-sized domestic appliance firm described what his firm had done to overcome the problem:

'I have always been taught that a foreman saw the employer's side as well as the employees' side. He was a man who, if not exactly erudite, exercised his discipline through superior mental powers, as well as knowing what the job was of every man in his department. He could probably do the job too. But here there was no such thing. If we got a foreman of the standard I have described, we threw our hats in the air. Consequently, we have had to undergo a long period of education to get them interested in cost. You might say they weren't even cost conscious at first. They were not conscious that in ordering up sets of materials for their men to use they were involving the company in expense. After the institution of budgetary control the cost accountant saw each foreman separately each month and showed him what the analysis was for each month of his expenses and compared it with the budget which the cost accountant had fixed. Gradually we got the foreman interested in the budget. Gradually he saw that the actions which he took were influencing the fixing of this budget.'

All these practices assist firms in maximising their productivity. It is not suggested that firms cannot be run without them, indeed they can be and many of the firms visited had been until quite recently. Nor is it presumed that these planning and control techniques do not involve management in fairly heavy expenditure. Again they do and the interviewers heard from several executives how cost had deterred firms from their introduction. However, the ability to combat competition and to ensure future growth will depend increasingly on intelligent planning and tight control. Budgeting, cost control and work study are some of the management tools used to achieve greater efficiency and higher productivity—others (such as critical path analysis) are becoming increasingly available to management. The thrusting management takes advantage of these techniques to transfer as much of the running of the firm from a basis of hunch and inspired guesswork to a basis of agreed objectives, careful planning and detailed control.

Plant Appraisal and Replacement

A second area of firms' activities relevant to cost reduction is the appraisal and replacement of their existing plant. This activity is of mounting complexity, first, because the fixed assets of firms have increased markedly since the war and, secondly, because the rate of technological change is increasing with the result that the working life of plant is becoming more difficult to predict. In order to optimise productivity a firm must use its plant as fully as is practicable and at the same time ensure by systematic cost studies that it could not improve its profitability by installing more productive equipment. To make the correct decision about replacement requires sound judgement in the light of certain pertinent information, which includes the cost of running the current plant, the practices of competitors and the likely cost of and benefits from operating new plant over its expected life.

In many of the companies visited decisions to replace machinery were frequently made without a full financial assessment of the consequences. The procedures adopted varied. In some firms production executives were annually allocated sums of money to spend on plant as they thought best. The interviewer's suggestion to one accountant that he might participate in the decision making process by producing some calculations was met by a timid 'that I wouldn't be asked to do'. At the other extreme a works director of a very large electronics firm with responsibility for several thousand employees was powerless to spend a penny. It was due, he complained, 'to the accounting mentality which always applied with boards of directors who can count money and capital'. However, a generalised account of what occurred in most of the firms visited can be given.

The actual responsibility for initiating plant replacement lay, without exception, with the executive in charge of production. At the sleepiest extreme he was activated by the actual breakdown of a machine, at the most thrusting by a detailed knowledge of the latest available equipment together with the total cost of running and maintaining each item of his present plant. Other factors bearing on his judgement were the expected life of new equipment, the availability of capital, the availability of labour—particularly for shift work, the attitude of shop-floor workers towards new plant, the ability of the factory to digest new machinery and the option of reconditioning. Once he had decided that a piece of machinery should be replaced, he had to present a case to the board. Sometimes this was done in collaboration with the firm's accountant and sometimes it was done without any financial justification at all, the case being pleaded only in terms of men saved or greater physical output.

In many instances the proposal had to show a very rapid pay-back period, usually in anticipation of obsolescence. In one domestic appliance firm a maximum of two years was laid down by head office, but the works manager told the research team that he personally liked to see certain pieces of machinery paid off in nine months. In other firms management hoped that it would be achieved in about five years. The technique of discounted cash flow was not mentioned in any of the firms visited.

Many of these points are worth examining in greater detail. The degree to which senior production management appeared thrusting in advocating new machinery varied widely. The yard manager of a large shipbuilding firm had little choice in the following situation:

'Well, if you've got a machine that breaks down you've got to get it replaced. . . . The flanger—that's the first machine I replaced—it kept breaking down.'

The same emphasis on using machinery as long as it is still reliable is present in the following remark of the works manager of a domestic appliance firm who appeared to have formed an almost sentimental attachment to some of his old machinery:

'Even if the machine was performing well and had been depreciated, there wouldn't be a case for replacement, would there? . . . It's earned its keep at work. . . . There's no case if it is producing effectively to say, "Well, look it's been a faithful servant. We've had it many years. We must get rid of it." I should say, "No. If it is a good performer, we'll keep it." '

Nor was this emphasis limited to just two industries. The production manager of a medium-sized machine tool firm described how junior works executives:

'. . . are looking for me to keep me in the picture as to which machines are now beginning to get on their last legs.'

From a very large earthmoving equipment firm the interviewer heard how the company was unwilling to discard undepreciated machinery. The works director said:

'We very rarely chuck out a machine tool because there is something better available. We would normally go to the normal length of that machine tool which is, say, ten years, and we will then replace it willynilly. If we find something better to replace it with, obviously we will, but if there isn't anything better then we will replace it with the same again.'

The sturdiness of British machine tools received special mention from the works manager of a domestic appliance firm when he discussed replacement policy:

'Well, we usually find that it's worn out, that it doesn't do its job properly. That doesn't happen very often you know because British machines, which mainly we've bought, are wonderfully robust and, if they are kept well, they seem to last for ever, these darn things! What we seem to mainly do is to buy new machines for additional work and then we do eventually scrap some of the older ones. We never run a machine until it's worn out and then buy a new one. We usually are in advance of that. We buy in advance of everything going out and then we decide later on, "Oh well, we'd better get rid of this thing."'

The most interesting set of reasons the research team heard for not replacing plant came from a shipyard managing director:

'I think modernisation in shipbuilding has become a fashion rather than a factual need. I think the pressure of efficiency experts and automation manufacturers has reached the point where it becomes a sales point that you're going to save two, three, four or five men, and the cost of saving is a terrible one. If this was carried to its logical conclusion, it is not only machines that would be automated but men too. . . . I would resent anyone telling me that in my industry I could automate and allow these men to go elsewhere. I can't mould or talk to a machine but I can take and mould men, and in the process be moulded myself. It is a reciprocal factor.'

None of these production executives can be accused of rashness in promoting replacement schemes. Their attitude seems to be one of 'let well alone', or, as one production director of a small machine tool firm put it, 'There's a lot of cock-eyed talk going on about replacing machinery after a very short period of time.' It contrasts forcibly with the attitude of a works manager of a large electronics firm:

'You must have someone who's looking and saying, "How can we do better? Is there any automatic lathe that will do this? Is there any automatic way of welding these things or an automatic way of pressing these things out?"'

The same point was made in a northern machine tool firm where the works manager commented:

'We have a methods engineering department and a production engineer. They are reasonably new recruits to the company so they are not steeped in the tradition of this locality or the company. They are young men who have been in other companies, have seen other things and have open minds.'

It was in this firm that production executives had a detailed knowledge of their plant and of the age of individual pieces of machinery. Machinery was classified according to its year of purchase and each year a thorough survey was carried out.

The thrusting attitude of some production executives towards their machinery is matched by their efforts to find better equipment at home or abroad and in particular to watch the practices of their competitors. The works director of a machine tool firm said:

'Every year I personally make it my duty to go out to another country. This year it was Switzerland. Last year it was Germany. A year or two before that it was America. Next year I shall be going somewhere else. That's to make sure that at least I know what's happening in other machine tool factories in other countries and to keep ourselves abreast of developments. We go to conferences, when we think they're suitable.'

And the director of a Scottish textile mill sketched his journeys:

'I have trekked all over as far as I can to exhibitions of machinery in Germany, Belgium, Switzerland, Italy. I have been to machine makers whenever we hear a whisper of something that's possibly turning out new. Some things—we're at it before it's hardly known!'

The contrast between sleepy and thrusting practices has so far been illustrated in terms of production executives' satisfaction or dissatisfaction with current plant. The difference can be further explored by examining to what extent a full financial justification is required before a piece of plant can be replaced. In some sleepy firms financial calculations are disregarded. To one accountant in the shipbuilding industry the suggestion that a financial appraisal should be undertaken was class-room theory. The part he played in deciding to purchase capital equipment was:

'Not very much. I'll tell you what happens, or, may I say, I'll tell you what *should* happen. The theorist says that when you want to introduce something, an appraisal is made. What is the capital cost? What is the life of the machine? How long do you have to write off the cost? What will it save? And therefore you make out this little thing which I call an appraisal. That's the theorist. A practical person says, "Let's take this yard." If we're talking in terms of modernisation, we're really dealing with things here which have another bearing, which is probably not financial. There's a run down in manpower. There's a shortage of manpower. One has to modernise to counteract that shortage. One has to modernise to survive. You modernise in order to sell—to make yourself more efficient. But can you just put figures on it? The bigger it is obviously the more difficult it is to put figures on it, and from an accountant's point of view, the more desirable it is.'

In another shipyard the company secretary explained that the amount which might be saved through the purchase of new machinery was studied but:

'You can work out a pious hope—that's all I'll ever call it. We study it of course with the maker—he always says, "You can save £25,000 a year with this machine", and you give him a hard, cold look and say, "We don't spend £25,000 a year on this work", but you eventually get some sort of idea of what you hope to achieve.'

In one large machine tool firm the accountant was unconcerned about plant appraisal. His reaction to the suggestion that he should be concerned was that the matter could be left to the method study department, who would work out the savings in time which new equipment would bring. As for calculating it financially:

'We haven't got it down to such a fine art as that for the time being.'

And the works manager added in a later interview that pay-back periods were not considered:

'We wouldn't get down to details like that necessarily. We should judge the usefulness of the new machine on the increase in output that we should gain from it.'

While these three firms did not think in terms of financial justification others did, but for one reason or another found it impractical or were only just initiating it. The director of a large wool textile mill played down the idea of routine appraisals of plant:

'Let me say what it [replacement policy] is not. It's not a regular review of equipment to say, "Should this go out and should this not?" It's usually something that grows . . . as for how we decide—we've no budget of expenditure. In other words, we're not told we can spend so much. . . . It's more a question of instinct, listening to managers talking about various machines—looking at the cost and also looking at high maintenance bills and generally just taking them piecemeal as they come along. There's no fixed plan of evaluation of equipment, if that's what you're driving at.'

In a midlands machine tool firm the company secretary was frank about the amount of cost information available for taking a rational decision on replacement:

'I'm not certain that we here approach this scientifically enough. I doubt whether we do sufficient analysis of repair and maintenance expenditure to keep a proper check on how much an individual machine is costing us in repair and maintenance. The works engineer must clearly have an idea that a given machine is costing a lot in maintenance, because of the number of times he has to send a man to do something to it, but certainly no figures are produced to show that, and I think this is probably a weakness.'

On the same subject the production controller of a very large electronics firm described how his company had only recently begun to keep detailed maintenance costs:

'We've got a complete plant record of the age, cost, depreciation, value. We're even now at the present time keeping records—we've only just recently started this; it is not a lot of value yet, but it will be—of the actual cost of maintaining this individual piece of plant. You see, many good machines don't justify themselves economically because a better machine is put on the market and the best thing to do obviously is to get shot of the old machine and buy the new one.'

The works director of a large earthmoving equipment firm compared the practices of his own firm with those of his previous firm:

'The other half of our replacement programme is what savings can be made by buying new machine tools compared to a machine tool we have here, supposing it was in first-class condition—the savings that are available, because of improved performance and techniques and horse-power, and so on, on a machine.'

Interviewer: 'How sophisticated a piece of accountancy is that?'

'Not very. We don't go to anything like the length that, for instance, my previous company do on replacing a piece of plant. I used to work for one of the largest manufacturing firms in the country. There you've got to be able to show a saving, a guaranteed saving, of 15 per cent on the product that you get up. We don't have that sort of thing. We normally are not very sophisticated. It's a matter of opinion. We normally take two or three jobs which go on the machine tool and we will ask the supplier of the machine tool to go through the job and see what time it would take him to do that job with his own method on a big machine. The smaller machines we just replace when we feel inclined.'

A more thrusting approach to the question of justifying the purchase of new plant in financial terms was found in a medium-sized domestic appliance firm. The works manager explained:

'We try and justify it—any purchase of that sort—on variable cost alone, if we can. If we can't, we look further afield to try and find another justification for it, which it may not be possible to evaluate purely and simply in terms of money, by the same methods. One thing we do try and avoid and that is buying machinery and equipment just because it looks pretty, but only because either it does a job better or it does the job cheaper or it does the job safer or something of that sort.'

Unlike the previous firm, an examination of total costs was made in another domestic appliance firm where the works director told the research team that his accounts department calculated all possible savings which would accrue from a new piece of plant:

'They go into everything—electricity, gas, light, heat, power, floor space, depreciation. They've got the whole issue all split down. We can say that, if we put that machine in there, instead of these, well, we're going to save that much floor space, and we can calculate pretty accurately what the savings are in terms of overheads and anything else. The accounts department do this and we have a special forecasting department who go through this thing with a tooth-comb and they do the financial justification for it. I don't do it. I've got a pretty good idea before I start that it's right but they do the eventual financial justification.'

Similarly thrusting was the combination of production and finance executives in an earthmoving equipment firm. The interviewer visited the firm at a time when:

'We have plans to replace six machines of a certain type by two machines of this latest and most modern kind. Now, the rates of depreciation on the old machines, their initial cost, the upkeep, the repairs in any one year, have been calculated and set against the initial cost and depreciation and tax allowance of the new one, and we decided that this is very much worth while. But I'm not doing this of my own volition, you understand? The decision to replace the machines is taken by the technical people because they have seen this new machine on the market and they are extremely interested, but I only justify what they would like to do.'

However financial calculations are prepared and whatever cost items may be missing from them or wrongly included, those managements that are using the pay-back technique for assessing replacement investments must decide on the length of the period. In many of the firms visited the period required seemed to be much too short and the return required therefore unjustifiably high. The two exceptions to this could be the electronics and domestic appliance industries. One managing director explained why in his firm certain machinery had to pay for itself in two years:

'With an expensive piece of machinery it is quite hard to make it pay for itself in two years. In the appliance market you have to look at the tremendous changes in the type of appliance that have been taking place in the last few years. Unless one writes off something in a really short period of time, one might find it outmoded. You take one of our machines, which really only enjoyed a really large sale for about three years and then tended to be superseded by another type of machine. If we'd taken say five years to write off the machinery we wouldn't have done it—it would have been spread over too long a period.'

In other industries there would seem to be less justification for a quick pay-back period. One shipbuilding firm mentioned a pay-back period of five years and an earthmoving equipment firm less. Its works director explained why:

'I think all the cases we have put up for new machine tools have been in the order of saving the purchase cost within three or four years. It may still be an economic proposition if in fact it takes ten years, but my general impression of machine tool development is really of such a nature that improvements in machine tools are being made fairly regularly. In other words, having got out two or three cases which produced savings, which have paid for themselves in three years, one looks a little bit old-fashioned at anything taking six years.'

Estimating the expected life of a piece of plant is an intractable problem. A revolutionary process can be introduced and firms may be left with relatively large quantities of obsolete plant which has not been paid off. Under this constant threat the tendency to play it safe must be very strong, but the fact remains that the shorter the pay-back period allowed the more difficult it becomes to present a case for buying new equipment.

One further factor which can lead to sleepiness in machine tool replacement is the effect on executives of knowing that an item of plant that they want to replace is not yet fully written off in the firm's accounts. Inland Revenue practice requires firms to write off fully in the year in which a piece of plant is scrapped the undepreciated balance of the original cost. Although complying with this requirement is no more than effecting a 'book' loss, the prospect of incurring such a loss sometimes appeared to deter senior management from introducing new plant until the old plant was fully written off, even if the difference in productivity between the new plant and the old was enough to justify the full cost of the new, less any amount that might be obtained by selling the old. The depreciation policy of firms can further aggravate this situation. In nearly all the firms visited the majority of plant was depreciated at the same rate. The company secretary of a medium-sized domestic appliance firm mentioned that machinery being worked on a two-shift basis was treated differently but:

'Most machinery we write off in ten annual instalments. That is the general run of machine tools.'

Asked why he chose ten years, he replied:

'It's just the accountancy training I suppose. Plant and machinery 10 per cent—that seems to be customary in this area.'

In a large shipbuilding firm the company secretary said that he had consultations with production executives on the expected life of individual pieces of plant. None the less:

'The general run of machine tools, and that sort of equipment, are depreciated over twenty years.'

This accountant thought that, although some pieces of plant had a short life and others a long one, a general average of all of them would provide a correct period of depreciation. In a few firms visited, however, the practice was found of estimating the life of each piece of plant and depreciating it over that number of years. The finance controller of a very large company explained:

'We've gone into estimating the remaining life of each individual asset and it is all worked out in the very greatest detail. I've got quite a big department, called the fixed assets department, which is concerned with the keeping of records of these blocks of machinery all through the organisation.'

It is clear that the practice of depreciating large quantities of machinery over the same number of years is administratively convenient but it produces accounts that are not likely to lead to optimum provision for plant replacement, which is best facilitated if the expected life of each item of plant is estimated separately and the item written down at the appropriate rate.

The survey referred to on page 31 showed that the majority of machine tools in British factories were over ten years old. While such a survey must be interpreted with caution, it does suggest that the productive equipment of the average British firm is not modern enough.[1] One reason for this that emerged from the interviews was the sleepy practice of failing to make regular plant reappraisals, indeed, of waiting until a machine is 'on its last legs' before replacing it. Another reason may well be the widespread failure to make such reappraisals on the basis of systematic costing. The thrusting practice is to appraise each item of plant regularly, and to replace it whenever financial calculations show that the profitability of the firm would rise by introducing a new piece of plant.

Purchase of Raw Materials and Components
On the subject of buying raw materials and component parts, most production executives interviewed expressed grievances against either the unreliability and indifference of their suppliers or the prevalence of price rings. These complaints were heard most vociferously from electronics firms and firms with American connections. Generally, it appeared that the forces of competition were slowly making themselves felt among industrial suppliers of all kinds. Many firms, however, did not seem to be expediting this process, and hence reducing costs, by placing special emphasis on their purchasing function. Despite the fact that the cost of raw materials and components was often as much as 60 per cent of factory cost, it was seldom

---

[1] A survey of obsolescence of machine tools in 1960 showed that in the ten years since 1950 new machine tools had become about 40 per cent more productive. This survey is mentioned in *Metalworking Production* Research Department, op. cit., p. 31.

suggested to the research team that they should interview the firm's buyer. One managing director gave a peculiar reason:

'We've got a very unsociable buyer. That's why I didn't introduce you to him—*I* wouldn't like to sell to him. Buyers are a race apart, I'm told, and they're awkward, lumpy men—as I think they should be.'

Within the management hierarchy it often appeared that the buyer was a relatively unimportant member of the firm and sometimes he was no more than a senior clerk with direct responsibility to a senior member of management, who might be the accountant, the works director or the commercial manager. The accountant of a large earthmoving equipment firm held an attitude typical of many senior managers:

'Buyers to my mind fulfil a clerical function only. They're told what to buy and how much to buy, and what time it's got to be in by. They're told all that by the production control department. They've then got to buy in the best market. They've got to know these markets. They've got to know who to talk to.'

None the less, this executive pointed out that buying was becoming a more professional activity:

'We're going out of the age of the old joke that, whenever two people met, a buyer and a seller, the first thing they did was to tell one another a joke. We're going now into a more educated sphere where what we want is more important than the old pals' act and slapping on the back and all this sort of rubbish, but a certain amount of that still goes on.'

Some of the executives interviewed placed all the emphasis on continuity of suppliers—a factor that clearly has to be taken into account in purchasing some articles more than others—and seemed too much inclined to play down the importance of price. The works director of a small machine tool firm talked about one of the firm's traditional suppliers—a foundry that had supplied them with castings for forty years:

'So far as I personally am concerned, it's as good as having our own foundry without the headaches. They know our job. They know what we demand and they can give it to us. . . . If you've got a good buyer, who's looking for 3d. a hundredweight off the price of castings and he has about a dozen foundries working for him, you're in real trouble. If you've got a concern that can produce good castings for you, that, we say, is the best way of dealing with it.'

And the works manager of a large earthmoving equipment company did not greet price reduction by suppliers with enthusiasm:

'You can't get into the rat race of just continually changing your suppliers because somebody has been sent out from a firm that's not doing so well and they've decided to reduce their prices. I think there's got to be confidence and an understanding between suppliers and buyers.'

Another firm, this time in the domestic appliance industry, told the interviewer that it was policy always to buy from British suppliers—thus denying themselves the possibility of cheaper materials from abroad.

In contrast to these three insufficiently thrusting attitudes, the research team heard of a variety of ways, mainly in the domestic appliance industry, in which firms had tried to reduce the cost of their supplies. The production manager of a very large domestic appliance firm described his attitude towards component suppliers:

'There is a much wider market for buying components and we do very widespread shopping before we decide on a particular supplier and that particular supplier is never given a long contract. He is always aware that he is up against the competition of the next man, and we do change our sources of supply and our terms of buying very considerably. The exercise at the start of a new product is really the key to the success of the product. It is a question of how widely you shop, because surprising differences are given on cost and surprising differences are given on tooling time, and it is a matter of going to sometimes a dozen different suppliers to find a satisfactory cost.'

Another domestic appliance firm had set up a purchasing office in Germany for six months to investigate the possibility of buying German supplies. The whole management team of one medium-sized machine tool firm had assembled together to pursue cost reduction:

'We've taken every type of machine we manufacture, built one and laid all the parts from another machine alongside it, and then everyone from the managing director to the chief engineer, the production engineer, the sales manager, the company secretary, the works manager, the superintendents, have gone through those items asking, "Why do we do this?" or "Why do we do that?", and in doing it we have gradually reduced the cost of materials for the machine and reduced the cost of manufacture. . . . Another thing we did, we listed all the people that we have accounts with, and then we grouped them into gross amounts—in other words, all the companies where we spend £10,000, all the companies where we spend £5,000, all the companies where we spend £3,000. We were very much amazed to find the number of companies we bought from and we set about reducing them by checking the competitive values of the various companies.'

In shipyards executives constantly quoted the fact that they seldom had control of more than 30 per cent of the final cost of a ship. Most were equally insistent that they were in the hands of their suppliers, who were unreliable and whose products were more expensive than their equivalent from foreign sources. None the less, little seemed to have been done to buy overseas. Sometimes it was claimed that owners' specifications nominated British suppliers only and left builders with no freedom of choice. One yard manager described his disappointment that falling order-books had not yet squeezed the firm's suppliers:

'It doesn't always make as big an impact as we hoped it would make. It is perhaps only going to come to light in the next year or two, when things are really tough. Up to the moment, at least up to last year, all auxiliary machinery suppliers for ships' machinery and so on had full order-books, so if one company left them it wasn't a tragedy to them. When we left them, they didn't throw up their hands in horror and come down begging us to reconsider, they just said, "All right, good luck when you go to the next man!" That's the danger, of course, you go away from one supplier and you fall into another trap somewhere else. You can only do that by trial and error, can't you?'

None the less, this yard had started purchasing overseas:

'We have bought various items of ships' auxiliary machinery abroad. Mainly machinery. We have in the last year bought the man-made timbers for internal bulkheads and so on. We've bought these abroad from Germany and imported them into this country. We have bought winches, through the winch suppliers. They have also supplied the electrics allied to these winches. Although we're only contracted with the one winch supplier, he in turn has brought in other electrics to apply to his winches to supply to us. So we have definitely explored the world market rather than just the British market.'

The advantages of buying overseas were abundantly clear to one works director in an electronics firm—his criticisms of the component industry were repeated by other executives in other firms:

'Unfortunately we have to use whatever is available on the market, but there's no doubt that one of the biggest millstones around this company's neck, and many others, is the British component industry. It is really appalling, if you compare it with American and German industry. The British component industry is still rolling along in the old war-time concept that: "They have to buy from us, because there's no one else to buy from, and therefore we can produce a minimal standard the whole time and they have to take it." And they are already feeling the pinch, because I'm not prepared to buy British components. I can buy much better American components and better German components, and, until these guys start waking up, we shall begin to do more and more of this.'

It was widely complained that there was not enough competition in many sectors of industrial goods; that for many years, suppliers had simply notified price increases by circular letter to buyers, who had been powerless to do anything about it. But the buyers are to blame at least to some extent. It was evident that some of them have tended to emphasise their inability to alter the *status quo* instead of taking steps to force price reduction or better performance on suppliers.

Conclusion

Costs can be reduced in the comparatively short term by modern techniques of budgeting and production control, and by an active and cost-conscious approach to the replacement of machinery and the purchase of raw materials and components. The interviews showed that some of the firms had high standards in these respects, and in particular that some of the thrusting practices had been adopted in the last five or ten years. Others had still to awaken to the possibilities that such practices offer in the way of greater efficiency and growth.

In the longer run, substantial or even spectacular results, in cost reduction as well as the development of new products, can be achieved by effective research and development. This, in relation, however, more to new products than to cost reduction, is the subject of the following chapter.

CHAPTER 7

RESEARCH AND DEVELOPMENT

Since the mid-1950s there has been a steady increase in the proportion of the gross national product spent on research and development (to be referred to throughout this chapter as R & D.)[1] In 1955 the figure was 1·3 per cent or £300 million. By 1961 it had risen to 2·7 per cent or £634 million: an average annual increase in real terms of 8·7 per cent. Besides a doubling in money terms of the resources devoted to R & D, there has also been a gradual change in the way in which the money has been used. In 1955 civil research expenditure was £115 million or 38 per cent of the total, the balance being spent on defence. By 1961 the amount had increased to £380 million or 59 per cent of the total. But, while no other country spends a significantly higher proportion of its gross national product on R & D[2] or devotes a greater proportion of its total R & D expenditure to civil research, it is by no means sure that such expenditure is distributed among British industries or firms to the best advantage or that they are making the best use of the results. The research team therefore examined the attitudes towards R & D in the firms visited.

In each of the firms visited, the managing director was informed that the study wished to interview that member of management responsible for R & D; thus, the onus for deciding which aspect of R & D should be the subject of discussion fell on the chief executive. In most of the firms the area chosen was that dealing with the development, design and introduction of new products and these topics will therefore predominate in the present chapter.

Wool Textiles

The research team heard, from executives in the wool textile industry, of a variety of efforts to introduce new or improved products ranging from creaseless cloth to spinning or balling machinery being developed with machinery manufacturers. As in the other industries,

[1] See the *Annual Report of the Advisory Council on Scientific Policy, 1961–1962* (HMSO), Cmnd. 1920, 1962, giving the results of the triennial survey on R & D in industry.

[2] The proportion of the gross national product devoted to R & D is roughly equivalent to that spent by the United States.

however, a number of reasons were given why a particular firm was hampered in its R & D activities. One managing director of a private firm employing about 400 people said that the disadvantage of being small was that the firm had not got the time or the resources 'to carry out big enough experiments to prove a point'. He went on to explain:

'It [R & D] has, due to the way we are running, to be to some extent rather a hit-and-miss job; plus the fact that you have the greatest difficulty—and this doesn't just apply to our firm, it applies all over the place—the greatest difficulty in getting people to try out new ideas as you want them to be tried out. I mean people in the mill, actually on the shop floor, if you like to put it that way—the foremen in particular.'

But the executive of another firm criticised the conservatism of his colleagues rather than that of the workers:

'This is the main difficulty that I have with people at top level. They cannot see that you've got to do a lot of playing about to get it right. They may admit this but they don't really believe it. They think it's a failure if it doesn't work the first or second time and they're resistant to change because it's a nuisance and because it's very risky. There's another thing . . . "What's good enough for my father is good enough for me", and there's something more to it than that—there's this inherent psychological, fundamental feeling of insecurity.'

The managing director of a firm producing cloth for the speciality and novelty trade was critical of his suppliers when he pointed out:

'I'm continually saying to spinners that they don't do enough research. The spinners should come to us with novelty yarns. They should give us a little more novelty. We shouldn't be left to do all the research, to say what we want. They should be finding out from the markets what's being developed on the Continent, what's being developed elsewhere in trends, and they want to embody that trend into their yarn much more than they've been doing in the past, such as the continentals do.'

A senior executive of another, medium-sized firm, answering a general question on the company's R & D policy, emphasised that if a firm was to stay in business it must always be looking out for improvements. It was particularly necessary to introduce new methods in the case of textile machinery yet it was here that he indicated a major weakness:

'One of the things that we certainly think is lacking in this country is that the machinery manufacturers are trailing along behind us rather than leading us.'

He went on to explain that his firm had had to go to an Italian company for certain textile machinery:

'We can't get it in England. I always say that we need a new aware-ness on the part of textile machine manufacturers of the need for semi-automation in this industry rather than going on with machines of a design and a principle that have been accepted for the last hundred years or so.'

The managing director of another firm, which made high-class tops, felt limited in his freedom of action by the conservative attitude of the small number of buyers who comprised his market. The energy which firms will put into diversifying their traditional output may be restricted if it seems to them that market reaction will be unfavour-able:

'The trouble is that you have a certain reputation for making tops of a certain general quality at a certain time. To maintain that standard is your first duty, at least it's what your customers look upon as your first duty. If it once got round that so-and-so was making a different kind of top, even though you were still making the others as well, they would immediately assume that the whole thing was changing. They would never accept the fact that you were diversifying and trying to move into another branch of the industry. They would immediately jump to the conclusion that the whole thing was slowly sinking quality-wise. It's ridiculous but I'm afraid that we must accept that as part and parcel of the realities of the trade.'

Such resistance, whether on the part of conservative-minded workers, management, suppliers or customers, was clearly widespread. Two of the firms interviewed had taken notably energetic measures to overcome it. In one of them, a small firm making top quality cloth, the importance attached to R & D had been clearly demonstrated in the last three years by the recruitment of an executive to take charge of it and by his immediate appointment to the board. He explained:

'I'm responsible for first of all knowing what is available and what is new in industry. That could be applicable to anything that we do now or anything that I could visualise that we will do in the next twenty or thirty years. The second thing I am responsible for is buying every new piece of equipment whatever it may be. If we can't buy a piece of equipment that we want, I am responsible for either making it ourselves here or developing it ourselves here or getting somebody else to do it for us. Then the last function that I am responsible for is the laboratory where we set out deliberately to produce new product ideas, like stain-resistant cloth.'

To speed the development of this stain-resistant cloth, the firm enlisted the help of a director of the raw materials suppliers and also of the local DSIR representative, and with their assistance successfully manufactured the complicated plant required to do the job.

Another of this director's responsibilities was to examine the firm's traditional method of deciding what designs should be produced each year. When he arrived he found this situation:

'We've always had as far as I can remember—certainly since the war—a committee whose job it is to provide the new range of patterns for the season. I suppose you could call this research and development, although it isn't really. All they do is inspired guess-work by some translation against known specified trends of the limited market research carried out by our salesmen.'

At this time, the governing factor for the firm was the attitude of its five most important customers. He suspected that these men were being too conservative in their interpretation of the needs of ordinary people, so he and some of his staff spent one or two days in the main square of a neighbouring city asking people what their reactions were to samples of cloth that they carried with them. Convinced that his interpretation of public demand was more correct than that of the buyers, the firm adopted a new policy:

'We will put better pressure on them [the five customers] through the man in the street by advertising. We will say, "This is X firm", to the man in the street. "This is the brand image of our firm. We're a firm in which science is married to craft and we're producing new attributes in cloth which we want you to have. Go in and ask for our cloth by name." '

Whatever degree of success firms may have had in planning and operating their research and development efforts, they spoke with one voice in their enthusiasm for the Wool Industry's Research Association (WIRA). (The industry is one of six which has a research

association supported by a compulsory levy.) The managing director
of a medium-sized firm, which spent no money on R & D, remarked:

'I would say that they are absolutely first-class. You see, none of us
is really big enough to run its own research department so that, as
you have gathered, we have more or less combined as an industry to
do it. Consequently it's done extremely well. Now, how far one
benefits from it is entirely one's own pigeon. It is a question of
whether one is perpetually pestering them, as we attempt to do, and
discussing things with them, our own problems, to see if they have
discovered anything of technical interest in their own research.'

This comment, despite its enthusiasm, was not untypical of opinions
heard in the other firms interviewed. The smallest firm of the nine
visited, which was a privately owned company, was just as anxious
to praise the research association. Its chief executive said that if he
had any problem at all he had only to approach the research association and they would try to solve it for him. As an example of their
helpfulness he described how he had been on the point of buying a
particular machine for testing the level of moisture in yarn, but
being slightly doubtful about its quality had asked WIRA to examine
it independently. The machine was found to be less accurate than
had been claimed for it by its makers, and he decided not to buy it.

A further example of how the research association helped firms
was given by a director of another small private firm. His company
had recently installed some automatic looms and was uncertain of
the optimum speed at which they should be run. On contacting
WIRA he was informed that a detailed study had been made of the
subject and that the best speed for an automatic loom was 105 to
115 picks per minute. Asked why he thought the Association worked
well, the managing director of another firm explained:

'Partly because it [WIRA] has the necessary financial backing. In
fact, it can really have as much as it needs—it's just a matter of
increasing the levy. Provided the results are there, we are only too
glad to increase the levy. And partly because, after all, we're critics
of it and therefore it is kept on its toes. It has all the necessary
financial resources it wants—it ought to be good.'

Machine Tools

Reference has already been made in Chapter 3 to the steady flow of
criticism to which the machine tool industry has been subject in
recent years. Two reports in particular, those of Professor Melman
and the Mitchell Committee, have been critical of many of the

industry's activities. Among the executives interviewed, reactions to the reports differed, although all were ready to admit that the industry had skimped on R & D. The managing director of one large private company said:

'I think it was excessively vigorous criticism, where a softer criticism would have been truthful. The vigour with which we were criticised was, I think, unjust, unfair and unwarranted.'

But later in the interview in answer to a question about the industry's past attitude to R & D he said:

'You see, the attitude in the industry towards research as a whole was, "Well, we've designed these machines for years. We know all about them." That attitude has changed very radically in the last few years.'

A positive view of the Mitchell Report was voiced by the R & D director of one small firm:

'Sir Steuart Mitchell, I think, did an excellent job. Many of the recommendations are things that people have been thinking about, as we often do, and then it needs this sort of sparking off. But it takes time, you've got to condition men's minds to accepting your ideas.'

All the firms visited showed signs of being increasingly aware of the importance of R & D and many of the ways in which they could use their new research association. A typical picture was drawn by the technical director of a medium-sized firm:

'I think in the last few years that new designs have been introduced at an increased tempo. I think the only way in which we can survive is by this policy of trying to anticipate future needs in this industry. . . . About six years ago, we decided that it was time that we had a section which could devote its time entirely to new machines and that we feel has been a very useful thing. . . . We have a number of draughtsmen including apprentices in the prototype design office and twice that number of draughtsmen in the other drawing office.'

A very large machine tool firm had always acknowledged the value of R & D but its efforts had been somewhat haphazard. The managing director explained:

'Previously each executive asked for specific amounts of money in his department to do specific tasks, but, while he would be desirous

E

of research being done on the project, it wasn't his prime function. It was the sort of thing that got done if he had time. Now we have an annual budget and we aim to work within that.'

In the last few years the firm has formed a centralised research division in the guidance of which all other departments have an interest. A regular meeting of the executives concerned ensures that production personnel can state their research requirements and keep in touch with the progress of the division.

A third example of increased R & D activity was found in a medium-sized firm which had paid scant attention to it in the past. As one executive said:

'We had allowed the design department side of our business to run down and in consequence had been trying to sell machine tools which were rather outdated, not only in design but in the possibility of economic manufacture.'

During the last six years a younger generation had taken over control of the company. One of them, an engineering graduate, formed a technical R & D department with himself as director. The immediate aim of the department has been the redesign of all the company's existing products in order to cut costs. The department's work is programmed two years ahead.

Not all firms, of course, have overlooked R & D in the past. One of the most successful owed much of its prosperity to its technical director whose thrusting attitude had kept it in the forefront of machine tool development. He had joined the firm before the war:

'As technical director, my duties were to invent machinery, most of it personally, draw it out personally, and get it made. These days the duties are still to invent it, still to think up the new ideas, still to think ahead of competition, still to think ahead of research. To get the "handle turning" done by subordinates, assistants, who are trained, as far as they can be trained, and eventually one of them must take this job I've got.'

His importance to this large firm was evident in the following remark, which contrasts with another executive's assurance that each department's expenditure was budgeted:

'We have a department but nothing is ever budgeted. What we spend on research and development is mainly what I think we ought to be doing for the future, as far as I can read the future, and, you see, public research is no use to me at all because in this competitive world I've got to know how to do the job before the nation knows how to do it, otherwise I'm no good.'

His record of success proves that he does 'know how to do the job before the nation knows', but he was in a minority in writing off the value of public research. The more usual attitude shown by firms was one of cautious welcome for their newly formed research association. Another research director explained clearly how he used outside research facilities, when answering a question on whether his company had any forward plan for research and development:

'We've now got a forward plan which includes a small section which attempts to forecast the type of our machines that will be wanted in thirty years' time, two generations away from present-day production. This small section should throw up very definite problems which at present have no solutions. Having found certain areas in which we're lacking in information and knowledge the intention is to throw these into the research organisations, either the Machine Tool Industry Research Association's building at Macclesfield, to be completed this year, or into one of the Government research establishments. And when we get answers back to some of these problems, which may take two, it may take five, years, this information should then be available for the next generation of machines. Furthermore, we can also enlist the help of universities: Manchester, Birmingham, London, Sheffield at various times have been asked questions in a very informal way, and we've had very good response. We've had very good help from the National Engineering Laboratory in East Kilbride.'

As in the wool industry, innovation by machine tool manufacturers can be inhibited by the conservatism of their customers, thereby creating a vicious circle in which neither maker nor buyer will take risks. Thus, the research director of a small company on being asked what was his toughest problem replied:

'The inability of a large number of people to realise that if you are going to make a commercial success of a product you must have a number of companies or Government establishments with sufficient competence to install an untried piece of mechanism. Only by field experience can it be proved completely that it will be satisfactory and thus build up a measure of confidence.'

On the whole, it may fairly be concluded on the evidence of the interviews that the machine tool industry has been responding to the stimuli of criticism by increasing its R & D effort, even if in many firms the process is still in its infancy. While it is argued that the Government and the engineering industry must, as the industry's customers, share the blame if it has failed to progress fast enough in recent years, machine tool manufacturers could not do better than share the attitude of the research director of one small firm:

'Machine tool makers ought to be not keeping parallel with the pace of improvement but ought to be leading the pace because they are the prime mover in production.'

Shipbuilding

In most of the shipyards visited it was the executive responsible for the design, estimating and drawing offices who answered questions on R & D. Generally the impression was gained that the R & D effort in these functions was haphazardly managed. Indeed, many executives claimed that R & D relating to methods of designing and estimating must by its very nature be intermittent; that it was inevitably linked to owners' enquiries and orders and each of these was different from the others; and that no shipyard could therefore allocate special personnel to these functions or budget for them on a long-term basis. It was, moreover, clear that R & D tended to be regarded as expendable whenever the pressure of work became too great. The designer of a medium-sized yard commented:

'We do it [R & D] to a very limited extent within our own organisation as far as the time at our disposal permits us. There are certain aspects of research into our own methods of construction, methods of design, methods of estimating which we develop in an endeavour to take short cuts but when at a time like, for instance, the present we are working particularly intensively on design and estimating to obtain the new orders which we have got to get there is a tendency to put the research into the background.'

A director of another large yard remarked on the casual nature of research in his firm when answering a question on how the work was financed:

'We decide what we want looking into as we go along and just meet the bill as it comes in. It's *ad hoc* absolutely. We don't have an advanced planning of design and development. We have to feel the pulse for the job as it goes along. You can't look ahead and say that you want to research on certain items in the oncoming year.'

Much the same account of how R & D was organised was given by the naval architect of one large yard when he explained that his firm did not have a long-term plan of work:

'No, it [R & D] is much more an *ad hoc* kind of thing.'
   Interviewer: 'Now, how in fact is this decision made? How do you decide that you will do research on whatever it is?'
   'That again is a very sort of chancy and hit-and-miss business. By conversations that we have with shipowners, for instance. From time to time we'll find out what their problems are and we'll find some of them are perhaps things we could be looking into. That's the only way that it's done unless somebody gets some ideas. I spend quite a bit of my time reading technical journals of one sort and another and we come across things in there which are worth following up, so the research on our side isn't really organised very much. It's very much a hand to mouth business.'

Any intelligent programme of R & D must be determined to some extent, varying with the nature of the industry, by a knowledge of the market for which a firm's products will be made. One firm, which had evidently tried to explore the minds of shipowning firms, spoke for most yards when its naval architect condemned owners for their lack of forward planning and research:

'I think what's wrong with all this business is that the shipowners don't do this research. There's an awful lot of research that they should be doing. They should be able to give us some ideas about what we should be looking into. We don't know about markets and all that sort of thing and it's up to the owners, I should think, to find out the kind of ships they ought to be having and the kind of things they should be having in the ships and that sort of thing. Those are their needs and they should be able to tell us. In fact, what has been happening is that the shipbuilders have been telling the shipowners what they ought to have, which is putting the cart before the horse in my opinion. I think the shipowning industry are very, very backward in this country in research themselves. . . . Our biggest problem, apart from technical problems, is handling shipowners and their technical staff. This may sound a very sweeping statement but, by and large, I think that the shipowners' technical staff or the people they send out to make day-to-day decisions aren't really up to the mark. They are not good enough. A lot of them haven't progressed in their ideas since they were apprentices. We find it quite difficult from time to time to get good ideas, or what we think are good ideas, accepted. Shipowners are very conservative and some of our methods, where we could save them a lot of money, are not accepted when put to them, because they are new.'

That the conservatism of owners has frequently been matched by that of builders is evident in the next quotation. The managing director of one medium-sized yard related how he had tried to persuade some of his directors that in the near future there would be bulk carriers of up to 25,000 tons operating at fifteen or sixteen knots:

'At that time I was laughed at. They preferred to think there would always be a market for the 10,000-ton ship . . . you see, well-established shipbuilders, as these people were, just could not foresee that the pattern of ships as they knew it and as they had built it for years could change so radically in such a short time.'

The British Ship Research Association (BSRA), which was founded in 1944 to undertake pure and applied research on behalf of the industry, appeared to play the main part in the industry's R & D work. Many of the executives interviewed were active on its various committees. Comment on it as a whole was favourable, though less enthusiastic than that of wool textile executives about their research association. A director of one large yard said:

'We use BSRA. They've got their intelligence service for extracting information from world-wide journals. If there are problems for which we haven't got the technical know-how, technical facilities, then they will handle it . . . and of course we use the National Physical Laboratory for testing models. That's a straight commercial transaction.'

While most firms did carry out a certain amount of R & D and all of them did make use of BSRA, another very large firm used its existence as a reason for not undertaking any R & D at all. The managing director of this firm said:

'We don't do anything as far as research in shipbuilding is concerned. I don't think there's any point. We contribute very handsomely to BSRA, and I can't see that we as a firm would gain anything by doing research on our own. I don't think there would be any sense whatsoever in us going to additional expense. I don't think we'd get the results from it.'

It is hard to believe that BSRA meets the special requirements of each yard to the extent of undertaking all the R & D that is worth doing in the industry, and it is hard to avoid contrasting this attitude unfavourably with the sturdy independence of the machine tool technical director who, in his determination to be ahead of the national average, appeared to go too far in the other direction by eschewing the use of any outside research facilities.

Until recently, the need for independent R & D was reinforced by a weakness of the Association which was emphasised by the naval architect of a large yard who remarked:

'To my mind, one of the great weaknesses of BSRA was that they were divorced from production, and you can do all the research in the world, but if you can't apply it to production, then, so far as applied research is concerned, it's just worthless.'

In 1962, however, the Association was re-formed and specifically directed to concentrate some of its activities on improving production techniques.

Research into methods of ship construction was outside the immediate province of most of the executives quoted so far. Some references were, however, made to it. One large yard had been ahead of others in starting a department to investigate production methods. The introduction of innovations and new methods of working was not without opposition from within the yard and the following comment of one yard manager is reminiscent of similar ones quoted by a wool textile manager:

'The methods which are being recommended by this department are now being accepted by foremen and workmen at a much faster rate than they were when we first started it. Sometimes at the beginning there was a lot of opposition to anything new. A man who had been hitting something with a hammer for thirty or forty years considered that no one else could possibly know as much as he did. That attitude has gradually changed.'

The naval architect of a large yard also related how the R & D effort had increased in recent years:

'I think we're a little more conscious of research and development than we were ten years ago.'
Interviewer: 'In what form does this consciousness express itself?'

'We do get projects approved and started, and things done, which ten years ago might have been considered a waste of money. Ten years ago we were turning work away from the door, our job was to keep the customers at arm's length. That is possibly one of the reasons why BSRA had a fairly thin time when it started. The ship-builders and the ship owners didn't really see that it was needed. They felt, probably, that they were wasting their money. It's only now that they're beginning to realise that, if they'd been willing to spend money ten or twenty years ago, they might have much better premises, much better ships, cheaper ships, and so on, now.'

Electronics

The electronics industry spends as much as 17 per cent of its net output on R & D. In one small firm the managing director showed how much importance he attached to it:

'I would say simply that, of all the money that was available, the first call on every money being spent that one can afford to spend is always in technical development. It is the prime function, as I see it, of an industrial company to spend every possible penny it can afford to spend on technical development.'

At the other end of the size scale, a technical executive of one very large firm described the scope of R & D in his company:

'We're spending a very great deal of money on it. I'm not talking about thousands of pounds. I'm talking about millions of our own money, never mind the Government's money. We're spending more of our own money in this outfit than we are of the Government's. No, research and development now is a major activity. I think we are extremely conscious of how much the future of the organisation depends on it. Well, in the group as a whole now there is something like 10 per cent of the total pay-roll working on R & D.'[1]

Another executive stressed the importance of being technically out in front:

'This has really been our whole philosophy, certainly in the field with which I'm familiar, that the only thing you've got to do is to be out in front technically. You can very often fail simply by taking a year or two too long to develop something. The other bloke has come

[1] This percentage includes those personnel working on Government sponsored R & D.

out with something which isn't quite as good but he's got it a year
before you have.'

A second incentive for R & D is the knowledge that through new
products a company grows. The technical director of an American
subsidiary put the matter this way:

'The [parent] company has found during the many years of its own
growth in the electronics instruments industry that it is almost
entirely dependent on the introduction of new products. We find
after a few years from the introduction of a new product that we
reach a plateau of sales. It is a remarkably stable plateau and it goes
on for a remarkably long time. But new growth is essentially built
around new products.'

The third reason frequently given for a company's R & D effort is
the ever-lurking fear of total American predominance in the electronics field. This anxiety about the American effort was found in
practically every firm visited. The chief engineer of a large firm which
was locked in fierce competition with a number of American companies stated this attitude quite baldly:

'My attitude has been all my life to say, "Well, I would like to have
a company which is competitive with the Americans." '

An important feature of this industry, motivated to a large extent
by the heavy Government support its American counterparts
received, was its attitude towards Government's relationship with
industry in the field of scientific research and development. The
larger companies unanimously believed that the only way in which
they could survive American competition, particularly in export
markets where certain American capital equipment has been making
serious inroads into traditional British markets, was by the Government giving more civil development contracts to the industry. The
statistic most commonly quoted in support of their attitude was that
IBM at present conducts two-thirds of the world's business in
computers. One research executive touched on the scale of the
United States Government's support for the American electronics
industry:

'The American electronics industry is pretty well, I should think, 70
per cent supported by the most massive programme of Government
R & D contracts which the world has seen or is likely to see. Well,
you can't compete with that sort of thing unless you're getting the
same sort of benefits. This is just a matter of common sense.'

One managing director was particularly critical of the 'no risk policy' which, he said, typified the British civil service and was engendered by 'direct reportability to Parliament'. As an example he recounted some recent negotiations he had had with Government officials:

'The Treasury now, for example, are saying that they aren't going to buy a computer for business data processing—they call it "computer"—lack of understanding again—unless it's been demonstrated working. They want to see it having run for three months on somebody else's premises. This attitude in one way is damaging enough, though semi-understandable to the lay mind—"Oh, you expect me to buy something that doesn't exist?" But I may say that all the advanced American computer developments have been done by the Government on a computer which didn't exist. . . . See, no risk! They want an absolute no risk policy! No risk, no advance, and this is how the Government doesn't back us.'

Another argument for Government support was the overdue modernisation of British industry which, executives argued, could proceed with vigour only if the Government backed key projects. IBM was again mentioned. This time its buying up of a paper mill in order to install automatic control equipment and demonstrate the resulting increased productivity was held up as an example of what the Government should do to speed up the pace of modernisation. The research director of a very large firm discussing this question said:

'It is highly desirable that the Government finances the uneconomical running of a full-scale chemical plant in order that the research be done to—nasty word—complete automation of such a plant. Somebody has to do it—O.K. Now, this is an immensely costly operation, you see, because full-scale plant puts stuff through at a fabulous rate and it goes down the drain. This is costly. What's more to the point, it is even more costly to the firm that's making it, if they're not able to deliver according to their schedule. This has got to happen. Now, if you've a firm in on the act, they're going to benefit, but on the other hand you cannot conceivably think that they are going to pay for it. They can't. It just won't be done. So the next thing you can do is think, "Ah well, we'll have a co-operative enterprise. We'll get everybody to agree"—and they won't. It won't get it done. And the Russians will do it, and the Americans will do it, through their own different ways of doing these things, and they will make the products—completely automated plants. We shan't. We'll go bust. End of chapter! Last final chapter, I think, in Glorious

British History. This is rather emotional but behind it there's a hell of a lot. And it's going to happen.'

To the managing director of this firm the Government had simply got its priorities wrong. He maintained that the Government bought aircraft which did not exist because they considered the aircraft industry more important than the computer industry:

'The air frame world just means whether you're in the air trade or not. The computer world covers whether you're going to be competitive right across the board of industry.'

Another executive in a similar firm with responsibility for selling a certain type of automatic equipment pointed to two industries which he argued could have been modernised if the Government had been anxious to promote industrial efficiency:

'If the Government was alive to what was going on in the shipping industry, it would have taken steps a long time ago and would not now have to put up £30 million. If it had been alive to what was going on in the cotton industry, it wouldn't have had to pay however much it did pay for the rationalisation there. And this is a crazy way for a nation to behave. Let your industries die and then pump money into them to make them turn over in their grave.'

The same executive mentioned that only 300 instrumentation computers (i.e. those used for controlling large-scale industrial processes) had been sold in the whole Western world. The number actually 'on line' in Britain was pitifully small—twenty-five to thirty-five.[1] It could not be too frequently argued:

'. . . that the management of British industrial concerns, British plants, have to change their attitude towards automation. They have to recognise that this is probably one of their only weapons left in competition against Europeans and perhaps even Japanese firms.'

In the larger companies considerable thought had been given to the organisation of R & D. Over the past few years most firms have developed a central research laboratory, or laboratories, which serve the various subsidiaries or divisions. The programme of work for the laboratory will be planned in broad terms up to five years ahead. Year-to-year decisions in greater detail will be taken at a meeting of

---

[1] These computers are mostly found in oil refineries, steel works, cement works and power stations.

managers of the subsidiaries or divisions that will be contributing
to the budget of the central laboratory, a representative of the main
board of the company, and the head of the research laboratory.
Within this framework one company's methods were described by
a director of a very large firm:

'Any engineer in the place is perfectly at liberty to put a proposition
forward. We encourage this, and in fact we allocate to each head of
laboratories sufficient cash to allow him on his own initiative to
institute work in his laboratory in order to, say, prove the principle
that will form the base of a proposition to the company. This
proposition, say to develop a new product, comes from the laboratory through to our research manager, who is concerned overall
with all technical activity. He is also my deputy, so he has this
entrée into all departments as well. He vets the proposal from a
technical point of view and, in effect, establishes an engineering
standpoint. He may reject it, in which case he would probably come
to myself and we'd argue about it. Generally speaking, we try at this
stage to establish an engineering standpoint and, technically, to give
a technical judgement as to whether the proposition is sound,
whether we support it overall-wise, and so on. It then goes to the
marketing manager, whose job in life is to assess whether the
market exists.'

As the last sentence suggests, the role of market research in this joint
endeavour of research laboratory and development team is somewhat
restricted. It seemed that most of the companies interviewed did not
feel that market research findings were of much help to them in
determining laboratory programmes of work. Instead the emphasis
appeared to lie on the laboratory and development sections throwing
up new ideas or products for which the salesman had to find a
market. Part of the explanation for the limited role of market
research was given by the technical director of a very large firm:

'Techniques which come up as a result of research very often have
no market until one has been discovered for them. This is where
technical advice rather than market research is needed.'

One very large firm, however, was altering its management structure
so that commercial and technical executives should have equal status
in future operations. In answer to questions on the relationship
between market research and development and whether the former
could set objectives for the latter, a senior research executive
commented:

'Now, in each of these product areas we've appointed somebody who has a major interest in the field as the technical manager. His functions again are largely co-ordination. We are also in the course of appointing another group of people who will be on the commercial side, product policy officers or something like that, who will co-ordinate the commercial side of the operation, working as a team with the appropriate technical manager. So in every product area you will have a senior technical executive, a senior commercial executive, who between them will try to co-ordinate and develop the business. There will be something like X of these pairs of people. In fact, they are already appointed. In fact, of course, I couldn't really operate without their help.'

The most positive approach was displayed by a very large firm which had recently started a marketing department and was increasing its expenditure on market research. One senior executive explained:

'We are tending to direct the market research along the lines of forward thinking and the overall market appraisals, as opposed to the detailed individual product market appraisals which are the functions of the divisional sales organisations.'

It is clear that the electronics industry, and most firms in it, devote a high proportion of resources to R & D and that this proportion is unlikely to increase much unless the Government does more to support it. Government policy in this respect is considered in Chapter 13. Meanwhile, the key problem for the firms is less how much to spend on R & D than, as one research director remarked, the choice of area in which to do it. If a criticism of the industry's effort can be made, it is that it remains doubtful from the interviews whether enough weight is yet given to market research and forecasting in selecting the areas for research or in discovering applications and markets for the techniques and products that are developed.

Domestic Appliances

All the six firms visited showed considerable interest in product design and development, though some of them had realised its importance later than others. The growing concern with design and development had several causes. One was that the market for consumer durables had grown at an annual rate of 9·3 per cent from 1954 to 1961, when it levelled off. During the years of expansion firms had struggled to satisfy demand, but latterly, operating below capacity, they have had to compete through improved products and price cutting. The extent to which the market has changed was stressed by an engineering executive of one medium-sized firm:

'A typical example of the short life of design is the electric cooker market. Now, one manufacturer's favourite boast was that a cooker designed before the war was selling very well right up to 1957, but he no longer makes that boast any more, and in fact he's having to change his design every year along with other electric cooker manufacturers—not necessarily change the basis of it but certainly add things or take things away and arrive at something that looks different and is, very often, different.'

A further reason for R & D activity was given by the chief design manager of a very large company. The respondent was in fact the only R & D executive to stress the point so explicitly:

'Well, cost reduction on existing products. . . . I set a target each year and this year it is just under 2 per cent of factory costs. That is the target, you see, throughout the whole of the standard lines that we have. Our target then, by design changes, is to reduce factory costs by under 2 per cent, which comes to about £X00,000 for this year.'

In their organisation of R & D some of the firms appeared to have integrated this function with production and marketing more successfully than firms in the other industries covered. In talking about the R & D department, one director discussed the mechanics of introducing a new product:

'The design department's job is to design the products, the mechanical design and the appearance design of the products. When any new product is contemplated the chap who leads the design team for that product or type of product will sit down with the marketing manager and they will draft a document that sets out the main features of the contemplated product. The document is then considered at a meeting which is attended by the managing director of manufacture, myself, and the designer for that particular product and his opposite number in marketing, and one or two other people, such as research men and so on, and the document is discussed in some detail and either accepted, or thrown out, or amended.'

Subsequent steps in the creation of a new product were the drawing up of a detailed engineering specification and full design drawings, the building of models which would then be looked over by the appearance designer from marketing, shown to the product planning committee for their approval, tested in the laboratories and finally distributed to a hundred staff and wholesalers for trials in their homes. Only when the new product had passed successfully through these stages could it go into full production.

Thus it appeared in some firms that design, production and marketing were all of equal status. The development manager of one firm felt that he could prevent conflicts between production and marketing by bringing their two requirements into balance where new products were concerned:

'Obviously one of the big tasks that I have is to prevent conflict between the commercial side of the business and the production side of the business, so far as I am able, in the field of new products. In any company there generally is this conflict for some reason which I don't understand, simply because the causes of the conflict, when you get right down to it, are very easy to isolate and recognise and deal with. I suppose the basic conflict is between the man who wants the new, and I suppose he wants the new on better terms than he had the old, and the man who wants to maintain a steady economic production. Well, these are chronically human sorts of attitudes and quite understandable ones. I have to do what I can, obviously, in preventing the sort of catastrophic situation which can arise if conflict does occur in the new product field, taking these two sides of the business.'

In some firms, however, the marketing side was deficient and failed to provide guidance to the R & D department. Thus, the chief engineering executive of a medium sized firm was uncertain why it was decided to make a product:

'Well, this is one of my main hobby horses, I suppose, but there is not enough market research done. I think we tend to decide things because the sales manager happens to like it personally or the managing director's secretary likes it. It is a little bit haphazard. I know it is very, very difficult, of course. I suppose there is no sliding scale when it comes to market research. You either have to do it properly or you leave it alone altogether.'

In another firm, long years of success based on patented products had enabled top management to do without both R & D and marketing executives, with the consequence that these products and their methods of manufacture had remained unaltered. One of several engineers who had recently been recruited described his first impressions of the firm:

'The interesting thing that I've found, coming into the company, is that, although their production has expanded, their techniques have not kept pace with that production. Their thinking has remained backyard thinking and, obviously, in this day and age, when other people are getting better and better, we can't afford to stay behind. We've got a very good sales force and that largely compensates at the moment for our lack of ability in other directions, but this can't stay with us, because other people are getting very good sales forces and we have obviously to develop our products along not only modern appearance lines but modern production techniques. We've got to get the cost down. We've got to get the volume up.'

To achieve sustained success in the competitive conditions of today a firm must be able to design and redesign products that are wanted and mass-produce them cheaply. This means that R & D must be closely linked with marketing and production, which calls for a complex and closely integrated management structure. In the six firms visited, it seemed that two were organised in this way, two were hastily trying to introduce such a structure, and the other two were unaware of its importance.

Earthmoving Equipment

Eight firms were visited in the earthmoving equipment industry. Most of them were British but a minority were either American subsidiaries or mergers of American and British firms. The attitudes and practices of these two groups of firms differed sharply in certain respects, though it was clear that the British firms were greatly influenced in their operations by their American competitors. One difference was that none of the American firms carried out R & D in this country because it was all done in their parent companies. A second characteristic of the American firms was that they laid great stress on the importance of market research, the findings of which were to be transmitted to their parent companies in the States and used for planning R & D as well as sales. A sales manager of one American subsidiary said:

'Well, market research is new to us here in Britain, something we've just started and something we are encouraging our dealers to start. You can't accurately forecast sales, recommend new products, new attachments, unless you know what your market is. It's probably a science which we don't know enough about yet. We are preparing plans and we are going to call on our parent company who have teams of experienced people to assist us in getting started. The parent company plans new models ten to fifteen years in advance and they rely on us for forecasts—what's going to be required, what size and its horsepower, which weight, what do they want out of it, cigarette lighter or that sort of thing. In order to give those answers properly we are going to have to have a history of market research, start building it up, so you can see the changes and trends.'

From interviews held in the British firms, three points are worth stressing: first, as in machine tool firms, the emphasis on R & D has increased greatly during recent years; secondly, the emergence of R & D activity has been, and still is, a battle in some firms; and, thirdly, the connection between market research and R & D is less positive than it is in the 'American' companies. A general picture of under-staffed and haphazard R & D is implicit in the following quotations.

One of a large firm's engineers commented:

'Going back about ten years, research and development was almost non-existent in this company and the department at that time consisted of about one man and two boys. And they didn't have a proper development shop. They were allocated to space in the corner of one of the other shops and they were kicked around. They were Cinderella.'

The engineering executive of another small earthmoving equipment machinery firm described what happens when R & D is left to chance. He is answering a question on whose job it was to keep the company ahead in their thinking:

'I don't think it is anyone in particular here. If anyone has a bright idea, it's studied and sorted out and it's decided whether there's anything in it, and, as a result, we don't have a committee on it, but often four or five of us in the drawing office might have a day or two on it going over all the advantages and disadvantages, and then, if we come across anything good, well, of course, we have to go down to the management and put the case. . . . There is always that difficulty, that future development never gets the backing that it should get. It always tends to be the unnecessary evil.'

Both of these firms had taken steps to upgrade the role of R & D; in one of them a new executive was due to be appointed to work specifically on future development. In a medium-sized firm, the chief engineer explained how he met criticism from the works side of the business after his appointment:

'There have been some quite definite attitudes, entrenched views between departments in this firm in the past. Particularly between design and production, when the producer, the man on the shop floor, tended to look on the designer as somebody with his head in the clouds, and unfortunately, I think, being right. One had a feeling of the two departments fighting each other in the old days. This was definitely my impression when I first joined the firm, that there was an enormous barrier between the works and design. The first action really on my part was to cultivate the works manager until we got on together and thereafter everything fell into place.'

But in one large firm, although expenditure is budgeted, the battle for full recognition of R & D activity was by no means won. One senior R & D executive said:

'We still hammer the table. We're still not satisfied. We still say where we must possibly spend some more money on research and development and on the engineering department. For example, I say we could do with an increase of at least one third in our labour force . . . but generally it's been a question of argument and putting forward one's point of view and trying to get across that my department in general is not the parasite that it's often been thought to be. That it does contribute a lot to the well-being of the firm.'

It has been observed earlier in examining other industries that part of the process of integrating R & D into a firm is to put its work on a long-term basis. An executive of one of the American subsidiaries mentioned that his parent company was planning equipment many years ahead of their likely production. The difference between casual and planned R & D is evident in the next two quotations. The first was made by a senior executive of an old-established firm with more than 1,000 employees. The department responsible for R & D did not employ any graduates and it had not grown at all during the last ten years. The interviewer heard how its size was determined:

'This becomes rather proportionate with the need, I would say. As the pressure increases, then the staff has to be increased. But, in fact, I think a very considerable amount of development work has been achieved with an approximately equal design force.'

In contrast, the technical director of another old-established firm discussed the advantages of having R & D on the basis of a long-term plan. During the interview this executive produced from the drawer of his desk the company plan, filled out six years ahead, and remarked that it was unlikely to be adhered to slavishly:

'This plan, as you see, extends for a term of six years. Now, I think it highly improbable that, in fact, this company's product development will follow this plan for the next six years. I think it improbable, but that's no excuse for not having a plan.'

One of the most marked contrasts between American subsidiaries and British-owned firms in this industry was in their attitude to the use of market research. The impression left after talking to R & D executives in British firms was that they wanted guidance from market research but still felt sceptical about its value. Certainly the executives concerned were anxious to try to discover what customers would like to see in their products and to consult them during the development of their new machines. One chief engineer discussed a typical scene from a meeting of his firm's committee on new products:

'In this particular company, in my opinion, we are very weak on market research. I think this is something which requires attention, and, therefore, as far as market research is concerned, in this company the engineering department does not get enough guidance, not enough help. I mentioned the committee. This is where the arguments about potential and so forth occur, mainly between the sales director and myself, and we have very strong arguments, and generally the arguments go something like this. We say to the sales director, "Well, you tell us what you want and we will do it." But then after a little while we say, "Well, obviously you don't know what you want, so how can we do it?" So this goes on. This happens in other companies. We have a market research division in the sales department, but we do not receive information from these people saying that here is a particular requirement in the industry, or in the contractors' industry, or wherever it is. "We consider that there is a potential for this type of equipment." This does not happen. Invariably we have submitted ideas to the sales people and said, "Here is a brief specification for a machine. We think that there should be a market for this sort of machine." In other words, it often works the wrong way round.'

In default of a firm's sales or market research department giving guidance on what the market requires, R & D executives have no alternative but to push their own ideas. Sometimes the after-sales servicing department falls under the control of the technical executives, enabling them to obtain a swift feedback from customers, which can be incorporated in new designs. In some firms customers are encouraged to call at the works and discuss their preferences for new machines. One managing director described how his executives went to earthmoving equipment exhibitions in order to keep an eye on developments so that when they have 'picked out a trend they can leap in at the appropriate moment'. The chief technical executive of one large firm described his work:

'My executive job is to try and peer into the future, to try and design something which will become a standard product tomorrow, and simultaneously to be having some sort of idea of what form it might take the day after tomorrow.'

He then discussed the 'dialogue' which the company has with its customers:

'Talking to prospective users and distributors and drawing them out on this, you don't often get somebody coming and saying, "Yes, of course, well, what we want is. . . ." It's far more likely to be—"We used the so-and-so and such-and-such a machine"—and so on. It's generally a case of piecing together a lot of information, some of it constructive, some of it destructive, and then backing a hunch and saying, "If we build a machine on these lines, this, we think, is what will give the most satisfaction and will ring the bell with these people who don't clearly define what they need." '

One further point which arises from this executive's description of discussions with customers is worth making because it applies to all the firms visited. It is that the earthmoving equipment and construction industries appeared to be more closely linked than any other pair of industries covered by the study. A specific example of what this relationship meant in practice was given by a chief engineer:

'We have various arrangements with customers of ours and friends of ours who have quarries and opencast sites and we put the machines out with these people.'

From different executives the research team heard that earthmoving equipment is subjected to exhaustive testing. Technical executives described the part played by customers in testing their machines as standard practice throughout the industry. Their references to it contrasted sharply with the fact that no executive interviewed in the machine tool industry mentioned a similar practice.

Conclusion

At the beginning of this chapter it was stated that between 1955 and 1961 civil research expenditure had risen from 38 per cent to 59 per cent of total research expenditure, which has itself more than doubled. In almost all the forty-seven firms visited there was evidence of increasing importance being given to R & D. Some firms had detached a number of personnel from the production department and had grouped them together in a separate R & D section; some had appointed executives from outside the firm to fill newly created research posts; some were making greater use of public research facilities; and others were planning R & D on a long-term basis and budgeting it accordingly. To have described the R & D department as the Cinderella of the average firm may well have been true of the mid-1950s, but today it would no longer be accurate. The interviews brought out, however, four main ways in which the effort appears to be misdirected or inadequate.

There was, in the first place, in every industry a wide variation in the effort put into R & D by the different firms visited, and it seemed that some firms were bound to fall behind unless the importance they attached to it increased. Moreover, while there are good reasons for variation in the scale of expenditure by different industries—with clear reasons, for example, why the electronics industry should be at the top of the list—spending in certain industries, and particularly in shipbuilding, still seems to be unduly low.

Secondly, in three of the industries—machine tools, shipbuilding and wool—R & D was inhibited by the vicious circle which seems to exist between makers and buyers on the subject of innovation. The research team heard repeatedly how innovation is delayed because the two industries concerned, be they shipbuilders and owners, or machine tool makers and users, were unwilling either to take risks or to collaborate effectively. Furthermore, each party knows that the situation is wrong but blames the other industry for not taking the lead.

Thirdly, executives in the electronics industry called vehemently for greater Government support in one form or another for civil R & D, and Chapter 13 indicates that there is reason to believe that this claim is valid, not only in electronics, but for a much wider range of industry.

Fourthly, there was in many firms an unsatisfactory relationship between the R & D, production and sales or marketing departments, and most of the R & D executives interviewed showed a negative attitude towards market research, ranging from outright disbelief in its use, through apologetic avoidance, to reluctant, and only occasionally enthusiastic, acceptance. The enthusiasts were found mainly in the American companies and in domestic appliance firms. Yet it is hard to deny that the efforts of R & D executives would be more profitably directed if they were based on the results of systematic market analysis and forecasting—which are considered in the following chapter.

CHAPTER 8

MARKETING

Productive efficiency is not the sole criterion of an efficient economy. It is also necessary that the goods produced should be what the consumer requires. Such a simple proposition would need no emphasis, were it not for the fact that in many British firms production is still carried on with small regard for marketing. Yet disregard for marketing hampers the nation's economic growth by making the economy unresponsive to the demands on it. This is doubly unfortunate in an economy as open as the British, where a failure to match our foreign competitors in meeting the requirements of consumers leads to increased imports and lower exports, and thus to balance-of-payments crises and the restriction of domestic demand and hence of growth.

The use of marketing techniques, moreover, enables efficient firms to maximise their sales, thus encouraging the growing points of the economy as against the more stagnant units.

The post-war sellers' market has by now disappeared for most firms. Such a situation still applied to only a few of the firms visited. Among them, the most common feature was that their attitude towards the techniques of marketing was one of apathy, if not of ignorance. The commercial manager of one large firm in the machine tool industry, which had a comfortably sized order-book, replied to the question, whether he ever estimated the annual growth of the market, by the comment:

'No. We have perhaps been spoilt over a period of years. We've on average been more than able to sell our output, and we tend to leave it at that.'

A similar situation existed in a small wool textile firm which did no market research and virtually no sales promotion. Resting on orders from buyers 'who are expecting us to call in on them', the sales manager of the firm believed there was no need to advertise.

For most firms, however, competition has been increasing, causing shorter order-books. For some of the firms which were visited the increased competition has necessitated a change in business methods.

In one medium-sized firm in the earthmoving equipment industry, for instance, the interviewer was told:

'We were a small company and our products had virtually no competition, so that, when a man went to build a dam, he just looked in the telephone book to see where he could buy one of our products and that was that. The last ten years, it's been such a competitive business that you simply can't do business that way.'

The Importance of Marketing

The gradual change from a sellers' to a buyers' market caused several managers to remark that selling was now the biggest problem their firm faced. The managing director of a firm in the domestic appliance industry summed up the situation:

'Yes, the biggest problem today in any business is not making the stuff. You can buy the plant and you can buy the brains to make it, but the biggest problem of all today is selling it. It's a very competitive market.'

A similar comment was that of the managing director of a small wool textile mill:

'Our main problem is selling our increased productive capacity. That's certainly our biggest problem and this is, of course, why, among other things, I have to interest myself so much more in selling than I do in other factors which are my equal responsibility. This is the key problem of the firm.'

It was not only in consumer industries that selling was thought to be the firm's biggest problem. The managing director of a medium-sized machine tool firm, for instance, said:

'Any fool can run a factory these days. There's a difference between running it and running it efficiently, but, generally speaking, it's a much more difficult thing to sell and to market than it is to run a factory.'

It is largely because of the increased importance which is now attached to selling that many firms, particularly those in consumer goods industries, are developing the marketing function. The essence of marketing is that a firm will make what it can sell rather than sell what it can make. Marketing therefore requires an assessment of consumer needs through market research and the orientation of all the firm's activities towards the satisfaction of those needs. This can lead to a very wide definition of the marketing function. Thus the managing director of a large firm in the domestic appliance industry, who was a marketing man himself, said:

'Somebody has to take the decision, you see. Who should it be? First of all, you've got to take the decision—what does the market want? The marketing man would know that better than anybody else. At what price must the product go to the public in order to attract the public purse? A marketing man, again, knows that better than anybody else. How many can the market take? It's the marketing man's job. It seems logical to me. The marketing director has the overall responsibility for the marketing of a product and seeing that the right orders are placed in the right factory at the right time. I have always said, "In a business of this character, God preserve me from the engineer and accountant!" I really mean this. I think that the success of a business of this kind must depend on the people who can say, "This is what I want and this is what I will do with it." I think it needs the help of the financial people, the accountants, to act as a guide in the matter of profitability and so on. I think the marketing man needs his production men and design men to get him to the point where he's got something to sell. To my mind the marketing man has got the responsibility of determining what the company has got to do. He contributes to the master plan—what is the best way to invest the company's money?—which is really the guide to everything we have to do.'

But the concept of the marketing function most often encountered consists of the application of techniques such as market research, advertising and public relations to the problem of sales. As the manager of a medium-sized firm in the domestic appliance industry said:

'Nothing will tick unless you make sure you get your orders. The whole operation is one of creating a climate for our wares and creating the sense of need. I regard the marketing aspect as being paramount. The mechanics of running a sales order office can be reduced to a technique, but the higher field of marketing involves understanding human nature and psychology. I regard this as being paramount because I always want to be one jump ahead of the others. Marketing is predicting future trends and, what is more, I believe, making future trends.'

It was not only firms in the consumer industries that had developed the marketing function. The marketing manager of one small firm making electronic equipment described why he believed his job to be different from that of the sales manager:

'A marketing manager should have full responsibility for all the selling operation, which would include such things as advertising, as the whole of the market research programme—a rather broader approach than I would expect the sales manager would have. The sales manager I would expect to have the direct selling responsibility, making sure that the sales engineers make the right number of calls and do all the right things in the field.'

The Use of Market Research

The key technique of marketing is that of market research. Information about a firm's market and its customers is collected and analysed in order to determine who buys the firm's products, why, when, and under what circumstances. On the basis of this analysis a marketing policy is evolved. Except when custom-built products are concerned, to attempt to operate without using market research is, to quote one executive, 'flying by the seat of your pants', and can be a strong contributory factor to failure. Many of the managers interviewed by the research team eschewed the technique and it is true that a handful of outstanding businessmen appear to be able to beat market research by what the executive quoted above described as 'an intuitive feel for the consumer durable business'. This flair, however, is the gift of only a very few. For others, market research is an essential basis for sound commercial policy.

There are four main sources of market research information: information which is available within a firm such as sales data; published information such as Government statistics or reports in newspapers and trade journals; information given to a firm on request, such as that which might be available through a trade association; and information which is collected by field enquiries. The field enquiry may be a sample interview survey of quite a large number of potential or actual customers for a consumer product; but for industrial products the number of potential customers is usually much smaller, and surveys frequently are better undertaken by somebody who knows the product and the industry well.

Several firms in the industries which were visited by the research team appreciated the importance of market research. An executive of one large firm selling to a mass market said:

'We have a market research executive so that we can examine the effects of our advertising or the acceptance of our products. We do a certain amount on our own. We've a field force of over a hundred people and do a certain amount of field work on a number of subjects. For example, the acceptance of a particular package is one that we've just been doing recently, but we employ market research companies to do any major work we want, finding out our standing in the market, or trends or anything like that.'

In contrast, an executive of another, medium-sized firm in the domestic appliance industry described what his firm had done about market research:

'We don't have a market research department as such. We're too small, for one thing. We pay lip-service to market research, but in fact we don't really do any. We're still on the basis, at the moment, of hunches and obvious signs that anyone can see.'

Nor had they made a practice of using market research specialists, to whom firms too small to have their own departments can always have recourse. Thus, new products had been introduced:

'. . . on a trial and error basis. We've produced many things, or half produced many things, that have never seen the light of day—with an occasional one coming out after someone else has already proved the market's there.'

This executive fully appreciated the value of market research but had not been able to convert his firm. He probably summed the situation up correctly for many firms when he said:

'But very often in these smaller companies the need for market research isn't realised. They pay lip-service to it but they won't really do it.'

A few of the companies visited, however, did not even pay lip-service to the idea of market research. The sales manager of a medium-sized firm in the domestic appliance industry believed experience was a substitute for systematic market research:

'We feel we have sufficient experience to give us all the types of information that we are likely to require.'

In the capital goods industries many of the firms visited used market research. The managing director of a small firm in the electronics industry explained:

'We look at our products and consider the total size of the market available to us, then we consider it is worth so many thousand or million dollars [the firm is the British offshoot of an American company]. We consider that we can take a given percentage with a certain amount of penetration per annum. We then set our targets in terms of time-scales and dollars. These are overall targets, we then break them down into products by market surveys.'

In another, large firm, in the earthmoving equipment industry, the sales manager described how his firm kept a watch over the progress of its competitors:

'We would use any possible figures that we could find that would tell us our competitors' position in relation to the whole. This would lead us, in turn, to know what our position was in relation to our various competitors.'

This latter company contrasts with a large machine tool firm, the commercial manager of which did not know his firm's share of the market, not only for the present year but for any single year. He estimated a figure but added, 'This is something I'm not wholly familiar with.'

Another, medium-sized firm, in the earthmoving equipment industry, conducted what market research it did in what the sales manager admitted was an 'amateur way', but he refused 'to employ any of the market research organisations' because he found 'they are too expensive'. Several of the firms which were visited realised, however, that market research was becoming increasingly important:

'I think we could do more in the market research field than we have done. We've relied up to now on the know-how of our sales managers. We've never really employed market research to any great degree. I think we've got to come to that, because we as a company are coming to the stage where we must really examine our products and decide what products we are going to continue with and what we ought to drop and what additional products we are going to take on. That can only be done by market research.'

A similar attitude existed in a large electronics firm in which an executive felt that one of the firm's chief problems was their unfamiliarity with their buyers:

'The man who buys is, after all, the guy who matters in the long run. If he doesn't buy, we don't exist. The first question to ask ourselves is whether we have necessarily got just the things that our customers wish to buy. I think we aren't necessarily sufficiently familiar with all the people who ought to be buying them and maybe we have a great big gap in our ranks here.'

These latter two firms relied to a very considerable extent on their own salesmen, agents and dealers for the limited amount of market information which they were obtaining. This practice was also apparent in a medium-sized firm in the earthmoving equipment industry. Asked how much market research the firm undertook, a senior sales executive replied:

'Market research? We're doing it all the time. We don't have anybody particular doing it. Our own sales staff, who are well chosen people, and indeed several of them are qualified engineers, they do the market research for us.'

There is, however, a severe disadvantage in relying for market information solely on a source whose prime function is selling. This disadvantage was indicated by the sales manager of a medium-sized firm in the heavy engineering industry:

'Remember that, if you are talking about penetration into a market, it's more important to know the sales you didn't get than the sale you got. If you have not got your own coverage in a market you're dependent on your dealer reporting to you what he did not get. Psychologically, he resists that.'

Dealers may resist it more than the firm's own sales staff; but the fact remains that the man whose job is to sell is often unable to be objective about the reasons for his success or failure, about his competitors, and about many of the factors that contribute to a proper assessment of the firm's prospects in the market.

Sales Forecasting

A senior executive of a very large firm manufacturing capital goods emphasised the importance of accurate sales forecasting:

'We emphasise to everybody how terribly important sales forecasting is. We budget for six months, twelve months and three years. The six months is easy. The twelve months a little bit more difficult, and

God knows what happens to the three years! But you've got to make an effort. That's the point! It's no good throwing your hands up in despair.'

Good sales forecasting enables the production programme to be scheduled in advance. In some industries this must be done a long time ahead:

'Making machinery like we do, you have to decide nearly a year before what you're going to make.'

In some of the firms visited a smooth sequence of operations started with market research, which yielded the information on which the sales forecast was based, and this led, in turn, to a scheduled production programme. Many of the firms which were visited by the research team, however, had not brought their marketing function to this stage. Frequently the result was that the production and sales departments were at loggerheads over two possible courses of action: should the sales department be charged with selling what the production department produced or should the production department produce what the sales department could sell? The way in which a research and development executive tried to resolve this conflict was recounted on page 143. The failure to resolve it in another firm was described very frankly by one of its executives:

'We either seem to be making what we can't sell or selling what we can't make. It's as bad as that. We have one product that's been going up and up for five years. Every year we've had a demand in the autumn. Every year our sales forecasting has been so poor that we have cut production down in May and June because everyone became alarmed at the way stocks were piling up and then in the autumn we suddenly discover that, with the rush in demand, which surely we should have anticipated, we're losing orders because we can't effect delivery until February or March. . . . Nothing is more vital than forward planning. It's far better for your sales department to forecast sales of 100 and actually take orders for 100 than to forecast orders of eighty and sell 120. . . . Our works manager was laying off people a short while ago. Now we have a desperate struggle to try and get more, to try and get production back. . . . We talk about market research! We don't know what the words mean, and so often when we are looking into the future, because there are elements of uncertainty, we just say, "Any guess will do", instead of trying to analyse the situation, breaking the thing down and really finding out at the point of sale what the possibilities are. We just say, "Well, the whole thing is so fraught with problems that there's really no point in going into it too deeply." . . . We decide to make, let's say, ten a month. Two months later they'll hastily change it to fifteen a month. The relationship between the works and sales department couldn't be worse at the moment. We've had cases where the works manager has driven his people to working over weekends, working late at night, to produce certain equipment and when it's ready on the date due, then, at the last moment, our sales department say, "Oh, the customer has changed his mind. He doesn't want it yet." Now, it makes our works manager so furious—also, of course, he looks a fool as far as his own department are concerned. But, as I say, forward planning is terribly important, and you'd be amazed at the extent to which it can, if it's bad, affect profitability. Unbelievable! Unbelievable!'

The same state of confusion was described by the works director of a medium-sized firm in the domestic appliance industry as:

'. . . one of those long battles that go on in every firm between manufacture and sales. Sales get a sudden intake of orders and expect manufacture to wave a magic wand and provide the increased output. If the orders stop they say, "It's not my fault", and expect us to suddenly switch it off. On the other hand they say, "We've got lots of orders. The customers are clamouring. Why can't you people in manufacture make these things?" And we, on the manufacturing side, tend to be rather a large clumsy fly-wheel that takes a long time to build up and a long time to cut down.'

In a small north-country wool textile firm the company secretary standing, as it were, on neutral ground between production and sales said:

'I keep asking the manufacturing side, "Why is it that sales say they want so-and-so and you haven't got it?" Then the next time it's the other way round, "Why is it that manufacturing have so-and-so and sales want something else?" It's a question I'd like the answer to myself, is that.'

In general, the thrusting attitude towards the relationship between sales and production is that where the marketing function determines the output from the factory. The sales manager of a large firm in the earthmoving equipment industry outlined the relationship which existed in his company:

'We decide how many of a particular model are going to be built, based on a forecast which comes in from our field people all over the world. Then we sit down with the merchandising people at a meeting and say, "Next year we're going to build so many of this and so many of that." If the production department says, "We can't do that because we can't get the material", we say, "Well, you've got to get it because this is going to be the demand." '

The sequence of operations within another large earthmoving equipment firm was described by the sales manager:

'The first and probably the most important factor is the control of the production, which means that we have to assess what the market requires. From the market research that we undertake, we then have to decide what machines we are going to build and when we want them, and how many we want, and the sizes we want. So, as an overall control of production we have a regular meeting and at this meeting we assess and review our forward production requirements. And we have a production schedule and production control, which comes from that meeting, which controls the whole of the production of the factory—we try to keep our schedule at all times covering two calendar years ahead.'

In addition to facilitating the planning of production, sales forecasting also enables a firm to introduce a number of other management techniques. The management of a small wool textile firm, for example, had been unable to introduce budgetary control because it believed it could not forecast the sales of its products:

'For the whole idea of this budgetary control of profit and expense, you have to forecast your sales for the following month. I don't think—in fact I'm sure—that we can't do that with any reasonable degree of accuracy.'

Sales Promotion

Two facets of sales promotion are advertising and public relations. Attitudes expressed by managers towards these two functions and other business techniques varied less according to their industry than to the nature of their firms. Sleepy attitudes towards advertising and public relations were found in firms manufacturing both consumer goods and capital goods. The sales manager of a medium-sized domestic appliance firm, for instance, explained why his firm did nothing about public relations:

'Our advertising agents have tried to interest me in it from time to time since 1960. You'll remember that until that time things were really swinging. Everybody was expending themselves on production capacity and since then, quite frankly, we have had to conserve our cash. We have to put our money to more direct uses rather than spend it on a nebulous thing like that. We're north-country people up here and our chairman just doesn't want a public image.'

Some managers believed that a high-quality product and an efficient after-sales service will sell themselves, rendering sales promotion unnecessary. The sales manager of a machine tool firm, for example, unconsciously repeated the Volkswagen advertising message when he remarked:

'Why has Volkswagen made such a hit in this country and the States? Because the first thing they did, before they allowed anyone to sell a machine, they insisted that they set up a service depot. Once they invested in that, they could then sell the car. The Volkswagen is popular, and so is the Ford, because you know jolly well that, if the thing blows up, you've only got to run into the nearest Ford dealer and that's it. I think it's more important, quite frankly, than publicity. Your service really is your publicity.'

In a shipyard the managing director also felt that public relations served no useful purpose. He said:

'We've had dozens of approaches from public relations people who want to take our business on. . . . I don't think much of them. The greatest publicity a yard like this can have is achievement. Every ship one builds must be an advertisement. You must be as proud of your ship as the owners are of it. And people talk and earn you a reputation.'

In another shipyard the managing director held quite a different attitude towards the subject:

'My father regarded the press as a confounded nuisance and as people who should not be tolerated except where you could not avoid it. We are now taking the view that the press is a necessary vehicle and that you have got to make the maximum use of it. You're very often better off if you get your name in the press in some scurrilous fashion than if you don't get your name in at all. You've got to get yourself into the public eye. We now have a full-time public relations man. We have an advertising agent as well.'

Some firms seem to undertake a little advertising merely because it is less trouble than ignoring it altogether. The owner of a small wool textile mill explained:

'Frankly, we don't believe that advertising of a top makes a buyer buy more readily than if we didn't advertise. Advertising has increased so much in the last thirty or forty years, we're just running along with the tide.'

One large firm in the machine tool industry which was visited apparently believed that advertising had some value, although it did not:

'. . . conduct sales campaigns as such unless we bring out some new development, in which case we just have a mild splash. We are brightening things up a little bit now but it follows a fairly steady pattern. We don't overdo it.'

Many of the companies which were visited, however, revealed a vigorous attitude towards sales promotion. This is particularly necessary in the domestic appliance industry, where the sales director of one medium-sized firm explained his company's policy:

'First of all, the manufacturer must not only make the product, he must create a sense of need for it. That is the premise on which I've always worked. We have said that we do not expect the wholesalers or retailers to stock our products, unless we create a sense of need amongst their buying public.'

He went on to describe the importance which the firm attached to advertising:

'Once I get my selling message right then it becomes an advertising message. I attach tremendous importance to that because we have to make our own place in the sun and we do it by arming the trade to the teeth. I've got to give the trade a reason for living and a zest for selling. I've got to give the public a real taste for our wares. You can only do that with a sustained selling and advertising programme.'

The idea of creating a sense of need for a firm's products was also in evidence in a very large electronics firm which had run courses for engineers to explain what the word 'computing' meant in everyday language. One senior manager of the firm said:

F

'We are trying at the moment to educate various people, trying to impress them and enlighten them as to what the computer represents. In fact, we're running a series of two-day appreciation courses which is designed for process people, instrument engineers, electrical and mechanical—everybody, managers as well—so that they can come and learn what is behind this word "computing" in everyday language. Our aim is to teach these people that a computer is not something miles up in the sky but it is something tangible . . . so our aim is to enlighten people.'

In one medium-sized firm making knitting wool the sales manager explained how they were running fashion-shows to publicise their range:

'We have recently started fashion-shows with a lady who is a specialist in putting on fashion-shows throughout the whole of the country. To get the crowds in, she will get in these television stars. . . . The proceeds from all these fashion-shows are for spastics. This also ensures there will be a good turn-up. These are running at least once a month all the time. Mind you, joining in with us in these fashion-shows are at least two of our competitors.'

The managing director of another, small firm in the wool textile industry, whose market was composed of a small number of multiple tailors, described how he was trying to persuade the multiples to stock garments made from his firm's cloth:

'We're trying a new marketing approach altogether to textiles. That is, by consumer promotion. The idea being that by persuading the public to ask for your branded goods by name the retailer will be forced to stock your goods as opposed to other people's, or, in our case, garments made from your cloth as opposed to garments made, say, from Italian or your competitors' cloth.'

The aids which can be enlisted to help to sell a firm's products are extremely numerous. One large earthmoving equipment firm hired an aircraft and flew fifty contractors to its plant in the north for a day's trip. The cost of this was £1,000 but, the managing director pointed out, 'it was a captive audience'.

Another firm, in the same industry, had:

'. . . started a programme here, which is not aimed at our customers at all, or people who are going to buy our equipment. It's aimed at the general public so that they become more aware of the need for better roads, and not only become aware of it but do something about it—speak to the government officials, Members of Parliament. This was done in another country, and a few years later the Government initiated this road programme. We feel that this has done a lot not only for ourselves but for the whole industry although, naturally, we do it for a bigger share in the market.'

The Selection, Management and Assessment of Salesmen

However good the sales promotion of a product, it has to be followed up at the point of sale by competent salesmen. In the majority of firms which were visited salesmen were selected by means of an interview with the sales manager. Most sales managers relied upon their experience to tell them which candidate to select, as did the sales manager of a medium-sized domestic appliance firm:

'I have been in the industry since I was sixteen-and-a-half and must have been with this company twenty-eight or twenty-nine years, and I think I must be conceited enough to assume that I can size up a man's ability by question and answer.'

Usually sales managers looked for certain qualities in their candidates. An executive of another medium-sized firm in the domestic appliance industry said:

'We look for personality and what have you. A person with sufficient drive and energy to fight the competition that exists but who will not be overbearing. So what we really look for is a person with personality, drive, conscientiousness, loyalty and a keen desire to sell.'

The personnel manager of a very large firm, discussing the recruitment of salesmen, said:

'We do not have psychological tests or anything quite so advanced as that. Salesmen have been recruited in the past from fellows who wrote in and said they would like to join our firm. We always interview a chap if he can write a decent letter to us, whether we've got a job to offer or not. That's basic, because you never know what you miss if you don't see these chaps, providing they can write us a decent letter.'

A drawback to the exclusive reliance on such methods of selection is that the qualities the interviewers are looking for, such as 'tact', 'initiative', 'a capacity to work hard' and 'loyalty', are all difficult to recognise with any certainty except by observing a person at work over a considerable period. Other relevant qualities can be assessed much more satisfactorily during the process of selection. Research studies have often demonstrated the fallibility of the hit-or-miss approach but only a few of the firms visited had appreciated the value of a more systematic method. Yet useful techniques have been developed that can help even the most experienced of interviewers to choose as well as possible and to minimise the number of wrong selections made. One very large firm, aware that its selection methods had been haphazard, was taking steps to improve them. The sales director of this firm said:

'We are more conscious of selecting the right man from the beginning and training him. Going back over the years, I'm afraid we haven't been anything like as good as that. If a man was a good clerk and knew how to dress and wash his face, we've tended to make him a representative. Now I think we've outgrown those bad old days. We do a lot more today than we've ever done before.'

Firms with a more sophisticated attitude towards the selection of salesmen naturally tended to be those which manufactured the most technically complex products. One small firm in the electronics industry put most stress on recognisable and measurable qualities. Its marketing manager explained that his policy was to look:

'. . . first of all for people who have a basic engineering qualification and preferably have had experience in R & D work. We like people to have spent several years in design and development preferably on instrumentation or some associated field. We also like them, of course, to have a feeling for selling. Ideally, we like to have people coming to us who have already had some commercial experience.'

The same firm also showed a thrusting attitude towards the management and assessment of its salesmen. The marketing manager went on to describe its operation:

'Targets are set up by discussion between myself and the sales engineer in a particular area. I usually look at the potential of an area in some detail. A complete breakdown by instrument type and by customer as well. A lot of work goes into this and we arrive at a number. We discuss this with the sales engineer and he agrees the target. This is done on an annual basis and we then divide it up on a monthly basis, and he gets issued with a sheet which will show him exactly what percentage of his achievement he has made in a month. This is a measure of how he does in a particular area and gives him an idea of how he is progressing. We also tell him what is the total cost of keeping him working in the field.'

This contrasts with more sleepy methods, which rely on the record of past performance and fail to produce any other yardstick against which the performance of salesmen can be assessed.

The Appraisal of Sales Methods

In the most thrusting firms this process of investigation in the area of selling does not stop at the selection and assessment of salesmen, but extends to continuous appraisals of all the methods of selling and distribution used by the firm. Other firms fail to make such appraisals: for example, the sales manager of a medium-sized firm in the domestic appliance industry told the interviewer:

'I personally see no reason why a time-tested method of distribution, which we have and which is very successful for the distribution of some of our products, should change. I think what must be done is that our present method must be added to—must be complemented.'

Despite the radical change from a sellers' to a buyers' market, shipyards in particular have been most reluctant to alter their time-honoured method of selling. The managing director of a shipyard described it:

'By and large, in shipbuilding the job of the managing director is that of chief salesman. That is really his biggest job. It's done, really, by keeping in touch. One has got to visit shipowners every three to six months and make sure that, if an owner does want a ship, he gives you an opportunity to quote for it. You might be able to persuade him to take one just like the ship you built for him last time, but, by and large, it is a question of going round and asking to be remembered—keeping him mindful of you—the things that you've done—technical achievements—making sure that he reads about the ships that you have produced and that sort of thing.'

One of the large yards visited had a particularly sleepy attitude towards selling. Its deputy managing director was still expecting to receive orders in a period of recession by using the same inactive methods it had used during the boom years:

'I don't know that we've developed any new methods of selling ships. I think I could explain it to you this way. We build merchant ships and, secondly, we build warships. Now, so far as the warships are concerned, we're on the Admiralty list. The Admiralty know what size of ship we can build so automatically we get an invitation to bid, so that we don't need to sell ships to the British Admiralty. When it comes to merchant ships, we receive almost automatically enquiries from certain sources. Automatically they ask us to quote. If it is the kind of ship they think we could build, they automatically come along and ask us to bid. Then in addition to that, of course, there are regular clients with whom we have built up a relationship over the years, and, if they've got a ship to build in which they think we would be interested, they may send us an enquiry or a letter asking us if we would be interested in quoting.'

In another large yard, however, the managing director seemed aware that the traditional method of selling ships would have to change. Asked how he saw the future of the shipbuilding industry, he said that he believed that there would have to be:

'. . . a different attitude towards sales. We will have a chairman or managing director who will still be the kingpin, but all sales contacts will not be left to him. We will have people who are doing the groundwork and following up the visits of the managing director.'

A small firm in the wool industry was, as the managing director explained, changing its methods of selling as a result of changing conditions:

'I do think our method of selling has got to change. I believe a revolution has got to come in this industry in this regard. This is partially caused by the fact that our type of customer is changing. We've got to adapt ourselves.'

Another, medium-sized, firm in the same industry had decided that its correct course of action was to eliminate the wholesalers and sell direct to retailers. It had done this partly because the 'wholesalers would probably buy the plums from our range' and partly because the wholesalers' representatives were unable to give the retailers the specialist sales talk which the manufacturer believed his products warranted. '. . . therefore the big changeover was made':

'Now we've got a specialist team. It makes a very big difference. The retail trade are surprised at the extent of our range. They'd no idea we did this. Some didn't know we had knitting leaflets. We've been doing knitting leaflets for thirty years but wholesalers thought leaflets were a nuisance. It may be that one would say, "We will just buy your baby wool", not knowing about the other fourteen or fifteen qualities that we had. . . . Now our men are going in and presenting the whole range very successfully.'

In many firms the changeover can be a difficult decision, but in one firm, at least, the better profits which would result from a change were the deciding factor:

'The board were probably frightened of engaging a large number of representatives to cover the whole country on the retail side. They were frightened of what the administrative difficulties would be, because, if you don't follow up your outstanding accounts immediately and have everything bang up to date, then you get into a mess in no time. . . . I think, by and large, it was a question of their having done this on the wholesale side for years and not wanting to change. Eventually they were forced into it because of the profit angle. Other firms in this industry were making bigger profits than we were. It had to come eventually.'

A small firm in the electronics industry abandoned its dealer network for the same reason, but it appeared that the decision had not been so hard to make. Discussing this problem, the marketing manager of the firm described some of the disadvantages of relying on agents:

'When you have an agent, however good he may be, he never really pulls out all the stops and sells your products as hard as he should do. He tends to set himself up as an adviser. He tends to sit by the telephone and wait for it to ring and, when somebody says they'd like an instrument to do a certain job, he says, "Yes—I think we've got just the sort of thing", and he will look through a catalogue. He's not really concerned whether it's one of our instruments or one of our competitors.' He will look through on what he maintains is an impartial basis, select an instrument, send off the data, and possibly take the sale. He hasn't in the past gone out to create sales. The essential difference between our approach and our agents' approach is this business of going out and probing, and promoting our range of products alone, and creating sales. We are doing this. We have already got a lot of customers that our agent didn't generate. We're increasing the business all the time. I think it's the only way to do this. We're getting very much deeper than the agent ever did, and we're going to progress along these lines. We shall certainly be pushing hard throughout the UK and our penetration will be without a doubt very much deeper than the agency, even looking at it, say, six months or a year from now.'

For some firms, however, there were considerable advantages to be gained from using agents. The sales manager of one medium-sized firm in the earthmoving equipment industry talking about the advantages of using agents for facilitating part-exchange deals said:

'One of the disadvantages of selling directly is that this business of ours almost always involves a trade-in. In other words, this means the re-purchase of used equipment, the price of which is offset against the price of new equipment. It's exactly the same in the motor-car business. Obviously you end up with a much better deal if you have an old car to trade in than if you simply go to buy a new car directly. Now, unless you set up a separate trading organisation, an organisation for handling second-hand or traded-in equipment, you cannot successfully compete, in my opinion, in this market.'

The Importance of Servicing

In an earthmoving equipment firm, the importance of servicing, which depended on the firm's agents, as an aid to sales was emphasised by the chief sales executive:

'I think you cannot divorce sales from service, because the greatest aid to a repeat sale is after-sales service. The first sale is not always easy, but the repeat order is much more difficult. A repeat order is almost impossible unless you have given service with the first sale, or following the first sale.'

The servicing aspect of an agent's work was also given considerable importance by the sales manager of a medium-sized firm in the domestic appliance industry who said:

'We allow what we consider to be a reasonable margin for the contractor who installs our product, because we expect him to do minor adjustments and repairs and, if he were not able to do so, we would seriously consider not supplying him with our goods.'

Some firms, of course, claimed they had an excellent after-sales service but did not use agents to maintain it. The sales director of one very large firm in the machine tool industry was convinced that the quality of his firm's service organisation was one of the two reasons for the firm's overall success:

'You can't give too much after-sales service. . . . You asked me earlier how we accounted for our successes. I think that skill and service are the two things that make a successful company, and we place a lot of importance on service.'

Asked how his firm's servicing compared with that of his competitors, he went on to say:

'Generally speaking, I would think that we leave everybody stone-cold. I needn't be bashful about it at all. We had a market survey a little while ago, and among other things we wanted them to find out about were after-sales service and so on. We were very pleased that we came out at the top of this poll.'

The marketing manager of one small firm in the electronics industry believed that one of the reasons why the firm could charge higher prices than its competitors was the quality of its servicing:

'We feel that we have rather better reliability in many cases. Very many of our instruments are identical in specification to our competitors' and, in general, prices are slightly higher. We don't feel this is a particular disadvantage. We are able to offer very good service. We are building a first-class service team here.'

These thrusting attitudes towards servicing contrast with a firm in the machine tool industry, in which servicing seemed to be undertaken on an *ad hoc* basis. The sales manager of the firm said:

'We don't get many serious complaints at all. We do endeavour to get a man out within a few days of getting a request—which is pretty good. We have a rota. Sometimes they have to wait a few weeks, but generally, if it's a breakdown, we get someone there more or less immediately.'

The Determination of Prices

Fixing prices according to what the market would stand was an almost universal practice in the firms which were visited. The accountant of one medium-sized earthmoving equipment firm spoke for many, when he said:

'Our selling prices in theory conform to the ancient rule that they are as much and no more than the maximum the market will stand and I think that is right. It's got to be right because, if you could sell for a £ more, you are not doing yourself any good.'

One small wool firm was being forced continually to cut its prices, because of the pressure of the market. One of its managers quoted the difficulties of another firm making a similar product as an example of the sort of problem his own firm was having to contend with. He described how the other firm:

'. . . produced a cloth and got an order for 1,500 pieces at 15s. 6d. a yard. This cloth was shown to another firm who immediately produced the same thing at 12s. 6d. a yard. Then another firm saw it and they produced the same thing at 10s. 6d. a yard. I think the last price was 7s. 9d. a yard, so nobody makes anything out of it. That is our problem.'

For some of the firms visited charging what the market would stand was synonymous with following a price leader. The managing director of a small firm in the electronics industry, for instance, said:

'We don't dictate selling prices as a company. They have nothing to do with us. They are determined by the leaders. X is the leader, and therefore anybody who wishes to sell dearer than them might just as well jump in the nearest river. Anyone who wants to sell a lot cheaper is most welcome to do so, but, if he sells a lot cheaper than they do, he is a fool.'

On the reverse side of the coin, one firm which was in a monopoly position commented that 'we try and raise the price whenever we can, of course', but this commercial sentiment was tempered by the qualification that the firm had 'some sort of public duty in the matter'.

The commercial manager of a very large electronics company explained how his firm decided the prices of new products:

'First of all, you must know what your works cost is. This is produced by the estimating department, who say, "We want so much labour content, so much material content, to produce this article." The managing director has already laid down a structure on the application of overheads and the amount of profitability he expects to get.'

The problem is then passed on to the commercial department which applies to the works cost the recovery of overheads, amortisation, selling costs and profitability to 'arrive at the price we should get'. At this point in the procedure another member of the management team comes into the picture:

'This is where the divisional head must have his say. He may say, "It's all very well, but at this price you're just not going to secure any hold of the market." Therefore he has got to be in a position to be able to recommend to the managing director if necessary that, instead of getting the understood profitability we were aiming at, we've got to accept something less. This is a decision which has to be taken at top level. This can depend very much on immediate circumstances. You may find two or three other companies trying to get into the market so that you've got to come down in price. On the other hand, you may find that the market will stand a higher price.'

Conclusion

This chapter has described the importance which is attached to marketing by some of the forty-seven firms visited by the research team. Certain of the selling practices which have been described in this chapter appear to be fairly widespread in British industry and have met with criticism from a number of commentators. One of the conclusions of a survey on buying and selling techniques in the British engineering industry carried out by the journal, *Metalworking Production*,[1] for instance, was that: 'Most manufacturers' overall selling efforts are far from what they could be. With few exceptions they undertake no market research. As a result the majority are unable to draw up a really effective sales plan or apportion the necessary promotion expenditure in terms of reaching their market potential.' This chapter has shown, by comparing thrusting and sleepy attitudes towards the various techniques of marketing, how selling decisions in some firms are made with reference to outdated practices and with little market information; and how sales promotion is considered irrelevant. In other firms marketing is the paramount activity and largely dictates the extent and order of the firm's operations. Such firms have escaped from the idea that they 'have a very efficient factory and a company in that position is unlikely to fall by the wayside' to the view, clearly expressed in one very large firm in the domestic appliance industry, where the managing director said:

'But after all, everything depends on selling. Without sales it's no good making anything anyway, and this is the major function. Everything stems from that. I think the emphasis in this firm has changed probably from the engineer to the marketing man.'

[1] *Metalworking Production* Research Department, *Special Report on the Buying and Selling Techniques used in the British Engineering Industry*, [1963], p. 20.

It has already been noted that the marketing approach is most strongly applicable to firms, such as those making domestic appliances, that sell to large numbers of consumers. But more attention should be paid to this approach through very wide sectors of British industry. It has become almost a cliché to say that much of British industry is too dominated by the production side, but the interviews confirmed that it is still, none the less, true. With the end of the post-war sellers' market, the need for a more thorough adoption of marketing principles and methods, properly adapted to the circumstances of each industry and firm, has been further reinforced.

CHAPTER 9

EXPORTING[1]

It was pointed out at the beginning of the last chapter that efficient marketing is particularly important for a country such as Britain which must be internationally competitive. Time and again since the war economic expansion at home has been curtailed because exports did not rise fast enough to keep our international accounts in balance. Rapidly rising exports are, therefore, probably the most vital contribution that British industry can make to economic growth.

NEDC has rightly stressed the need for more buoyant exports. Its March 1964 report, *The Growth of the Economy*, increased from 5 per cent a year to 5·1 per cent its estimate of the rate at which exports will have to grow if the British economy is to expand by 4 per cent a year. NEDC has also emphasised that the level of exports is determined by selling methods, quality, design, service and delivery as well as by relative costs and prices.[2] This serves as a reminder that exporting is merely a special case of marketing, in which there are certain special problems due to the differences and distances between Britain and the export markets, as well as great opportunities for expanding a firm's sales. This chapter accordingly starts by considering the reasons that induce firms to export, and then shows how firms deal with some of the problems that are peculiar to marketing abroad rather than at home.

The Reasons for Exporting

The reasons given by firms to the research team for being in the highly competitive business of exporting were mainly economic. Predominant among the reasons was the limitation on output and, in turn, overall profitability if selling were confined to the home market. Many firms in two industries, earthmoving equipment and wool textiles, have found themselves in the situation where, in order to survive, they have had to export. An executive of one firm in the earthmoving equipment industry commented:

[1] PEP published in November 1964 a broadsheet, 'Firms and their Exports', based on a survey to which reference is made in this chapter.
[2] *The Growth of the Economy*, pp. 43 and 45.

'We haven't any choice. We have a very limited home market in this earthmoving business, so we really live on the export market.'

Another executive, in the same industry, whose firm exported about 80 per cent of its output, made a similar remark:

'The position here is that these works would shut if it wasn't for exports. One way and another, either directly exporting from the works or supplied to our customers for export, the very great majority of the goods go for export.'

The economic forces which have caused firms in the earthmoving equipment industry to export have also been operating, usually for a much longer time, in the wool textile industry. The chairman of one small firm explained:

'The Scotch wool trade has never lived on home trade. It's always been mainly export trade. About 90 per cent of the Scotch wool trade went to Germany pre-1914.'

The same underlying reason for exporting was discernible, to a lesser extent, in the electronics and machine tool industries. The managing director of a very large electronics firm which exported 50 per cent of its output was very conscious of the need to export in order to reduce the unit cost of production and so be in a position to meet American competition:

'We believe that we can only stay alive by exporting because, if you take any one of our products, the American market is ten times ours. American competitors designing a new piece of apparatus can estimate a volume of sales about ten times ours. It may not be as much as that, but it's very big. They can spread their R & D over that. We say that our little market here is so small compared with the Americans that we couldn't possibly design such a good instrument if we didn't believe that our sales could be increased considerably throughout the rest of the world. So we believe that, if we're going to produce these sophisticated products at a competitive price, we've got to export.'

This firm was a traditional exporter but the wish to reduce unit costs by expanding the market was found in a machine tool firm which had been exporting for only a few years:

'Industrial efficiency depends, of course, on a good market. The larger your market, the more efficient you can become. This is particularly true of the auto industry—the larger the market, the better the production techniques, the more research, the higher the profits, the greater the plough-back into the industry. We, as an industry, must have a larger market—a world-wide market.'

One of the principal reasons why one very large domestic appliance company exported was the conviction of the managing director that competition in this country would, over the next few years, become more internationally based and only by exporting to meet that competition now would he be sure that his products were invulnerable. Some other firms visited exhibited this wish to be aware of the calibre of foreign competition. The sales director of a very large domestic appliance firm commented:

'Unless we can compete and do well in the markets of the world, we don't really know if we are efficient and competitive at home in our own market.'

In a few instances firms exported because their sole market for a particular product was overseas. One firm visited by the research team made a piece of equipment used on tropical plantations and naturally exported 100 per cent of its output. Another company, in the wool textile industry, which had formerly sold its output to local worsted spinners, had found that 'many people abroad are now putting in their own spinning plants' and the firm, in order to retain its outlets, had had to 'get into the spinners abroad'.

In these cases the decision to export has been taken as a result of calculations regarding the profitability of the firm. In some of the firms which were visited, however, the managements appeared to have inherited an exporting tradition almost without question. One small wool firm visited was exporting about 85 per cent of its output, and its managing director admitted:

'This is the stupid part about everything—it would be much simpler for us to sell on the home market and have less worries. We could finance it much easier, and we could sell just as much on the home market. But, because our background has been export, this is something that gets into your blood. So, we have become export-minded. I can't answer why, really, because life for me would be much pleasanter if I sold on the home market.'

Tradition is not the only non-commercial reason given for exporting.

Two of the firms visited exported because their managements believed it to be their patriotic duty. The company secretary of one large engineering firm explained that the difference in profitability was of secondary consequence to his firm which considered first 'the well-being of the country', while the chairman of another, medium-sized engineering firm considered it was in the national interest for his firm:

'. . . to put all its efforts into exporting rather than into the home market, whether it's good for the firm or not. I have been brought up in that way of thinking.'

A senior executive in a machine tool firm said that official persuasion had induced his firm to put effort into exporting:

'I'm saying that the Government, in fact, did this through their reports and through the press. We as an industry are aware now that we must export and, solely due to this awareness, we have established here a large and progressive export unit. Up to a few years ago there wasn't an export department. If we had an export order, it was in some ways a damned nuisance. Expensive! But I think we must be made aware of the need to export. Propaganda, publicity, whatever it may be, we have been made aware of it and it has had its effect. The answer lies with the industry. Being made aware of it, it is up to us now and I think the solution is with us and we can do it.'

Market Research

There was a wide spread of attitudes towards the systematic survey-ing of export markets, just as there was towards market research at home. Only a few of the firms that were visited discounted the value of research into export markets altogether. In more of them there was a realisation that such research had been neglected but that the fault had to be rectified. A director of a small wool firm explained that it was:

'. . . really a new subject which we haven't explored at all. We're only at the beginning. I would like to tackle this thing further, but at the moment we have done little or nothing about market research as such.'

A number of the firms visited deployed their export efforts into relatively narrow fields, which were indicated by market research. Thus, a senior executive explained how his machine tool firm selected the markets to concentrate upon, although if, as he indicated, they relied entirely upon information from agents, each of whom has an interest in his own market being selected, their policy is a questionable one:

'We are selecting now a number of countries in which we are making the maximum effort and that depends upon the demand for machine tools. This comes from information being fed from our agents on industrial activity, and the countries we're concentrating on at the moment, where the demand is the maximum and is likely for the next two years to be the maximum, are Japan, Australia and Germany. A maximum effort is being made in those countries. We find that, with the limited resources and technical brainpower which we have and the limited cash that we can plough into exporting at the moment, we must concentrate in a number of major countries rather than spend a little and achieve very little in many other countries.'

For a firm manufacturing consumer goods and making sample surveys the cost of overseas market research can be considerably higher than that carried out at home. A number of the consumer goods firms visited, however, had no hesitation in taking this step. For a medium-sized domestic appliance firm, the first step in marketing a product overseas was a research programme concerned with:

'... the finding of the market, the discovery of the product that will sell, and then a great deal of discussion back at home here to see if we can produce it economically and at a profit.'

Another firm, in the wool textile industry, sent a small team of men to six continental countries to make a sample survey. To reinforce these data it commissioned some continental market research agencies to furnish statistics which were not readily available. This approach was not confined to the consumer goods industries but was found in others. A sales executive of a medium-sized machine tool firm, after prefacing his remark with a warning that research findings had to be interpreted cautiously, said:

'We try to collect what the potential is, what machines are actually installed in the country, the possibility of replacement, the possibility of expansion in our particular small, narrow market. Those are the figures we try to get at.'

Some managers regarded export market research as important

and specialised enough to warrant their own personal attention. Thus, the chairman of one small wool textile firm spent a lot of his time abroad because:

'The difficulty about market research in this industry, as I see it, is that it's almost impossible to do it except on an expert basis. In other words, you can't send somebody in who doesn't know about cloths. It's very difficult to hire somebody. I'm not saying that it can't be done, but I think that in a smallish set-up such as ours it's infinitely better done personally if at all possible.'

The Organisation of Export Sales

It may not necessarily indicate a thrusting attitude towards exports that a firm should have a separately organised department to deal with exports. If a firm, for example, exports up to 80 per cent of its output the case for such a department is weak. Where firms export around half their output, however, the absence of a separately organised export department is very often an indication of sleepiness. A medium-sized machine tool firm exporting 40 per cent of its output which was visited by the research team, for instance, described its sales office organisation in the following way:

'When the mail comes in the morning the export and the home sales are jumbled together',

—while their export salesman also 'looked after part of the midlands territory'.
    Equally sleepy in its attitude to export selling was a shipbuilding firm, the deputy managing director of which is quoted on page 166 using the word 'automatically' four times in a short description of his yard's sales policy. This company had passive methods of obtaining overseas enquiries:

'. . . through a broker in London. But in addition to that, of course, there are embassies that have their commercial attachés, and they've got their ear to the ground for all types of business in which the UK is interested, and of course shipbuilding is one of these. Therefore, through the embassies, through Government sources in this country, through the Board of Trade, we get informed of enquiries for ships or requirements for ships in countries all over the world.'

Another source of information about possible purchases of ships is the shipbuilders' trade association, the Shipbuilding Conference. Not all the shipbuilders, however, relied only on these sources. One managing director of a yard, commenting that 'the most important thing was to have your ears to the ground', kept 'running up and down to London', while another firm had opened offices in several overseas countries where they expected to find orders.

To set up such an extensive export organisation takes some time, as a senior executive of a very large electronics company explained:

'We're having to build up an export organisation. We've now got a number of technical representatives abroad. We have one in Germany, one in Italy, one in Beirut—the Middle East—another one in Malaya for the Far East, and we're about to open up in Latin America. But all this is long term. It takes a long time. You put a man in a particular area, and it will be a couple of years before you get any real return from him.'

In the electronics industry, 'technical representatives go out for something like two or three years at a stretch and, within six months of them going out, they are virtually out of date as far as the technical side is concerned'. Many electronics companies therefore operate a two-wave selling attack. One executive, describing his company's approach, which was typical, said:

'The agents or the representatives are men that are chosen for their connections or their ability with language, their ability to get on with people, their ability to latch on to almost anything. For instance, in the bar of the new Nile Hilton in Cairo, if they heard something, they would be able to pick it up. They would realise that big money was going to be sent there or something like that. They would latch on to that, you see?'

When a possible order has been located a high-powered team of engineers is flown out to try to obtain it.

The problem of breaking into overseas markets is always considerable. To do so effectively many firms have had to build up separate export departments staffed by the best men in the organisation. One sales director of a firm which had enjoyed considerable overseas success commented:

'Our managing director decided quite rightly that it was impossible to build overseas business unless we in fact creamed some of the best members from each of the departments.'

The Organisation of the Overseas Sales Force

The organisation of a company's export sales force was more often than not a pointer to the thrustfulness or otherwise of that company's attitude to overseas selling. One earthmoving equipment firm instigated an enquiry conducted from its head office in the United Kingdom each time an overseas order was lost. Another company, in the same industry, kept a list showing against each salesman's name his schedule of overseas visits over the next twelve months. In this company there were:

'. . . fourteen people going visiting. There's the manager, the export manager, and the assistant manager, plus the sales engineers. But we all visit.'

Not all the firms in this industry, however, had a positive attitude towards overseas selling. An executive of another company, which relied almost wholly on agents 'to feel pretty closely in touch', explained that:

'Touring is carried out probably more intensively if things are quiet on the home market. One of our directors does have special responsibility for India and Pakistan. He goes out every winter.'

Most of the firms believed that a knowledge of at least one foreign language was essential to an export salesman. The managing director of a wool textile firm commenting on the importance to the overseas buyer of having someone travel out from Britain to meet him said:

'This is getting more and more important as more and more organisations abroad become big and are apt to buy with buying committees, which is the most horrible thing I've ever come across in my life. It is therefore necessary to have somebody of considerable stature and, of course, at the same time he must speak the language. This, of course, is frightfully important and is something that has not been enough realised in this industry in the past.'

Only one manager believed that a foreign language was unnecessary for an export salesman. He thought that, although knowledge of foreign languages is 'very nice if it is confined to personal matters and meeting people and so on', the technicalities of a subject frequently defeated the amateur linguist:

'So often people say they speak a language but, when they come to technical discussions, they can find themselves in very deep water and they can—and I have seen it—involve a company in difficulties and in loss of money. So personally myself I conduct important technical meetings always in English, if necessary with an interpreter.'

One Yorkshire wool textile manufacturer confessed:

'I only speak sufficient German or Italian to get me around. We're in a very, very fortunate position in this respect, because all our continental customers speak English. It's nothing to be proud of.'

The methods used to make overseas sales vary from industry to industry. A typical organisation of the sales force in the electronics industry has already been described. In other industries, however, the limitations imposed by rapid technological advance clearly did not apply and a hard selling approach was adopted from the time the salesman set foot in his overseas territory. The executive of one domestic appliance manufacturing firm described how his sales department had adapted itself to American conditions:

'The very nature of their sales system over there necessitated our own salesmen going over to the United States regularly and, for long periods, doing the work of the commission salesman while training one who was with him. . . . And he bought himself a station waggon, loaded it up with samples, and he was briefed to lay on a hotel display in every city of the country where the population exceeded a quarter-of-a-million people.'

But whether the export salesman is selling electric kettles or landing control equipment for airports, his life is not one of moving, leisurely, from palm-fringed beaches to exciting foreign capitals. Talking about his job, one sales executive made this comment:

'I myself have come home sometimes and almost kicked the garage door in, you know. . . . Whether the supersonic aircraft will help or not, I don't know. For instance, if you come back from New York or Canada you catch the overnight flight. It's six-and-a-half hours. You leave there about eleven o'clock and arrive in London about seven or eight in the morning. You can't sleep. Frankly, you can only try. If your company sends you first class, you do have the opportunity to lay out. If you go tourist, you don't. But you can't sleep—I mean, the vibration and everything. Then you're in London at the crack of dawn, and you have got to get the report written and you're back at work. . . . You've probably only been away for three or four days, but it upsets your food—everything. . . . I was last out there in their winter and our early spring and I found the temperatures all wrong and wasn't too happy at all on that.'

Selection and Management of Agents

At least as important as the selection and management of export salesmen is the selection and control of overseas agents or dealers, who are a vital link in the sales network of many exporting firms. The sales manager of one firm in the earthmoving equipment industry, for instance, described the attention which his firm gave to the selection and management of overseas agents:

'Selling overseas really comes down in the long run to your dealer. You appoint a dealer and he buys as a principal and re-sells, and you stand or fall on his efforts, reinforced by anything you might be able to do yourself with people who have buying offices in this country—crown agents in the colonies, for instance—but basically you depend on your dealer. The only way of making a dealer concentrate on your line, if it's a difficult seller, is to go there. In my opinion you must travel. You've got to sit on his doorstep. He's got to take you out to lunch. He's got to get your specification sheets in front of his shop. He's got to spend a little time on your products, thinking about them.'

In another firm, in the machine tool industry, the export director outlined his criteria for selection of an agent:

'In countries where we've had no agent before we would use the Board of Trade Export Services Branch. Alternatively, we would take the opportunity of a public exhibition and go there under our own steam in order to attract not customers but dealers and agents or would-be agents, and then we select them by delving into their affairs. We usually sit down with the prospective agent and ask him what he thinks the potential for our product is. We ask him how many people he's got and so on. And try and form a judgement whether he's talking through his hat, how seriously he's prepared to take our line, how much money he's prepared to invest at the beginning. We want those people whose interest goes really deep. . . . Our product is for a process in an engineering plant—it is frequently necessary to have a knowledge of other processes which might affect the performance or use of our own equipment. An agent must always have that kind of background information.'

These two quotations illustrating thrusting attitudes provide an interesting contrast with the selection of agents in other firms:

Interviewer: 'If, by some misfortune, one of your agents dropped dead tomorrow morning, how would you set about finding another one?'

'My answer to this would be that I'm quite sure that over the years Mr X has had other people applying for the agency and I've no doubt that amongst his files he's got these recorded. Because, you will appreciate, we get requests from people to represent us not only in this country but also in other countries. They write in.'

The passive approach to selection of selling agents was also evident in a small wool textile firm where the sales manager felt that changing agents would be simply too much trouble:

Interviewer: 'Have you ever thought of changing your agents?'

'Yes, we have, but once again it's a case of probably a little knowledge is a good thing, in that the agents we have have handled our type of stuff. Whereas if you start with somebody completely from scratch who doesn't know a thing about it, you're going through the whole mill again, which can be awfully tedious.'

The difficulty of finding good, as opposed to indifferent, agents abroad should not, however, be underestimated:

'We not only have difficulty: we have no selection at all. It is a most difficult thing to day to get a good agent. We had trouble in Germany with our agent, and I went to the consulate in Frankfurt, where they were most helpful. They did everything they possibly could, but in fact did not succeed in finding anybody who was really interested in selling what is a comparatively unknown brand of English wool in Germany to German shopkeepers. I finally got our present agent through the introduction of our agent in Italy, who recommended us, as being rather nice people who produced quite nice yarns, to a friend of his in Germany. This is the sort of difficulty that one is up against to find the good agent. He's worth his weight in gold.'

Political factors may increase the difficulty of finding good agents. An executive of an earthmoving equipment firm complained that one of his major problems was East Africa where, 'owing to the wind of change, conditions are difficult and distributors are actually pulling out'. An executive of an electronics firm referred to the difficulty of keeping his agent in countries with unstable governments, where agents sometimes have to be dismissed for political reasons:

'This was not always due to our fault or the agent's but due to the different political pressures in the country, which do play a major part in who you appoint as an agent in a country like Syria or Iraq. Where there are political upheavals every few years, or every few months sometimes, you get an agent who is well in with the government, then the government gets overthrown and he's just no use to you with the new government that comes in. We have had to face that a number of times.'

There are also considerable differences in the way that agents, once appointed, are managed by the parent company. Some of the firms which were visited appointed their agents by letter and then neglected to exercise any active control over them or, indeed, to specify clearly what the agents were expected to achieve. This attitude may be contrasted with that of the sales manager of an earthmoving equip-ment firm who was constantly bombarding his agents with telephone calls and cables:

'This is the sort of programme that is going on all the time. We have one sales engineer whose whole purpose in life is overseas travel and he is hammering these distributors, taking out our latest development machines, training their sales personnel in how to sell our machines, hammering them for confirming their orders that they gave us provisionally perhaps three months ago, and this we are chasing the whole of the time.'

A part of the effective management of agents consists not only in visiting them regularly but in many cases in bringing them back to the factory in this country in order that they may be acquainted with new methods. A director of a domestic appliance firm did this:

'We encourage them to come to our factories. Last week I was at the factory with our Dutch representatives, the directors of the company and one of their salesmen—one of their top-flight salesmen—doing just that. It was time for them to be reindoctrinated so to speak, not that their enthusiasm had waned but because they had produced some handsome results, but I knew they were capable of more, so we invited them across to Britain. They came for the whole week and we did a tour of most of the ways that we sell in this country. Though we realise that what is good for Britain is not necessarily good for Holland.'

An executive of another company felt that it should do more along those lines:

'They don't come quite as often as we'd like. We'd like them to come for refresher courses, which would be ideal, but it's all time and expense, I suppose. We have had the salesmen, and also their service people, which is more important. We have a service fellow over, let him spend a few weeks in our works getting to know a little bit more about the machines. . . . What we try to do is to invite somebody in the company over perhaps once a year. Unfortunately we don't get this. We might see somebody for two weeks and then we won't see anybody else from that company for two or three years. This is really a thing we could do more about.'

The Importance of Servicing

In two of the industries particularly, machine tools and earthmoving equipment, it is essential for the manufacturer to have agents or distributors overseas who are able to give the prompt service a customer will require. The export manager of an earthmoving equipment firm explained that:

'For our line of business we could not possibly sell our equipment without a distributor, because it isn't a question of selling equipment these days—it is a question of what you are going to do after you've sold this equipment. The distributor has to hold spares to certain values. He has to hold a machine in stock and he has to give prompt service which could not possibly be carried out from this country. We have thought from time to time of setting up our own organisation in Europe, but here it is knowing the country in which you set up your own organisation—the language problems, psychological problems and all kinds of problems which we feel are far better handled by a good distributor who is really doing his best for you.'

The ability of a British manufacturer to give a quick service is obviously important in the supply of earthmoving equipment which may be used on a large construction job. Such speed in servicing can often be a decisive factor when the customer re-orders. This is true too in other industries. The sales manager of a machine tool firm explained why servicing is even more important for export than for home sales:

'The man in France will buy a French or even German machine because he knows that someone can jump into a motor car, put something into a van and get it there quickly. When a Frenchman buys a machine from England, he's got that little stretch of water to cross and this frightens the user, so you have got to guarantee the user that he will not only have as good service from us as he would in France, but better. And then having sold him this, you have then got to prove it, and he will watch this most closely. A big user in France bought from us last year one machine. They didn't need it—they just bought it to see how we would perform. We realised this of course. We whipped them the machine across, straight into the customer's works and the next day we had a service engineer there. This year they have bought ten machines. They will buy an order for twenty machines towards the end of this year. You must have after-sales service. This is the most important thing.'

The Profitability of Exports

Most of the firms which were visited claimed to know the level of profitability of their export trade. There were a few exceptions to this, mainly the firms that had no effective costing for any of their production or sales, whether home or export. A particularly sleepy approach to export costing was displayed by one of the small firms visited where an executive complained that his firm's policy was:

'In our overheads we cost commissions, we cost carriage, we cost packing and paper, and that is included in the cost of every piece whether we sell it to Canada, South Africa, to Leeds or even to the man down the road.'

Because the costs of selling overseas are necessarily higher than those of selling at home many firms claimed that the profitability of sales in all their export markets was lower than that of home sales. Only in a few firms was exporting found to be more profitable than home sales. An executive in a wool textile firm said:

'There is a higher profitability. There is an opportunity to include a profit in your price for export, whereas in your home trade it's almost impossible. I think proof of that, to some extent at any rate, is to be found in one or two companies in Bradford, public companies whose accounts were published. They have a better profit record than ours. They do at least double the exporting that we do.'

Not all the wool textile firms, however, shared this enviable position. Other firms, along with the firms in other industries which were visited, did suffer from lower profit margins on export sales, but for at least two of these firms the importance of the 'Made in Britain' tag and the 'snob appeal of the imported article' which it produced did mean that they were able to retain their share of the market. The accountant of one wool textile firm commented:

'There again, of course, there's this very big thing—that foreigners are still, particularly in the textile trade, very much influenced by the trademark "British", or a British name to the goods. So we are able to sell at a higher price than local products are selling, but even so the margins that we are able to get are insufficient to enable us to make a profit on the total turnover of the export market. It varies by market. In some markets we might be able to get decent prices and a fair margin. In other markets, to get in and stay in we have perhaps to reduce our margins.'

Most of the firms visited varied their prices in order to attempt to hold their own either against other foreign competition or against tariff barriers. The export manager of a domestic appliance firm recounted his company's practice:

'The margin will vary from country to country. Obviously, since we've got a very high duty barrier to climb, if we're going to get into that country we must sacrifice here to compensate for that high duty. Equally, if there's a market with a tremendous potential—Germany is an example—then even if it is a low tariff country we are prepared to work on a much smaller margin, knowing full well that the price is going to make a big difference in the end result of our total sales—not perhaps in two or three years but in five or six years' time.'

The ability to accept lower profits demands that a management should always know precisely what its costs are rather than be dependent, as one small machine tool firm was, on a system of 'costing in arrears' and therefore of not knowing 'exactly just what our profitability figures are until after the event'.

Price was important not only in the craft-based industries but also in the technologically highly advanced electronics industry. A senior executive of a very large electronics company replied to the suggestion that for such equipment it was perhaps not the price of a product but its quality that was the determining factor:

'I don't subscribe to that at all, not in the export market. Unless you get a well-established overseas customer, I would say that price plays a very large part in any overseas negotiation.'

It is interesting to note at this point that the PEP questionnaire referred to in the footnote on page 173 showed that for all firms, regardless of size, the three greatest hindrances to exporting were, in order, tariff barriers, price competition and the low profitability of exports against home sales. In the case of the last, when factory capacity is fully occupied by the home market, the incentive to export is, of course, considerably reduced if the profitability is lower.

Conclusion

Despite the problems of price and profitability as well as the special difficulties of marketing abroad, several of the firms visited were boosting their own growth and that of the country by rapidly increasing the proportion of their output exported. The attitude, in respect of both pricing policy and marketing, that makes this possible was forcibly expressed by the sales manager of a medium-sized machine tool firm which has had an outstanding export record:

'One has got to be prepared to offer attractions in the form of competitive prices to such an extent that initially we might even lose money to become established. Good deliveries, good service, reliable machines, efficient commercial organisation—these are the things needed!'

CHAPTER 10

THRUSTERS AND SLEEPERS

The purpose of the last five chapters has been to report and evaluate through the extensive use of quotations the salient attitudes and practices encountered in the research. Frequently, in order to provide a direct contrast, quotations have been 'paired'. So that the contrasts may be more easily remembered, a summary is given below of the main thrusting and sleepy characteristics, each one of which has been, where possible, illustrated by a quotation.

Provision for effective management	Thruster	Sleeper
1. Recruitment of potential managers	Open-minded on all potential sources of management material —creating spirit of opportunity within the firm	Ignoring potential supply—little attempt to foster such spirit
2. Recruitment of middle and senior management	Ready to buy up other firms' top management without undue regard to feelings	Inaction because of understanding with competitors not to poach
3. Management education	Regularly using outside training courses or internal equivalent	Haphazardly indulging in occasional training, if any
4. Management development	Considered of great importance and planned	Little or no attention paid to it—probably caught napping
5. Treatment of existing management	Ready to retire early, demote or overlook second-class management to make way for first-class	Unwilling to be so tough
6. Delegation by senior management	Appreciates importance of delegation of responsibilities	Clings too much to day-to-day operational work

Provision for effective management	Thruster	Sleeper
7. Management structure	Individual managers' responsibilities defined in written job specifications. Organisation chart exists and is used	Managers uncertain of individual responsibilities. Organisation chart non-existent
8. Management communication	All members of management, including foremen, informed and consulted where practicable on firm's policy	Members of management haphazardly informed and consulted. Management demarcation exists or managers deliberately misinformed and not consulted

Broad assessment of firm and its future

	Thruster	Sleeper
9. Management consultants	Aware of all activities of consultants—felt to be of great help in assisting firm	Regard consultants as charlatans—at best contribute more paper work
10. Interfirm comparison at home and overseas	Belief in learning about and from others	Such comparisons meaningless
11. Market share	Aware of market share	Unaware of market share or the importance of assessing it
12. Objective of firm	Determined to grow	Not growth conscious
13. Assessment of performance	Measured in terms of profits, assets, turnover, square feet, number of scientists, etc. Aware of industry trends	No sure knowledge of 'performance' statistics or relative position
14. Statement of accounts	Important indices published	Minimum required by company law published
15. Diversification	Prepared to consider diversification or have diversified	Diversification not considered
16. Future of firm	Planned in terms of specific medium and long-term objectives, i.e. share of market, sales expansion, return on capital, research and development effort, labour relations improvement	Thought about in terms of coping with immediate problems

Broad assessment of firm and its future	Thruster	Sleeper
17. Long-range planning	Carried out by special department or individual executive	Ignored
Operational control of firm		
18. Use of budgetary control	Budgetary control in use with great emphasis attached to its importance	Not in use
19. Reviewing of operations	Regularly undertaken, feedback exists, control exercised where necessary	Spasmodically carried out and no proper system of feedback
20. Capital budgeting	Undertaken together with full assessment of capital projects and alternative use of funds	No such forecasting or analysis carried out
Marketing at home and overseas		
21. Marketing	Seen as key aspect of firm's organisation	Same as sales or meaningless concept
22. Market research	Seen as vital activity the results of which help to determine the scope and direction of the firm's activities	Thought to be inapplicable or impossible
23. Sales	Forecast	Not forecast or estimates based on guesswork
24. Relationship of sales to production	Production based on sales requirements	Production dominates sales
25. Method of home selling	Assessing and experimenting with traditional methods of selling	Present and probably traditional methods of selling accepted uncritically
26. Salesmen	Selected for definable, assessable and proven abilities and qualifications	Selected on basis of vague generalisations with reference to such things as loyalty, energy, enthusiasm
27. Advertising and public relations	Seen as useful in creating public image of company	Belief that product will sell itself if good enough

Marketing at home and overseas	*Thruster*	*Sleeper*
28. Export motivation	Wish to be world-beater	Exporting because of tradition or not interested in exporting
29. Difference in profitability between home and export sales	Known from calculations **as** far as possible	Guessed or known intuitively
30. Method of export selling	Actively assessing and experimenting with various methods of exporting	Unwilling to change traditional methods
31. Management of agents	Attempt to assess agents' efforts	Little or no assessment

Production

32. Capacity, efficiency and productivity	Are known	Are assumed to be appropriate or excellent
33. Plant	Regular assessment of plant with regard to cost and innovation	Systematic cost studies not undertaken. Plant kept in service until depreciated or broken down
34. Shift working	Ramifications of shift working assessed. Introduced where economic and possible	Ramifications unassessed. Not introduced
35. Buying function	Carried out by a member of management	Undertaken as a clerical activity
36. Suppliers	Pays special attention to and carries out analysis of suppliers to select best/cheapest	No such close examination carried out. Tends to remain with traditional suppliers
37. Decisions to buy out components and/or sub-contract	Taken on assessment of reliability, quality and price of components in conjunction with production schedule	No assessment carried out. Traditional methods continued
38. Operational research techniques	Uses various operational research techniques to assist in optimising plant efficiency	Unaware of such techniques or regarded as irrelevant

Labour relations	Thruster	Sleeper
39. Responsibility for creating positive labour relations	Belief that all management is responsible	Blaming history and/or labour force
40. Assessment of good labour relations	Numerous methods employed — sickness, accident, lateness rates, labour turnover, strikes, product quality, etc.	Number of strikes or other single indicators used
41. Grievance procedure	Carefully worked out, agreed by all parties, and adhered to	Roughly drawn up and not always followed
42. Unions	Regarded as having constructive role to play	Discussed in terms of actual or potential nuisance
43. Workers' output	Belief that men will give of their best when treated as being responsible	Belief that men are lazy and must be browbeaten
44. Consultation	Exists and is seen as healthy and functional	Does not exist or has been abolished or is discussed in terms of nuisance value
45. Personnel function	Matters affecting all personnel dealt with at senior managerial level	Does not exist or duties confined to welfare work
46. Training and education of work-force	A variety of training schemes and/or people sent away on courses	Limited facilities for training—largely concentrated on apprentices. Little use of outside courses
47. Staff/works differentials	Have been ended or are being progressively reduced	Little or no action taken to this end
48. Labour relations research	Curious about other firms' practices — carries out investigations	Insular, ignores other firms' practices
49. Shortage of skilled labour and/or other labour	Action to train up unskilled or acquire extra labour from abroad if necessary	Acceptance of shortage as limiting factor

G

Labour relations	*Thruster*	*Sleeper*
50. Method of payment	Actively assessing and experimenting with various methods of payment — flat rate, piece rate, merit system, bonus system, profit sharing and share owning	Present and probably traditional methods of payment accepted uncritically
51. Revelation of financial results	Regularly and frequently given to shop floor workers	Restricted to top management
52. Employees	All employees considered to be actively contributing to success of firm	Staff (non-production workers) regarded with suspicion—an overhead

Research and development

53. Overall plan	Decided in consultation with marketing	No research and development carried out, or on an *ad hoc* basis
54. Research association	Uses research association or other sources of advice, viz. universities, technical colleges	Ignores research association and alternative sources
55. Relationship of research department to production	Research and development activity departmentalised, budgeted and represented at board level	Research and development is dogsbody of production
56. Taking out and granting licences	Both actions regularly examined with regard to all benefits economic or otherwise accruing to the firm	Either or both possibilities ignored

General

57. Problems of firm	Managers' readiness to blame themselves for any shortcomings	Readiness to blame others (Government, unions, labour, Communists, junior supervision) for lack of progress

General	Thruster	Sleeper
58. Unprofitable products	Ready to cut out unprofitable products unless case for retention demonstrated	Unwilling to be so surgical
59. Competition	Regarded as healthy, necessary and functional	All right as long as it does not hurt, otherwise unfair

As most of the points in the 'thruster' and 'sleeper' specifications have been illustrated by a quotation, it is of some interest to examine a breakdown of the quotations included in the last five chapters. Altogether 396 quotations have been used—165 and 149 to suggest thrusting and sleepy characteristics respectively and eighty-two to illustrate attitudes and practices which fell outside the thruster and sleeper concepts as they were explanatory of an industry's or a firm's particular situation. The quotations have been selected fairly evenly from each of the industries covered in the survey. The following table shows the breakdown by industry:

TABLE 10.1

Breakdown of Quotations by Industry

	Thrusting	Sleepy	Neutral	Total
Wool textiles	29	30	10	69
Machine tools	30	36	15	81
Shipbuilding	10	35	24	69
Electronics	39	6	16	61
Domestic appliances	24	22	6	52
Earthmoving equipment	28	20	10	58
Other industries	5	—	1	6
	165	149	82	396

Any interpretation of this table must be undertaken with caution as the decision to select a quotation from a firm in one industry to illustrate a general thrusting or sleepy characteristic rather than from another firm in another industry may have been due only to the succinctness or intelligibility of the respondent. None the less, the pattern of the quotations' sources does suggest that the most thrusting attitudes and practices were present in the three newer industries—electronics, domestic appliances and earthmoving equipment—while the most sleepy were found in the old industries and in shipbuilding in particular.

The quotations were also selected fairly evenly, though to a lesser extent, from all the firms interviewed: 12 firms contributed a minimum of 2; 22 firms between 6 and 10; 12 firms between 11 and 15; and one firm 16.

Hitherto, the terms thrusting and sleepy have been applied to those attitudes and practices which have been illustrated by quotations. Together they account for only a small proportion of all the attitudes and practices encountered in the forty-seven firms visited, and their analysis cannot therefore be used to answer the question whether it is legitimate to describe certain firms as thrusting and certain others as sleepy. This can be done only on the basis of a full assessment of all the interview data. In the course of analysing each firm's transcripts the research team graded firms according to the attitudes they displayed and the practices they employed, using the same standards for all of them irrespective of industry. This grading was carried out on the basis of each firm's performance in the more important areas of its activities, as depicted in the two specifications at the start of the chapter. Each firm was then numbered and placed in one of three groups depending on whether its attitudinal grading was: good—A; medium—B; or poor—C. These gradings are shown below:

TABLE 10.2

Firms' Attitudinal Gradings

	A	B	C
Wool textiles	3, 4, 5, 6	1, 7	2*, 8, 9
Machine tools	10, 13, 14	12*, 16	11*, 15
Shipbuilding		17, 21, 22	18, 19, 20, 23
Electronics	24, 25, 26, 28*, 29	27, 31	30*
Domestic appliances	34, 35*	36	32, 33, 37*
Earthmoving equipment	39, 40, 41	38, 43	42, 44, 45*

* Firms whose financial results were not available.

The grading of firms in this way immediately raises the question of whether there is any correlation between firms' attitudinal ratings and their commercial performance. It was stated earlier that Moodies Services Ltd was asked to analyse the published accounts of all the firms it was intended to visit. This was done both to provide the research team with basic information about the companies and also to make possible a comparison of the firms' attitudinal and commercial standings. But, before any appraisal is undertaken, several points must be made about such comparisons. The first concerns the relevance of past commercial performance to current attitudes and practices. To understand how a firm has fared commercially it is necessary to examine more than one year's accounts. Opinion will differ about exactly how many years should be considered but it is clear that while a firm's commercial record may in many ways be better assessed by including extra years, its relevance to attitudes which have been recently ascertained will diminish. Thus, executives who were responsible for the last five years' financial results may not be the same as those who were interviewed, or an overhaul of the firm's management or practices may not have had time to bring its full results. The second point is that, in the short run at least, the comparison of a firm's attitudinal grading and commercial performance should be seen in the context of its industry, otherwise it may be facilely assumed that a thrusting firm in a static or declining industry is somehow 'worse' than a thrusting firm in an expanding industry, where opportunities for growth and profitability are greater.

The remaining points concern the financial information published by firms and the treatment of this material. The main problem concerns the treatment of a firm's assets as the figure it publishes in its accounts may well bear little relation to their true value. The possibility of substantial undervaluation led Professor B. Tew and R. F. Henderson in their *Studies in Company Finance*[1] and Dr I. Little in his article 'Higgledy Piggledy Growth'[2] to exclude profitability calculations based on assets. It is none the less all that is available and most experts in this field have reluctantly concluded that any assessment of firms must make use of it.[3] From annual accounts it is possible to prepare a number of indices by which firms' financial performance can be judged. The main ones are:

1. Growth in earnings (pre-tax profits);
2. Growth in total assets or capital employed;
3. Record of profitability.

Others are growth of fixed assets and cash flow. In assessing a firm's financial results a combination of yardsticks is necessary because otherwise a firm with unbalanced financial growth, say in profits at the expense of assets,[4] would be made to appear in an unrealistically strong position, as would a firm which boosted its turnover by price cutting to the detriment of its continuing profitability.

[1] Brian Tew and R. F. Henderson, *Studies in Company Finance* (Cambridge University Press), 1949, p. 259.

[2] I. M. D. Little, 'Higgledy Piggledy Growth'', *Bulletin of the Oxford University Institute of Statistics*, Vol. 24, No. 4, November 1962.

[3] See for instance A. S. Mackintosh, *The Development of Firms* (Cambridge University Press), 1963, and Tibor Barna, *Investment and Growth Policies in British Industrial Firms* (Cambridge University Press), 1962.

[4] In the short run at least a firm can run down its assets whether human or physical. Preparation for management succession can be ignored and the replacement of old machinery waived.

Given a detailed calculation of the three main yardsticks there are still many problems concerning their application and interpretation:

1. Over how long a period should comparison be made?
2. Which base year should be chosen?
3. What combination of yardsticks should be used?
4. How should growth be expressed, in terms of averages or year-to-year increases?
5. What relative importance ought to be given to different yardsticks?
6. Should any allowance be made for the 'lag' in ploughback?[1]

In its summaries of accounts Moodies Services Ltd was requested to show for each of the last ten available years each firm's total assets, capital employed, and pre-tax earnings. Where a firm was either exempt private or only recently incorporated or when a division of a large company was being visited, no summary could be made available. In these cases the research team later wrote to the companies and requested their financial results, which were sometimes forwarded and sometimes withheld.

In the analysis of financial information below (Table 10.3 *et seq.*) calculations have been based on the financial results of two periods—the most recent ten years for which figures are available, and the last five years. Most series therefore start in 1953 or 1954. A longer period would have included the immediate post-war years, the economic conditions of which were sufficiently different from those of the 1950s to justify their exclusion. Their inclusion would also have involved the likelihood of two generations of management. In order to strengthen the connection between the present management's attitudes and practices and the past financial results, the analysis has concentrated on the last five years' results, using figures from the last ten years to supplement the interpretation where necessary. The difficulty concerning the choice of a base year has been met by taking an average of the first, second and third years, and the fifth, sixth and seventh years of the series, thus reducing the possibility that the results will be biased because they start from an exceptional year. Of the available financial indices, two main yardsticks have been selected and two subsidiary ones. The primary yardsticks are growth in capital employed and earnings on capital employed. The former, which is defined as total assets less current liabilities, has been used in order to reduce the inequities caused by differing accounting

[1] The time required before earnings ploughed back into a business generate fresh profits,

methods,[1] and to obviate to some extent the problems of differing financial year ends and volatile stock and commodity price movements. The latter[2] has been employed because consideration of profits alone is misleading. The subsidiary yardsticks are growth in total assets as shown in the balance sheet, and earnings related to total assets. These have been used as a check on the primary yardsticks and as a source of additional interpretative material.

The method of expressing growth was to calculate, for the specified periods, the compound average annual increase of capital employed and of total assets[3] and the average return of pre-tax earnings to these. Averages were calculated rather than year-to-year movements because the research team wished to examine how firms had performed over a number of years. In studying the results, no attempt was made to lay down general rules comparing the relative weights of the growth as opposed to the profitability yardsticks. For a full assessment of a firm's performance both must be considered. A steady growth in capital employed or total assets indicates that a firm has been constantly adding to its resources, though it does not necessarily mean that investment is occurring in fixed assets. A firm is, however, most unlikely to increase its productivity or its production in the long run without such an increase in its resources. The ratio of earnings to capital employed or total assets, on the other hand, shows the profitability of the firm and should in the long run reflect the level of its productivity. It is through a record of high profitability that a firm is enabled to sustain its growth of productivity, which is likely to require the expansion of its total assets either by ploughing back part of earnings or by raising fresh money from the public or other sources. Thus profitability is used as a criterion to judge whether a firm's expansion has been soundly based or not. On the question of the 'lag' involved in ploughback no allowance has been made in calculating the yardsticks, but the interpretation of results takes it into account.

An examination of firms' financial results should also be con-

[1] This is especially noticeable in those industries where long-term contracts are the rule. In shipbuilding, for example, the total asset figure in a company's balance sheet can vary substantially depending on whether the amount received on account of ships under construction is deducted from the stock and work in progress or shown as a current liability.

[2] Earnings are defined as profits before tax and before debenture and loan interest and minority interests but after depreciation, directors' and auditors' fees, regular pension fund contributions and other expenses considered legitimate charges against the revenue for the year.

[3] In the few firms where assets have been revalued the continuity of the series has been assured by adjusting earlier figures in the proportion that the revalued assets bear to the assets after deducting the revaluation surplus. In this way pre-revaluation trends are not distorted.

sidered in the light of the experience of manufacturing industry as a whole since the war. One of the outstanding features of the post-war years has been the secular physical expansion of the industrial company. Figures produced by Moodies Services Ltd for 475 very large industrial companies, which are of course among the fastest growing, show that their net tangible assets[1] have increased fourfold since 1948 with the pace of expansion hardly varying. Some of this growth is accounted for by the swelling of the monetary value of assets by inflation, but a great part of it has been growth in a real sense.

The profits derived from these mounting assets have been more irregular in their progress. Until 1957 the ratio of pre-tax earnings to net tangible assets varied between 18·1 per cent and 22·3 per cent. From then onwards profitability was sharply curtailed with the ratio falling as low as 13 per cent in 1961 and 1962. There were several causes for this collapse in profitability, one of which was the official policy of 'restraint' initiated to safeguard the country's balance of payments. Latterly, matters have been improving and company results which have been published in 1963 and 1964 suggest that profitability is once again rising.

[1] There is virtually no difference between the rate of growth of net tangible assets and of capital employed.

TABLE 10.3

Analysis of Firms' Financial Results*
A: Based on Capital Employed
(*All figures are expressed as a percentage*)

Firm	Attitudinal grading	Compound average annual increase in capital employed		Average return of earnings (pre-tax profits) to capital employed	
		10 years	5 years	10 years	5 years
Wool					
1	B	2·3	4·3	12·8	12·5
2	C	n.a.	n.a.	n.a.	n.a.
3	A	9·7	6·2	25·1	24·6
				(9 years)	
4	A	4·2	1·5	14·0	8·6
5	A	16·5	24·5	6·1	5·1
6	A	1·8	2·5	11·7	8·8
7	B	5·3	7·6	12·4	12·2
8	C	Decline	Decline	5·9	Loss
9	C	1·3	Decline	10·5	3·2
Machine tools					
10	A	8·3	8·9	25·6	22·0
11	C	n.a.	n.a.	n.a.	n.a.
12	B	n.a.	n.a.	n.a.	n.a.

* The two firms where no industry comparison was available have been omitted.

TABLE 10.3—continued

Analysis of Firms' Financial Results

A: Based on Capital Employed

(*All figures are expressed as a percentage*)

Firm	Attitudinal grading	Compound average annual increase in capital employed		Average return of earnings (pre-tax profits) capital employed	
		10 years	5 years	10 years	5 years
Machine tools					
13	A	10·4 (7 years)	3·1	20·8 (7 years)	19·8
14	A	10·6	9·8	23·4	21·8
15	C	9·1	3·8	23·2 (9 years)	18·9
16	B	6·4	7·4	13·0	8·8
Shipbuilding					
17	B	7·7	2·9	10·4	10·8
18	C	7·2	5·6	9·8	6·9
19	C	6·2	4·0	12·7	11·7
20	C	2·7	Decline	7·6	7·5
21	B	6·9	15·8	17·9	16·9
22	B	5·2	2·7	21·8	17·2
23	C	0·03	Decline	39·1	32·7
Electronics					
24	A	10·4	16·8	14·5	14·2
25	A	33·4	52·6	15·7	15·2
26	A	35·2	30·1	12·9	12·8
27	B	5·6	2·8	29·3	30·5
28	A	n.a.	n.a.	n.a.	n.a.
29	A	19·8	28·3	29·4	32·6
30	C	n.a.	n.a.	n.a.	n.a.
31	B	15·2	19·2	14·3	13·0
Domestic appliances					
32	C	7·4	4·3	13·0	8·9
33	C	13·7	17·8	34·6	41·0
34	A	n.a.	36·9	n.a.	60·6
35	A	n.a.	n.a.	n.a.	n.a.
36	B	23·4	16·5	11·7	14·3
37	C	n.a.	n.a.	n.a.	n.a.
Earthmoving equipment					
38	B	14·9	10·2	12·6	10·0
39	A	9·1	13·0	13·7	12·4
40	A	33·2	24·8	12·0	6·7
41	A	14·7	0·3	29·4	18·5
42	C	1·1	1·9	6·6	5·9
43	B	6·3	5·2	21·0	17·6
44	C	1·2	Decline	10·7	4·9
45	C	n.a.	n.a.	n.a.	n.a.

TABLE 10.3

Analysis of Firms' Financial Result
B: Based on Total Assets

(*All figures are expressed as a percentage*)

Firm	Attitudinal grading	Compound average annual increase in total assets		Average return of earnings (pre-tax profits) to total assets	
		10 years	5 years	10 years	5 years
Wool					
1	B	2·4	7·0	9·1	8·8
2	C	n.a.	n.a.	n.a.	n.a.
3	A	13·3	12·9	14·2	12·8
				(9 years)	
4	A	4·2†	1·5†	14·0†	8·6†
5	A	13·0	20·9	4·8	4·3
6	A	9·0	14·7	7·8	5·4
7	B	5·4	8·4	10·8	10·5
8	C	5·2	10·5	2·3	Loss
9	C	1·3†	Decline†	10·5†	3·2†
Machine tools					
10	A	6·3	8·4	19·5	17·6
11	C	n.a.	n.a.	n.a.	n.a.
12	B	n.a.	n.a.	n.a.	n.a.
13	A	13·0	8·5	16·8	16·0
		(7 years)		(7 years)	
14	A	9·1	10·6	15·9	15·4
15	C	7·3	2·4	18·5	15·5
				(9 years)	
16	B	8·9	11·8	10·5	6·8
Shipbuilding					
17	B	Decline	Decline	4·4	5·9
18	C	6·1	4·7	6·5	4·7
19	C	5·9	3·8	10·5	9·8
20	C	5·1	5·6	5·3	5·2
21	B	2·9	6·5	6·3	6·0
22	B	2·7	Decline	7·3	5·7
23	C	Decline	Decline	15·2	15·5
Electronics					
24	A	8·5	12·4	8·9	8·8
25	A	31·7	52·2	12·3	12·1
26	A	33·1	28·2	9·1	9·2
27	B	13·6	12·9	13·4	12·5
28	A	n.a.	n.a.	n.a.	n.a.
29	A	19·8†	28·3†	29·4†	32·6†
30	C	n.a.	n.a.	n.a.	n.a.
31	B	11·1	12·5	9·2	8·9
Domestic appliances					
32	C	6·5	3·1	11·5	8·0
33	C	13·9	16·3	26·8	30·7

† Based on capital employed.

TABLE 10.3—*continued*

Analysis of Firms' Financial Results

B: Based on Total Assets

(All figures are expressed as a percentage)

Firm	Attitudinal grading	Compound average annual increase in total assets		Average return of earnings (pre-tax profits) to total assets	
		10 years	5 years	10 years	5 years
Domestic appliances					
34	A	n.a.	45·0	n.a.	39·8
35	A	n.a.	n.a.	n.a.	n.a.
36	B	22·5	14·7	7·3	8·9
37	C	n.a.	n.a.	n.a.	n.a.
Earthmoving equipment					
38	B	12·8	9·1	10·4	8·4
39	A	8·2	11·8	9·5	8·3
40	A	32·0	13·8	7·2	3·9
41	A	11·5	Decline	22·2	14·6
42	C	1·3	3·7	4·9	4·4
43	B	5·8	5·7	16·8	14·2
44	C	0·8	Decline	7·1	3·3
45	C	n.a.	n.a.	n.a.	n.a.

For all the reasons that have been given any interpretation of the financial analysis of firms' results and of the attitudinal gradings must be treated with great caution. Some interesting and significant observations can nevertheless be reached on the basis of the information shown in Table 10.3 above.

Wool Textiles

There is a sharp division in financial performance between firms 8 and 9, which were rated C, and all the firms rated A or B. Both C firms suffered a decline of capital employed in the last five years, during which time one made a loss while the other made the smallest profit recorded by the wool textile firms. Among the other six firms for which financial results are available there is, however, no clear evidence that the A firms performed better than the B firms. Firm 5, which was rated A, did indeed grow the fastest, but its capital employed was given a boost by a big fire claim, without which its results would have been less good than those of some B firms. After firm 5, firm 7, with a B rating, grew the fastest in the last five years, while sustaining a fairly high rate of profit. It was followed by an

A firm, number 3, which grew steadily but with outstanding profitability, a performance attributable to two factors: it is a company run by a very able executive, and it manufactures limited amounts of high-quality fashion cloths. Firm 1, rated B, grew reasonably with good profitability whereas firms 4 and 6, both rated A, had fair profitability but showed only slow growth in capital employed in the last five years. The latter two were, however, in fact more successful in growing than these indicators suggest: firm 6 had a very rapid build-up of its total assets (mainly in stock and work in progress) in 1953 to 1957, when it was taken over, and rapid growth started again in 1960–3; and firm 4 also enjoyed fast growth up to 1957, after which the expansion flattened out.

Thus, there is no clear dividing line between the performance of As and Bs, as there is between these two categories and the Cs. It may be supposed that, in an industry whose prospects of expansion are limited by sluggish demand, there is at present inadequate scope for the A attitudes to reap the rewards which can come to them in some other industries, but that in a competitive atmosphere the C attitudes do bring bad results.

Machine Tools

Here the best results are clearly shown by firms 14 and 10, both rated A, with growth rates of 9–10 per cent in capital employed and profitability of some 22 per cent over the five-year period. Firm 16, rated B, was not far behind in growth of capital employed but was considerably less profitable. The A rating of firm 13 might appear anomalous in view of the rather slow growth of its capital employed in the more recent period, but this was a period of digestion after the extremely rapid growth of the previous three years, following on a takeover and a large infusion of capital. The accounts since 1960 show a swift rise in profitability and a healthy expansion of total assets coupled with the paying back of the loan capital. Thus, the foundations appear to have been laid for a high rate of growth in the next few years.

If the three A firms can, then, be classed as highly expansionary and the B firm as satisfactorily so, a comparison between the attitudinal rating and the financial results of firm 15 shows an apparent anomaly that is not so easy to explain. Although rated as C, this firm had high average profits in both the ten- and the five-year periods, and the growth of its capital employed, and also the growth of its total assets, were very high during the first five years, although this levelled off in the second five years. Two comments may be made about this discrepancy between attitudes and results. First, the very rapid growth in the former period and the high profitability were achieved during a period of boom for the industry. In such conditions the absence of modern management techniques in a small firm need not impede growth. Secondly, the levelling off of growth in the more recent period may well be the consequence of failure to implement modern management techniques which have been made all the more necessary by the relatively difficult period through which the industry has been passing. This supposition is strengthened by the most recent financial results, which show a slight decline in capital employed and in assets, and a sharp decline in profit.

Shipbuilding

It will have been clear, from those quotations in Chapters 4 to 9 which are attributable to shipyard executives and conveners, that modern attitudes and practices, such as are becoming more widespread elsewhere, were rarely found in shipbuilding. This is reflected in the attitudinal ratings for shipyards: four Cs, three Bs and no As. Yet some of the financial results shown in the table are far from discreditable, particularly in the context of an industry known to be facing considerable difficulties.

Thus, firm 21, rated as B, shows high profitability and a very high growth rate. Firm 18, rated C, shows growth in capital employed that would be satisfactory in most industries, as well as an adequate rate of profits. Firms 19, 17 and 22 show some growth in capital employed and substantial profitability, with 19, rated C, performing, if anything, better than 17 and 22, which are rated B. Firm 20, rated C, showed a decline in capital employed in the more recent period and has since encountered serious financial difficulties. Firm 23, also rated C, averaged extraordinarily high profitability over both periods.

It may be accepted that the shipbuilders have, historically, suffered from a violent trade cycle that has embittered labour relations and placed long-term planning by management at a discount. It may also be granted that modern management practices are harder to apply here than in most firms. Thus, it is not difficult to understand that managers in the more efficient shipyards have been slower than managers in most other industries to modernise their methods, and this may account for a comparatively good performance on the part of managements with attitudes and practices that would in other industries be associated with mediocre results. In an industry where it is particularly hard to break out of old habits, above-average financial performance may be realised by firms that have been only partly successful in doing so.

Yet it may still be asked whether the industry will prosper, or even survive, unless vigorous action is taken to modernise its management. In all the firms visited, except firm 18, sharp falls in profits were shown in the years following 1960. This was especially marked for firm 23, which had previously enjoyed very high profits while allowing its assets to run down. Government help may temporarily breathe some life into the industry, but its revival cannot be permanent unless it becomes internationally competitive; and this is unlikely to be achieved without further and far-reaching progress towards modern methods of production and of management.

Electronics

If shipbuilding is outstandingly an industry in which a long and stormy history has left a legacy which makes it hard for new attitudes and practices to take root, electronics is outstandingly the opposite. Here the rate of expansion and the technological progressiveness of the industry provide an atmosphere in which modern practices may be expected to flourish in conjunction with exceptional rates of growth and of profitability.

Thus, firms 25, 26 and 29 were all rated A and each had an annual rate of growth of capital employed of over 25 per cent in the five-year period—in two of these cases, admittedly, partly as a result of take-over bids—together with a ratio of profits to capital employed that was both high and consistent. Firms 31 and 24, rated B and A respectively, had rather similar records of growth (15–20 per cent in the last five years) and of profits (13–14 per cent). Firm 27, rated B, although it had profits of 30·5 per cent, had a slow growth of capital employed; but other capital indicators—property and plant and stocks and work in progress—increased fast and it is clear that the firm was very far from stagnant.

Although, therefore, there is no clear-cut dividing line between the results of A firms and of B firms, those of A firms were in general outstanding and those of B firms moderately good. Financial results for the one C firm were not available.

Domestic Appliances

In domestic appliances, firms 34, 36 and 32 are rated A, B and C respectively, and show outstanding, good and moderate results. The difference in results is most noteworthy since 1960: the profits of firm 36 fell sharply in 1960 and 1961 but showed a significant recovery in 1962; those of 32 were steady at a fairly low level right up to 1963; while the profits and the capital of firm 34 forged ahead remarkably through each of these difficult years.

Firm 33, rated C, on the other hand, shows anomalously good

results, with high growth and excellent profits. With a sharp increase in competition in 1963, however, profits have fallen steeply.

Earthmoving Equipment

In earthmoving equipment, again, results correspond well with attitudinal ratings. Firms 40 and 39, rated A, showed growth in capital employed of 24·8 per cent and 13 per cent respectively in the last five years, and profitability of 6·7 and 12·4 per cent. Firms 38 and 43, rated B, had growth in capital employed of 10·2 and 5·2 per cent and profitability of 10 and 17·6 per cent. Firms 42 and 44, rated C, had negligible growth or a decline in capital employed, with profitability of 5·9 and 4·9 per cent.

The table shows that firm 41, rated A, was virtually stagnant in the latter five-year period, but this conceals the fact that a very large dividend was paid to the American parent company during these years, thus reducing the assets and the capital employed. If this special factor is taken into account, the company grew fast throughout the period, so that its result corresponded well with its attitudinal rating.

Conclusion

This analysis of the relationship between financial results and attitudinal ratings, then, shows in general a discernible connection between attitudes on the one hand and growth at adequate or good profit levels on the other. In the wool industry there is, admittedly, little to choose between the results of A and of B firms; in shipbuilding some Bs and some Cs have done well in difficult circumstances; and in other industries there are discrepancies in the case of a few firms, owing usually to special factors that came to the attention of the research team. But the correlation that emerges is strong enough to justify the assumption that thrusting management attitudes and practices, as defined and listed at the beginning of this chapter, are considerably more likely to lead to high and profitable growth than are the sleepy attitudes and practices with which they are contrasted.

Thus, even if the comparison and interpretation of the firms' attitudinal and financial records which has been made is purposely limited it is sufficient to show that, while thrusting attitudes do not always pay, sleepy attitudes generally engender financial results which are less good than those managed by thrusters. The point here is not that sleepy attitudes will lead to ruin—several sleepers had been making a comfortable living—but that the firms concerned could always be more profitable if they adopted thrusting characteristics. To a lesser extent the same capacity for raising profitability existed in many of the other firms visited. Moreover, although the present report only covers six industries, it is a reasonable assumption that, wherever there is an industry the firms in which vary very widely in profitability, scope must exist for improving the profitability of the worst firms through the adoption of thrusting characteristics. That there are many other industries where firms vary very widely in performance has been conclusively demonstrated by the work of Inter-firm Comparison, reference to which has already been made in Chapter 4.

The fact that many firms throughout British industry could in-crease their productivity faster poses the general question of how the level of performance can be most quickly raised. In the course of the interviews the research team found several answers to this question. One way of increasing productivity is by a physical up-rooting. One of the wool textile firms visited was burnt down a few years ago and with the insurance money was able to build a new mill lovingly planned by the executive in charge of production. A second method of swift change is the acceptance of management con-sultants' recommendations, although, as Chapter 4 reported, man-agement consultants are very seldom invited to survey an entire firm. Another answer is the take-over bid, followed by the expulsion of the old management and the introduction of the new one. Much the same result can be achieved by a parent company changing the management of one of its subsidiaries.

A drawback to each of these ways of bringing about increased productivity is that they occur haphazardly or insufficiently through-out the economy and therefore cannot be guaranteed to act quickly enough or across a sufficiently wide sector of industry to ensure that the efficiency of British industry as a whole matches that of its foreign competitors.

The traditional answer of laissez-faire economics has been that the pressures of the market are such that a firm will either increase its efficiency enough to compete successfully or be driven to the wall. In the course of the interviews considerable evidence was found to suggest that competition can indeed act as a catalyst of change. One shipyard manager commented:

'Competition is a stimulant, a very necessary stimulant. That applies equally to the men on the shop floor as well as to me, to the manage-ment and to everybody. No matter how one might talk, the facts of the matter are that you run faster if you are being chased, and this applies all the way through the place. These difficult days of heavy competition have certainly spurred us on to tremendous efforts.'

However, it is noticeable that this quotation comes from an industry where demand has been declining for several years. As the interviews show in relation to the early 1950s, competition operates far less well in conditions of high and increasing demand (which will invariably accompany a high growth rate), when even sleepy firms can easily prosper. The option of liberalising imports to compete with home products is sound in theory but cannot be practised too drastically because of the likelihood of running a balance of payments deficit larger than the country can afford. An additional weakness of depending on competition alone to increase efficiency is that, even if Government policy allowed market forces to operate more fully, the process by which firms would be compelled to improve themselves would be a relatively slow one.

In order to speed up the process of raising productivity, therefore, it is desirable that the industrial climate should become more conducive to the introduction of greater efficiency and in particular of modern techniques. Such a process is one to which the nation as a whole, and industry in particular, must contribute; the Government can, however, play a major part in it. All firms do at present operate within a framework set by the Government, from company taxes to Factory Acts. Few of these edicts have been put on the statute book with the intention of augmenting efficiency, but this should certainly be a major criterion in any legislation affecting industry. Part Three which follows, therefore, considers various ways in which official action could help efficiency and productivity, in particular by making available certain services for firms in key areas of their activities.

Chapter 11 deals with industrial training and in particular with the new industrial boards which are being established. Chapter 12 examines management education, explains its importance and tries to meet the problem of the lack of interest which the majority of existing managers show towards this essential subject. Chapter 13 covers methods of improving the dissemination of relevant technical innovations especially to small and medium-sized firms. Chapter 14 looks at the question of manpower planning, which in British industry at the moment is in an embryonic stage. Chapter 15 examines the general nature of the environment which has to be created if firms are to become more growth conscious and the sort of institutional framework which would provide firms with assistance in a form that they will be ready to assimilate.

PART THREE

THE ENVIRONMENT FOR GROWTH

CHAPTER 11

INDUSTRIAL TRAINING

The purpose of industrial training should be to fit *all* workers for the job they are doing and, in a rapidly changing society, to prepare them for the jobs they might be doing in the foreseeable future. This definition is wider than that normally given and it draws attention to two important points: that training patterns ought to be as various as the different jobs in the economy, and that the people who require industrial training are all those whose job performance could be made more efficient. This includes almost everybody who plays any part in industry. It is significant that management education, the part of industrial training which has received most attention from the universities, is already seen as a continuous process, altering in content as the manager's job changes and develops.

Present Inadequacies in Training

As the interviews showed, this broader concept of industrial training is still foreign to many firms. To many employers and trade unionists 'industrial training' is synonymous with apprenticeship. The Industrial Training Council, established in 1958,[1] has tried to change the attitude of firms and unions in this respect, but the overall picture remains the same. There is still a tendency, even among people who at times take a more sophisticated view, to equate improved training with more apprenticeships.[2] At best, this is an over-simplification and, at worst, it can do positive harm to the cause of economic efficiency and to the job careers of many young people.

Over the last few years the opinion appears to have been gaining ground that the system of industrial training in Britain needs to be reorganised. Dissatisfaction seems to be felt equally by employers, labour leaders, academics and politicians.[3] The criticisms are not

[1] See p. 217 *et seq.*

[2] See the address of (the then) Mr John Hare, then Minister of Labour, to the BACIE conference in January 1963. (British Association for Commercial and Industrial Education, *Cmnd. 1892: The Next Step. Report of the BACIE Conference, London, 15 January 1963*, p. 5.)

[3] The following are examples of criticisms of the apprenticeship system, picked at random. They could be multiplied many times: (1) Mr Austen Albu, M.P. (Labour), stressed in a debate on 30 June 1960 'the need for improving training

always identical—in fact the failings attacked by one group are often vigorously defended by another—but they are sufficiently numerous and coherent to make it clear that there is room for improvement in every facet of the present system, whether this is taken to include merely apprenticeship, or the training of all entrants to industry, and still more if it is meant to include a total and continuous attempt to fit the worker for his job.

Although many problems are common to all forms of industrial training, different difficulties predominate in different fields, and it is therefore advisable to examine industrial training in three parts: apprenticeship training; non-apprentice training for new entrants to industry; and retraining of people whose job is changing. Naturally, since training is so complex and ill-defined a subject, these categories are not sharply exclusive and the second, at least, can be said to contain so many heterogeneous elements as to make generalisations very difficult. Management training is properly a part of industrial training but it is of such crucial importance and of such complexity that it will be dealt with in a separate chapter to itself.

Apprentice Training

The wide variation between the practices of the best firms and those of much of the rest of industry is mentioned elsewhere (see Chapters 10 and 15) and this is illustrated perfectly in the field of training; as a result few generalisations can be made which are entirely accurate. First, 'apprenticeship' as normally understood in industry means 'craft apprenticeship', but there are also other methods of introduction to industry or commerce which are (confusingly) called 'apprenticeships'; the most widely used of these are technician, student, graduate and commercial apprenticeships. In this chapter 'apprentice' is used in its normal industrial sense of 'craft apprentice', since the question of the so-called 'higher apprenticeships' is more relevant to management training, while commercial apprenticeships

methods in view of the bulge'. (*Hansard*, Commons, 30 June 1960, col. 1562 *et seq.*) (2) A resolution was passed at the conference of the Confederation of Shipbuilding and Engineering Unions at York on 13 September 1962, saying that many apprenticeships were too long and too rigid. (3) The Association of British Chambers of Commerce submitted a memorandum to the Government on 17 September 1962, saying that steps should be taken to eliminate the narrow craft basis of apprenticeship and that the opportunities in this direction given by the 'bulge' had been missed. (4) On 1 February 1963 Mr Wilfred Proudfoot, M.P. (Conservative), introduced a Private Member's Motion to call attention to the need for better training. (*Hansard*, Commons, 1 February 1963, col. 1285 *et seq.*) See also the speech of Mr R. E. Prentice, M.P. (Labour), in the same debate. (Col. 1348 *et seq.*) (5) In February 1963 Lord Hailsham declared that apprenticeships were too long. (*Hansard*, Lords, 11 February 1963, col. 804.)

are a facet of the training of white-collar workers, which will be dealt with later in the chapter. Secondly, even craft apprenticeships vary greatly in character from industry to industry. A small number of industries, such as the retail meat trade, require only a three-year apprenticeship, while a much larger number, such as baking, catering and, in some regions of the country, building, require four years. Nevertheless, it is true to say that the majority of apprentices, especially in the engineering industry, serve five years, while some (e.g. in printing) serve six. Similarly, some industries (e.g. the gas industry) require their apprentices to take a public examination before qualifying as skilled men, but the great majority of industries demand no such standards, although, of course, many individual firms do encourage their apprentices to pass such examinations. The limitations on age of entry are equally varied. It is usual for a boy to be allowed to enter full apprenticeship only between the ages of sixteen and seventeen but many industries (e.g. agriculture, catering and building) will take boys of fifteen, while some boys of over seventeen are taken in the engineering trades.

In spite of this diversity, there appears to be general agreement on certain points:

1. Many apprenticeships are far longer than is required by the nature of the job the boy is learning, and this disparity may often be expected to become greater as modern technology reduces the skill needed to perform precision tasks.[1]
2. The lines of demarcation between different trades, which the present structure of the apprenticeship system helps to foster, are far too rigid, and often reflect an industrial structure which has long since been made obsolete by changes in technology.[2] Even where present lines of demarcation do coincide with the existing methods of production, their rigidity means that the adoption of any radically new and improved technique in the future is likely to be inhibited.
3. There is too much variation between the training standards of different firms, and little possibility, at present, of making an objective assessment of the quality of a firm's training. Few trades compel all apprentices to pass a public examination and no inspection of firms' training arrangements yet takes place. This means that,

[1] Fitters and turners are approaching this situation in the motor industry, and the introduction of industrialised buildings will produce it for various construction trades.

[2] Modern methods of printing need a labour force patterned on a quite different structure from that of the present British printing trade unions and the same is rapidly becoming the case in such industries as shipbuilding and construction.

although there is general agreement that the best British methods of training produce excellent craftsmen, the potential of many apprentices is never fully realised because they are not scientifically trained.
4. In many firms there is not enough forward planning as to the quantity of apprentices to be taken in the succeeding year, nor enough use made of pre-apprenticeship tests, Youth Employment Service recommendations, or the other means whereby an employer could ensure that he chose boys of the right quality as apprentices.

Although most or all of these flaws in the apprenticeship system have been pointed out many times,[1] it is rare for a sufficiently wide conclusion to be drawn from them.

Training Non-apprentices

Only a minority of entrants to industry are apprentices—about a third of all boys, and hardly any girls.[2] Most apprentices have something in common, however tenuous, in so far as their jobs almost all contain what can be described loosely as a technical content, and therefore the concept of apprentice training can be expected to have some general meaning. On the other hand, no common thread unites non-apprentice training. At one extreme, this category includes trainees in the chemical industry, who are given two years' rigorous training, probably demanding greater skill and intellectual attainment than most apprenticeships, while at the other it contains such jobs as shop assistants where the training period is short and little technical knowledge is needed. Between these extremes are such categories as the semi-skilled operatives, such as the machine-minders in light engineering, and the large and heterogeneous group of white-collar workers. Clearly no generalisation can cover this inchoate mass.

In general, the more skilled the non-apprentice trainee, the more attention is paid to the techniques of training him. However, at the semi-skilled level, most non-apprentices can be said to face the same major training problem—that many employers are not convinced of the utility of formal training schemes for operatives. The dichotomy in Britain's industrial structure between the skilled (i.e. apprentices) and the remainder gives the impression that only apprentices need any form of systematic instruction. The common method of introducing operatives to their jobs is to place them next to an experienced worker and tell them to pick up the job from him or her. Once again, it must be stressed that no rule can be laid

---

[1] See Gertrude Williams, *Recruitment to Skilled Trades* (Routledge), 1957; John Wellens, *The Training Revolution* (Evans Brothers), 1963; and many others.
[2] See Table 11.1.

down to cover all operatives in all trades. Nevertheless, there are very few jobs where workers do not gain in efficiency and flexibility from an organised training programme, and in some, the difference in productivity that results from proper training is immense.[1]

In at least one respect, it is far simpler for a firm to remodel its operative training programme than to do the same for its apprentice training. A smaller percentage of operatives and white-collar workers are trade union members than is the case among men who have been apprenticed (where unionisation is often almost total). Further, if a non-apprentice joins a trade union it is usually one of the non-craft unions, which are all very much in favour of training and put no barriers in the path of employers who wish to train their operatives, either by limiting numbers to be trained or by imposing minimum training periods.

Retraining Schemes

The retraining of adult workers to adapt them to new jobs or to new techniques in their present jobs is even more haphazard. Some Government training centres exist, whose function is to retrain unemployed adult workers for skilled employment, but they can only deal with a very small proportion of the labour force and, for reasons which will be examined later, it seems unlikely that, under present conditions, they can play a major role in the permanent training process which must necessarily accompany a dynamic economy. Most retraining takes place within firms and usually concerns workers already employed there. It is impossible to give an estimate of the number of firms with planned internal retraining policy, still less a guess as to whether they succeed in taking full advantage of the available opportunities for technological innovations. What is shown quite clearly from the interviews is the divergence between the methods adopted by different firms and the lack of knowledge of many firms about external bodies who could advise them on this matter (e.g. the Industrial Training Service, Industrial Welfare Society, etc.). It is noteworthy that in the interviews no manager ever mentioned the work of any such body in this connection nor was there any suggestion that external advice was helpful in establishing a planned retraining policy.

There can be no doubt that a well-conceived retraining programme can work quickly and effectively and with little friction. This would require management to engage in forward planning and advance

---

[1] For examples of large productivity increases due to management consultants showing firms more efficient means of training their workers, see J. Johnston, 'The Productivity of Management Consultants', *Journal of the Royal Statistical Society*, Series A (General), Vol. 126, Part 2, 1963, p. 237.

consultations with labour, in order to minimise their workers' fears and suspicions about possible large-scale redundancy, fears which are often magnified when the climate of labour management relations is bad and distrust is rife.[1]

Background to the Industrial Training Act

Until the middle of the 1950s, it was widely held that training was essentially a matter to be decided between management and labour without the interference of the Government.

The immediate cause of greater Government interest in training during the late 1950s appears at first to have been not so much a concern about the existing standards of training as a desire to ensure that adequate apprenticeships were created to cater for the large increase in school leavers due to begin in 1960 (see Table 11.1).[2] The Carr Committee was set up in 1956 to look at this question, and its report kept to this brief. Its criticisms of the *status quo* were carefully muted, possibly in order to achieve unanimity. It came to the conclusion that, while all firms should be encouraged to take as many apprentices as they could and give them a good training, this was a private decision, and the Government had no direct role to play in fostering industrial training. Nevertheless, in order to help to persuade firms to provide enough apprenticeships to take care of the 'bulge', the Government gave a subsidy to an organisation set up jointly by the British Employers' Confederation, the Trades Union Congress, and the nationalised industries. This body was called the Industrial Training Council although, significantly, the name which the Carr Report suggested for this body was the National Apprenticeship Council.[3]

By the time the Industrial Training Council was established, its sphere of interest covered a far wider field than apprenticeship. Its objects, as stated in its terms of reference, were: 'To keep under review the recruitment and training of workpeople, to provide encouragement and help to industries in dealing with the training of workpeople, and to collect and disseminate information about aspects of training common to more than one industry, including information about training practices in other countries.'[4] To this end, it set up a subsidiary, the Industrial Training Service, with a regional network of officers, whose main function was to help firms with

[1] See Chapter 5.

[2] See the Carr Report—Ministry of Labour, *Training for Skill* (HMSO), 1958, opening paragraph and paragraph 18.

[3] Industry and the Government each contributed £75,000 to the Industrial Training Council over a five-year period ending 31 March 1964.

[4] Industrial Training Council, *First Report* (HMSO), 1959, p. 2.

their training problems, to inculcate more scientific training methods and generally to make the average employer and trade unionist more 'training conscious'. As far as action to meet the 'bulge' is concerned, the Industrial Training Council can be said to have been moderately successful. The total number of boys accepted as apprentices rose throughout the period 1958–62, although it fell in 1963, partly as a result of the recession at the beginning of the year, but, possibly, also partly as a reaction to the extra pressure put on employers in 1962 to take more apprentices.

TABLE 11.1

Young Persons Entering Craft Apprenticeships
(Great Britain)

	BOYS		GIRLS	
	Number	% total entrants	Number	% total entrants
Average, 1950–1958	93,426	35·1	16,755	6·6
1959	98,701	33·6	20,631	7·4
1960	103,004	36·0	19,951	7·6
1961	114,729	37·9	20,547	7·2
1962	121,517	36·2	21,243	6·6
1963	101,708	33·5	15,361	5·5

Source: Ministry of Labour, Youth Employment Department.

In spite of its moderate success in persuading firms to take more apprentices, there is little doubt that the Industrial Training Council helped to create in much of industry a climate of opinion more favourable to training, and that it increased the amount of attention focused on the techniques of training for non-apprentices as well as apprentices.[1] Thus, the Industrial Training Council could fairly claim to have exceeded the expectations of the Carr Committee in respect of its work in industry. Nevertheless, there is a general consensus of opinion (shared by the staff of the Industrial Training Council) that, on a deeper and more important level than the Carr Committee's deliberations ever reached, the Industrial Training Council has not been successful. The Industrial Training Council deliberately set out to improve training in Britain at all levels, and in this enormous work it has been able to make little headway. It is important to understand the reason for this. It has not been due to a lack of enthusiasm or ability on the part of the Council's personnel, nor to

[1] See the Industrial Training Council pamphlets, *Training Boys in Industry—the Non-Apprentice*, 1960, and *Training Girls in Industry*, 1962.

any particular shortcomings in the training schemes advocated. The trouble has simply been that the Industrial Training Council has usually found itself preaching to the converted and unable to reach the unconverted. In spite of the Industrial Training Council's best efforts to bring water to the horses, many have resolutely refused to drink. Those firms whose training practices were worst, and who were therefore most in need of the Industrial Training Council's help, were exactly the ones which the Industrial Training Council found it most difficult to influence.

Faced with this situation, the Government had two choices: either it could spend a great deal more on publicising the Industrial Training Council and improving its services, or it could ensure by direct action that firms had a strong financial incentive to provide adequate training—or more accurately, impose a financial penalty on those who provided inadequate training. The first alternative might well be successful in the long run[1] but more direct pressure is almost certainly required to change the worst training practices within a reasonable time. This opinion was clearly revealed in the white paper, *Industrial Training*.[2] This proposed that industrial training boards should be set up to organise proper training facilities and to inspect firms' own training schemes to see if they were adequate. Each board was to be financed, at least in part, by a compulsory levy on the employers in its industry. At the same time a grant was to be given to firms whose own training facilities reached the standard required by the boards' inspectors.

The Industrial Training Act, 1964, embodies many of the principles of the white paper. Its purpose is to 'establish industrial training boards, and to give to those boards certain responsibilities for the promotion of training'.[3] To meet these responsibilities, the boards are to provide, or ensure the provision of, such facilities as are required to give sufficient training to meet the industry's needs. They have also the function of publishing recommendations as to the nature and length of training needed for various jobs in the industry, and the minimum qualifications trainees should possess before they can be classed as properly trained. The responsibility for appointing all members of the boards rests with the Minister of Labour. The Minister of Education and the Secretary of State for Scotland will, however, suggest the names of certain members of each board, while the relevant trade unions and employers' organisations will each nominate an equal number of members as representa-

[1] The Agricultural Advisory Service is a good example of how effective such a policy can be.
[2] Cmnd. 1892, 1962.
[3] Explanatory memorandum to the Industrial Training Act.

tives of the industry concerned. The boards will be financed by a levy on firms in their industry. This levy will be raised on principles which the individual boards will decide for themselves in consultation with the Minister of Labour, and only representatives from the employers' organisations and trade unions will be permitted to vote on this issue. There is no indication in the Act as to how widely an industry is to be defined for the purpose of setting up a training board. The first four boards which have been founded are to cover the engineering, construction, steel and wool textiles industries, which suggests that, wherever possible, a wide definition is to be taken. As important as the size of the industries covered (which is important from the point of view of the Government's financial control over the boards) is the liaison between and within the different industrial boards. This is important because the complex nature of industry makes it impossible to prevent the same board from having to cover widely separate activities (e.g. the engineering board will encompass both the motor car and the watch-making industries), while other trades (e.g. plumbing) would cut across the activities of numerous different boards. It appears that the Act will be implemented so that training for a 'cross-industry' trade will be the responsibility of that board whose industry contains most workers in the trade (e.g. training plumbers will be the responsibility of the construction training board), but that this board should maintain constant liaison with other boards from industries which have a requirement for the workers concerned. In this way it will be known how many trainees are required, and whether technological change makes it advisable to alter the training syllabus in any way. Boards may deal with sub-industries by forming *ad hoc* committees whose members have specialised knowledge of training in the area concerned. The Act authorised the establishment both of committees within a board and liaison between committees on different boards.

Obviously a careful co-ordination will be needed if the scheme is to work effectively. At the executive level, it is intended that this function should be exercised by the Ministry of Labour since it is the Minister who is finally responsible for the efficient operation of the Act. To advise him on this, and on other general policy matters, the Minister has set up a Central Training Council. This Council has six members each from the trade unions and employers' organisations, two from the nationalised industries, six chairmen of industrial training boards and twelve members appointed by the Minister of Labour, six of whom were appointed in consultation with the Secretary of State for Scotland and the Minister of Education. The exact functions of this Council remain obscure, but it is reasonable to assume that its use will be to draw in influential men to help to spread the gospel of better training, rather than to take an active part in the formulation of training policies. Much, however, depends on the force and quality of the chairman and members of the Council.

It is clear that this Act showed a considerable change in Government thinking and represents a far more positive attempt to eliminate the defects in the present structure of industrial training. There is scope within the Act for the introduction of almost every practicable improvement to an industry's training programme that could be advocated by the severest critic of present conditions. There remains, however, a doubt which must weaken confidence in the effect which the Act will have in improving the structure of Britain's training. Many sections of the Act are of necessity permissive rather than mandatory, and vague rather than precise. It would be easy to adopt a conservative interpretation of its provisions, which would lead to few real changes in the way in which most firms undertake their training commitments. The question is whether the boards can succeed in operating as instruments of radical change, in spite of the pressures that are almost certain to be generated to cause them to become merely means of marginal improvement. Perhaps the major factor in a board's effectiveness will be the quality of its full-time chairman. It is apparent that people within the Ministry of Labour are aware of this and it is to be hoped that the right sort of chairmen can be attracted. Another factor favourable to change is the general agreement by articulate opinion, inside as well as outside industry, that the present training structure needs reform. This has not prevented, and will not prevent, the strongest resistance to almost any specific change but it does strengthen the hand of the Ministry of Labour if it presses on with major reforms.

It is advisable to examine the present inadequacies of Britain's industrial training, as outlined earlier in this chapter, to see what improvements are practicable and what would be achieved if the 1964 Act were applied as a genuine intrument of change.

Future Possibilities—(1) *Apprenticeship*

It is clear that certain of the present defects inherent in the apprenticeship system are likely to remain untouched, at least in the short term. Negotiations between employers and trade unions are under way in the engineering, building and various other trades with a view to shortening the present period of apprenticeship, and a certain amount of progress has been made, but the advance is slow. Discussions which are taking place at a regional level are least effective in those regions of the country where there are already most abuses. There has still never been an admission in general terms by any part of the trade union movement that length of apprenticeship and conditions of entry should vary with the craft being taught and that most apprenticeship periods should be considerably shorter than they are now. The reduction of some apprenticeships from five years to four is an advance but this does not alter the fact that with modern teaching methods many apprentices could become proficient in two years or less.[1]

In our present form of society it is, however, likely that little can be done to improve this situation in the short term, even though many leaders of the trade union movement are as anxious as the Ministry of Labour or the employers to rationalise apprenticeship training and to end the compartmentalisation of crafts which leads to demarcation disputes.[2] This is especially true of those who fear that restrictive and apparently unfair labour practices will tend to alienate public sympathy. However, many skilled workers, especially in older industries, are deeply imbued with a sense of the uniqueness of their particular craft, an attitude which is heightened by the fear of redundancy if the labour market in their skill should become glutted. This results in the perpetuation of small unions dedicated to the preservation of a particular craft and its particular training methods, while even in the larger craft unions, such as the Amalgamated Engineering Union, the decentralised structure gives full scope for local conservative influences which are preventing changes in the older patterns. No precise Government legislation could hope to deal with the intricacies of apprenticeship and industrial structure, and there are no means, comparable to an industrial training levy on employers, whereby unions can be influenced to alter their ways. In the long run a considerable improvement could be made by union amalgamations and a more effective TUC[3] but, in general, as long as a large number of workers feel strongly that they need the job and wages protection which the present form of apprenticeship appears to give them, such restrictions are likely to remain embedded in the industrial structure of the country.

Although the Government might find that a direct attack on union practices would precipitate an intolerable degree of labour unrest, this does not mean that it can do nothing to ease the situation

[1] Thanks to new teaching methods, the RAF has reduced a training course in trigonometry from eighteen months to seven weeks.

[2] As shown by Mr H. Weaver in his presidential address to the Building Trade Workers in 1961 and Mr George Woodcock in his address to the annual conference of the Incorporated Association of Headmasters in January 1963.

[3] See Bernard Donoughue, Alan Oakley and Janet Alker, *The Structure and Organisation of British Trade Unions*, PEP *Planning* No. 477, 2 December 1963.

or alter the climate of opinion so that agreement with the trade unions becomes easier. Skilled workers feel threatened by a shortening in the period of apprenticeship or by a relaxation of the rules as to who is or is not entitled to do the work of a skilled man. They are far less sensitive about the details of the training an apprentice receives, and most trade union leaders are in favour of their members possessing as many external qualifications as possible.[1] Thus, the most acceptable method by which the apprenticeship system could be improved would be by raising the level of the instruction given, and the industrial training boards could be ideal instruments for this purpose.

If the boards in each industry (or sub-industry) worked out, in conjunction with the further education authorities, a model training course for a particular kind of apprenticeship, and the boards' inspectors approved grants only to those firms whose training policy reached at least those standards, several of the defects of the present apprenticeship system might to a considerable extent be remedied. First, the long tail of firms in many industries whose training procedures are frankly unsatisfactory should be diminished, especially if the levy is high enough to make it worth firms' while to gain a grant. Secondly, the present system, whereby the nature of further education in a particular trade in a particular area depends on *ad hoc* arrangements between local businessmen and the technical college, should vanish. Instead, much more systematic forms of training could be developed. Thirdly, the divorce between training, especially first-year training, and production could be ensured. Training youths in the place where production is being carried out is bad both from the point of view of training and from that of production; this is especially true where some system of piecework or incentive payment is in operation. Nevertheless, until there is greater co-operation between local industry and educational establishments, there will often be no alternative to an apprentice learning in the production line. Finally, individual employers need no longer be in doubt as to the best external training for a given craft and the best way in which they could co-operate within their firms. There are many voluntary bodies now which can advise firms on this subject if they ask for advice, but most do not. A body with statutory powers to provide a strong incentive for firms to accept its advice is the only short-term means of breaking through this barrier.

Technical colleges are not the only external bodies capable of helping to train apprentices. An alternative method of helping firms, which some employers seem to prefer, is being pioneered by Govern-

[1] Although any move to institute a compulsory examination at the end of apprenticeship would meet with strong union opposition.

ment training centres, where there are complete first-year apprentice courses in engineering, radio and electrical and sheet-metal work. These combine a practical approach with a wide appreciation of the subject concerned and they appear to provide an excellent grounding for apprentices. Unfortunately, apprentice training is only a small part of the functions of Government training centres and normally not more than twenty or thirty apprentices per year are accepted by each centre. This means that their present contribution to the problem is numerically negligible, but they provide a model, and could perhaps even provide a nucleus, for a much more extended coverage in the future.[1]

One of the most promising recent contributions to the development of training is the 'Crawley experiment'. This was initiated by Crawley Technical College, which set up a special industrial training centre and is running a course for first-year apprentices in co-ordination between the centre and the college. This allows many more apprentices to be taken than would be possible at a training centre alone, while allowing them to use machinery at the training centre, the purchase of which would have been a large and rather wasteful cost on the technical college. It is difficult to generalise from a single example, and in many other parts of the country the environment may be less favourable for such a project, but with the proposed expansion in the number of Government training centres (see Chapter 14) and the possibility of training boards setting up their own training establishments, there should be many more opportunities for co-operation, which could prove most fruitful. In any case, if the new Act is effective, all methods of apprentice training are likely to be severely strained, as a considerable increase in the numbers requiring organised instruction must be expected, but the great increase in demand for technical training and education could well provide an opportunity for useful experiments.

Future Possibilities—(2) *Non-apprentice Training*

If applied with sufficient stringency, the provisions of the new Act should cause an even greater revolution in the methods of training the young operative than they will in apprentice training. It is easier to make extensive changes in methods of training non-apprentices since the unions raise far fewer objections. At the same time, most firms have probably devoted even less attention to operative training than apprentice training. The interviews show that nearly all firms who have apprentices have some sort of external help in their apprentice

[1] The Government training centres' syllabus of training for engineering apprentices has been published: *Handbook on First Year Apprenticeship Training in Engineering* (HMSO), 1964.

training, even if they do not make as much use of external examinations as they ought. It is, however, comparatively rare for firms to ask for outside assistance in running an operative training programme, which they too often regard as a matter of the shortest period required to allow an operative to begin work on the production line without being so inefficient as to lower the output of the line as a whole. The major difficulty up to now has been to persuade the less progressive firms to try out new methods of non-apprentice training. Here, once again, the incentive of a grant on the compulsory training levy, to be given only if adequate training is provided, should influence large numbers of firms who hitherto saw no reason to change their training methods, if any. Since it is obviously impossible to lay down general criteria for training non-apprentices, the degree of training suitable for any kind of job can only be determined by people with considerable and detailed knowledge of an industry and its peculiar problems, and, once again, this could be provided by the industrial training board.

Although most operatives can be trained best within their own firms or industries, external courses can play a most important part in training certain non-apprentices, especially those likely to achieve positions of responsibility or those in white-collar occupations. Many specialised colleges already exist to help certain sorts of operatives and white-collar workers (e.g. the Distributive Trades College) and there are national examinations for office staff, for which technical and other colleges give training. However, it is probably true to say that these have received too little attention from either industry or the Government. Certain industries, such as iron and steel and cotton, have shown what can be done to train operatives and new boards could learn a great deal from their example. If industrial training boards succeeded in emphasising the value of such courses, they would be taking a considerable step towards increasing productivity, especially in such growing sectors of the economy as the service industries. As a corollary to this propaganda work, the boards will need to make systematic attempts to improve the standing and increase the number of commercial courses. It is in the field of non-apprentice training that the boards could probably most quickly make a significant difference to the efficiency of industry.

Future Possibilities—(3) Retraining

It is in the field of retraining that the deficiencies of the Act, as it is likely to be administered, appear most clearly. Of course, the improvement in general training practices which the industrial training boards should produce will affect older people as well as

H

youths. Nevertheless, it is probable that the administration of the Act will deal primarily with the entrant to industry who has just left school rather than with the adult trying to adapt himself to a new job. This emphasis is easy to understand. It is far simpler to inspect and evaluate a youth training scheme than it would be to try to ensure that every firm operated an effective development programme to widen the scope and facilitate the promotion of its workers. This in part explains and justifies the gap in the Training Act, but it does not remove the necessity for a reasoned assessment of the retraining position.

Much of the discussion about retraining is rather confused by a failure to distinguish between retraining and redundancy. Many people who are redundant do not need retraining: they may need instead to be made more mobile by the offer of accommodation elsewhere in the country or by a greater resettlement grant. Similarly, and even more important both for the economy as a whole and the purposes of the Industrial Training Act, a man does not have to be redundant in order to be in need of retraining. The whole question is dealt with in greater detail in Chapter 14, but it is worth pointing out here certain factors which, even if the industrial boards were perfect, would limit the effectiveness of the Act in providing adequate retraining. In the case of men who have to change their work, either within the same firm or by moving to a new firm, there is no institutional barrier preventing the retraining of an adult for a non-apprentice trade, but in the so-called 'skilled' trades the position is quite different. Few apprentices are taken on after the age of seventeen and it is difficult for anyone who has not served a proper apprenticeship to become a member of a craft union. In effect this means that a large number of remunerative jobs, where labour may be in short supply, are difficult of access to most workers. In practice, unions in prosperous regions of Britain governing crafts where there is and is likely to remain a severe labour shortage take a more lenient view than those in depressed areas. However, it is precisely in these latter areas that there is a pool of unemployed workers capable of acquiring comparatively complex skills comparatively easily. In the short term, the industrial boards can do little about this problem, except by improving the climate of relations between trade unions and employers. As a first, necessary condition, its solution would require the elimination of pockets of high regional unemployment and the maintenance of full employment nationally, both of which depend on Government action.

Another overwhelming difficulty in the way of providing an adequate retraining programme in order to avoid or minimise redundancy within a firm is largely the result of the refusal of workers to think of redundancy in rational terms. Many are too young to remember the 1920s and 1930s, but the attitudes generated in that period are firmly embedded in the working-class consciousness and are intensified by the great difference between the average earnings of an employed man and the amount he receives as unemployment benefits. The major damage is done by the attempts of people who have jobs to make sure that they keep them. One reflection of this has already been discussed—the determination of craftsmen to restrict entry to their craft so as to ensure that there is always a labour shortage. Another example is the general suspicion of new machinery, especially when it is labour-saving in character (see Chapters 5 and 14). This is also perhaps the major reason why Government training centres, as they are now constituted, are unlikely to play a significant role in retraining large numbers of people for skills which are causing a drag on the economy because they are in such short supply. At present, workers associate these centres with the idea of unemployment. To ask a worker to become redundant voluntarily in order to acquire a skill which is in short supply is usually asking too much. The ambitious individual might be prepared to do this, but such people are likely to be too few in number to provide the reservoir of talent needed to keep the country abreast of changes in technology.

Clearly the ideal solution is to have retraining without redundancy. This is achieved in industry all the time, whenever a firm accustoms its workers to a new process or shifts an employee from one job within the firm to another. Unfortunately, it is very doubtful whether such small piecemeal changes are sufficient to meet the demands of a quickly changing technology. Over the next few years, considerable changes can be expected in the quantity and quality of labour which firms require and, unless planned steps are taken in advance, the prevalent complaint in industry about being hamstrung by a shortage of skilled labour[1] will be heard even more frequently in the future. One way in which the present provisions of the Industrial Training Act can be expected to ease this situation in the future is by emphasising and insisting on flexible training for all skilled, and even semi-skilled, workers. This would make it easier for them to alter their mode of work as techniques changed. However, at best this can only solve part of the problem and is essentially a long-term measure, as it will be many years before workers trained under schemes approved by industrial boards make up a sizeable fraction of the labour force. Apart from this, the new Act offers no help on this vital industrial question.

---

[1] See p. 88 *et seq.*

The Administrative Machinery

To criticise the retraining aspects of the Act does not detract from its importance in the development of training in Britain. It embodies what is in many respects a revolutionary principle, possibly capable of a much wider application than one confined to the field of industrial training. The basic idea of using the industry as the unit whereby changes can be made to permeate through to individual firms seems eminently sound, as no single central authority could have the knowledge and experience to settle every difficulty that arose in each unique set of industrial circumstances. However, although a central Government organ cannot deal with individual problems, it is needed to lay down general lines of policy and guidance to which the various industrial boards can and must adapt themselves. It is then up to the Government to create an environment in which individual firms feel a sufficient incentive to co-operate with their industrial boards. If it were applied in this spirit, the Act should help not only to bring Britain's industrial training standards up to those of its continental competitors, but even to improve on them.

The successful working of the boards depends on their fulfilling three conditions. First, they must be fully conversant with the working and structure of an industry with regular access to leading personalities in it. This is likely to require the participation on the boards of influential representatives of both sides of industry—a principle embodied in the new legislation.

Secondly, the boards must be effective administrative bodies. If they are to have any hope of achieving the difficult task of bringing order and progress into the confused and often archaic field of industrial training, they must have the resources to collect all relevant and available facts about the firms in their industry and about the factors in their environment which are likely to affect them significantly. An inspectorate would have to be established to examine whether the training facilities offered by firms met the requirements stipulated by boards as a condition of earning a rebate from the levy. The need for outside experts on the governing bodies is perhaps less obvious, but none the less it exists. There is already provision for educationalists to be co-opted, but, if effective training is to be carried out, a great deal must be learned about the technical and economic conditions which the industry faces, and economists and engineers would certainly be required for this purpose. Finally, the secretariat must be able to communicate its conclusions freely and effectively even if this means offending powerful forces within the industry. A situation such as that facing NEDO, which can publish nothing without the prior agreement of its Council, could lead to some contentious but important subjects being ignored or discussed only in platitudes. There is a danger that if they are too careful to offend nobody, they will fail to sponsor the sort of changes that are required. It is far from certain that the new legislation takes sufficient account of this danger. The Act requires the industrial training boards to publish their recommendations[1] and the Central Training Council to bring its report to the Minister of Labour, who has to lay it before Parliament, but, as the position now stands, it appears likely that criticism from boards dominated by the representatives of the two sides of industry might be so muted as to lose much of its point and that advice on delicate topics such as the adoption of labour-saving machinery might be stifled.

The third criterion for success is the provision of a sufficiently strong incentive for firms to follow the guidance of the boards. A compulsory levy can provide such an incentive, but only if it is sufficiently heavy to make firms anxious to gain the offered grant. In particular, since the training practices of smaller firms are generally the worst, the levy should be so designed as to affect them considerably. As long as it pays a firm to avoid its training obligations, there is every reason to assume that it will do so, and only a strong Government initiative can make the socially responsible course of action also commercially profitable. In this respect the new Act will have to be interpreted with care. There is provision for a compulsory levy on industries, but the reason given for instituting the levy is simply to finance the work of the boards and their provision of training facilities. If this is the only purpose of the levy, it is possible that firms in an industry will put strong pressure on the boards to reduce their costs to a minimum, and there may well be an equally strong temptation for the boards to collect the levy in the way which gives the greatest financial return for the least effort— and this in effect means concentrating on the large progressive firms, who are usually willing to contribute to what they believe are good causes.[2] However, a levy run on these principles will almost certainly fail to provide the incentive for less progressive firms to reform their training structure, without which the boards might share the fate of the Industrial Training Council. This danger is not lessened by the fact that the sum and allocation of the levy is to be decided only by the industrial members of the boards, who might well be under considerable pressure to assess the industries' contributions as lightly as possible. This danger might never materialise. The Ministry of

[1] Clause 2 (1) c.
[2] As in the amount of voluntary support large firms give to co-operative research associations from which, in the nature of things, they can expect little direct benefit.

Labour has many means of putting pressure on boards to ensure that they apply the spirit of the Industrial Training Act as well as the letter. Nevertheless, the Ministry may have to be prepared to act energetically to ensure that a board is ready to stir up the training practices of its industry.

Even if the boards satisfied the three conditions, a great many practical problems would remain. In part, these are matters of detail which could only be settled by trial and error—for instance, the allocation of responsibility for training craftsmen who are widely dispersed over different industries, or determining how widely any particular industry is to be defined. There are bound to be such teething troubles but they can be overcome. Even an imperfect system of organised training would achieve more than the present unplanned system does. However, such criticisms do point to the necessity for good co-operation between different industrial boards and for a co-ordinating body to ensure that this takes place. The structure of industry is immensely complex and rapidly changing and the effectiveness of the boards and their various sub-committees to adapt themselves to these conditions will have to be judged pragmatically.

A further consideration that would still remain unresolved is whether the principle is being applied widely enough to give the maximum assistance to British industry. It seems unlikely, for instance, that the improvement of management training is to be included specifically among the boards' tasks, at least for a considerable number of years; as the next chapter suggests, however, it would be possible administratively, and a perfectly logical step, to bring this function in. Beyond this, the possibility of adapting industrial boards to help firms in a wider variety of ways should be examined, and this report attempts such an examination in its later chapters. The importance of the Industrial Training Act in improving the quality of training, great though that could be, might even be exceeded by the value of the precedent it sets for further development along the same lines. This Act is an implicit admission that at least part of the plan for industrial development councils envisaged under the Industrial Organisation and Development Act, 1947, is worth applying under present circumstances, and it may reopen the question whether there are other parts of this wide-reaching plan which are similarly applicable in the many sectors of British industry where, as Part Two of this book showed, help is needed if firms are to achieve the full productive efficiency of which they are capable.

CHAPTER 12

MANAGEMENT EDUCATION

The previous chapter argued that the purpose of industrial training should be to fit all workers for the jobs which they are doing or which they are about to undertake, and also to prepare them, by providing a broad training, for jobs they might be doing in the foreseeable future. While training is necessary for an operative, it is even more so for a manager because of the greater responsibility and complexity of his job. Like the training of operatives, systematic training of a manager involves both attendance at courses and a planned programme of practical training. Ideally, a manager should be able to find opportunities for wide experience in his job and to supplement these by further opportunities for development through formal courses of education and training. Only a small minority of firms, however, have well-considered schemes for management development, and for the majority of managers in British industry the provision of the proper opportunities is still a matter of 'the luck of the draw' rather than the result of a management development programme. The need for training managers within the context of a management development programme has been clearly demonstrated by reports by such organisations as the Organisation for Economic Co-operation and Development (OECD), NEDC, and the Federation of British Industries (FBI).[1] The purpose of this chapter is to make a necessarily cursory assessment of the provisions for the present training of managers in this country and to suggest possible ways by which more managers might be trained, in order that the gap between the best firms and the rest may be diminished.

The Variety of Management

Any broad discussion of management courses must take into account the wide range of managerial functions and the widely varying degrees of responsibility. Firms vary enormously in size and this

[1] OECD, *Issues in Management Education*, 1962, and *The Training of a Body of Management Teachers*, 1963. NEDC, *Conditions Favourable to Faster Growth* (HMSO), 1963. FBI, *Management Education and the Training Needs of Industry*, 1963.

variation demands different approaches to management problems. It is equally true that the difference between a scientifically based industry and a traditional one also postulates a different approach. Further, there is the question of the manager himself. Is he a young man moving into a lower management position or a middle-aged one with considerable specialist experience moving into top management? Is he a manager who some years ago reached his promotion ceiling but who should be made aware of certain new management techniques or is he a man taken off the shop floor to be trained for what will probably be the only managerial job he will have? Equally, the level of general education and—for some management techniques—the mathematical training which a man possesses will affect the type of management course most suitable for him. Such variables as these—and there are, of course, many more—lead to a great number of possible combinations, all of which require a different approach to management training.

It is therefore necessary to distinguish at the outset of this discussion between the different types of education and training which are currently available. Immediately, a distinction has to be drawn between education for business in general and education for management as such. Although the precise constituents of an education for business may vary slightly, their selection should be based on the knowledge which anyone entering business requires about the economic, political and social framework within which a firm operates. This demands some knowledge of economics and sociology together with some mathematics and some economic and social history. Management training and education, on the other hand, involve both training in techniques such as budgetary control, costing, and organisation and methods, and also the education of the student so that he is aware of the way in which thinking about management has evolved and of the application of both the social sciences and quantitative techniques to management problems. After the basic distinction between business studies and management training and education has been drawn, a number of different courses which lie within the broad field of management training and education must be distinguished. Courses concerned with techniques for specialists differ from those for non-specialists, and general courses for managers drawn from all types of firms and industries differ from courses for those engaged in a particular firm or industry.

The Present Pattern of Management Education

It is because of the great variety of management situations that it is difficult to decide what form of management training and education is most suitable for this country.[1] Certain features are, however, generally agreed. The widespread American practice of adopting management studies as a subject for a first degree has largely been rejected in this country on the grounds that the study of management requires a degree of maturity in the student which is frequently not found in undergraduates. In its second report NEDC commented: 'In the United Kingdom it is generally accepted that academic education in management as such should come after the undergraduate stage.'[2] *The Times*, reporting the controversy over what form management education should take, found that there is little support for undergraduate studies,[3] and the FBI has stated that management education 'should be acquitted at the post-graduate stage, in the sense that it should come after gaining a first degree or professional qualification, or in the concluding stages of the latter'.[4]

It is at this point that the distinction between education for business in general and education specifically for management is important. Experienced teachers of management have frequently found that, while it is unsatisfactory to teach many of the subjects dealt with by a management education course to students of undergraduate age, the fact remains that the study of management in depth either at the level of the new entrant to industry or at that of the experienced manager requires more time than companies are usually prepared to make available. It is, therefore, desirable that, whenever possible, there should be, as an addition to a good general education some pre-entry education on business subjects, and such a course has been recommended by the report of the Crick Committee,[5] an advisory sub-committee of the National Advisory Council on Education for Industry and Commerce. The report suggested that there should be a nationally recognised qualification in business studies at honours degree level and suggested that it should be equivalent in standard to the existing Diploma in Technology and similarly organised on the sandwich basis, consisting of academic work in college associated with practical experience in industry and commerce. The report suggests that the basic subjects should be economics, mathematics and sociology.[6]

Turning aside from business studies designed for younger students, there is also a large measure of agreement on the broad principles of

---

[1] See the Robbins Report (Committee on Higher Education, *Higher Education* (HMSO), Cmnd. 2154, 1963) and also *British Business Schools*, Report by Lord Franks for the BIM, November 1963.

[2] *Conditions Favourable to Faster Growth*, p. 5.

[3] *The Times*, 8 June 1963.

[4] *Management Education and the Training Needs of Industry*, p. 15.

[5] *A Higher Award in Business Studies* (HMSO), 1964.

[6] This type of course is currently provided by at least four colleges.

management training and education. Both Lord Franks's report and the FBI report have emphasised that management training and education is a continuous process, the career of the manager within the firm being reinforced at different levels of seniority by different management courses. Both these authorities have recommended that the younger manager should make a study of the framework subjects, such as applied economics, sociology and psychology, together with the skills of management techniques, especially those involving quantitative methods, such as financial and cost control, quality control and production planning, to name only a few. The essential common feature shown by both these reports is the belief that the best preparation for general management is a grasp of the basic disciplines together with a working knowledge of more than one management technique. The same broad path was trodden three years before both these reports, when the Arnold Working Party on Management Studies presented to the Ministry of Education the syllabus for the proposed new Diploma in Management Studies.[1] This recommended a six-months' full-time or three-year part-time course (with other block release and sandwich combinations between these two extremes) divided into two parts. In the first part the student of the resulting Diploma course concentrates on at least three of the following subjects: applied economics, business law, finance and costs, marketing, purchasing, production, statistics and human aspects of judgement. In the second part all students cover three subjects: management principles and practice, higher business control and industrial relations and personnel management.

These suggestions for the training and education of managers take into account two certain developments in management. First, rapid changes in both management techniques and industrial processes are now normal and managers should ideally have some appreciation of the forces and trends of scientific development which are at work. Secondly, in all but the smallest organisations, the manager himself will find an increasing interdependence between his work and that of others. He may be a specialist but many of the new developments will be on the frontiers of different specialisations and the requirement will be less for control from above and more for co-ordination by the specialists among themselves.

Any attempt to describe or assess the effectiveness of management courses is bedevilled by the inadequacy of statistical data. One estimate is that 'of the 450,000 managers in industry today, less than 1 per cent have received any form of external management training; among larger companies it has been estimated that about a fifth have a systematic training scheme, while among the smaller ones

[1] Ministry of Education, Circular 1/60, 28 March 1960.

there are hardly any'.[1] Even if this were a gross underestimate it is difficult to believe that more than a fraction of managers have received any systematic training. The only reliable statistics which are readily available relate to those students attending the courses for the Diploma in Management Studies which has already been referred to. From these it appears that the Diploma was able to attract for the academic year 1963–4 some 3,000 students as against 1,150 two years earlier. This represents, however, only a minute proportion of those young managers qualified to take the course. Of these 3,000 only 5 per cent were attending full-time courses while 29 per cent were attending evening classes only, despite the statement in the Ministry of Education circular of March 1960 which gave the details of the new Diploma, that 'courses of part-time evening study are not satisfactory for this purpose'.[2]

In most discussions of this kind comparisons are drawn with the United States where the scale of the operations of the graduate business schools and their standing with the American business community have impressed most European observers. The evolution of centres such as Berkeley, Chicago, Harvard, Massachusetts Institute of Technology and Stanford—though they do not function without criticism—has undeniably contributed to the confidence shown in them by American businessmen. This has not happened in this country. With the exception of a single course at the London School of Economics, which has been established for thirty years, and of some of the university summer schools, which have been in existence for ten years, the universities have only very recently and very hesitantly entered into this field and have not yet won the confidence of industry with the result that, even with their present very limited facilities, the majority of their places are unfilled.

The failure of the universities to play, so far, a major role in this field has meant that the greatest single contribution in terms of number of students has been that of the technical colleges. It is only recently that some of these, and particularly some of the colleges of advanced technology (CATs), have begun to acquire the resources necessary for the job they have been endeavouring to perform for many years. To this paucity of resources there has been added over the years a proliferation of courses and sponsoring organisations. There are two independent management colleges, the Administrative Staff College at Henley and Ashridge College. The remainder of the courses, which add considerably to the total, are provided by a number of different types of organisation, such as management

[1] Estimate of a leading management consultant quoted in the *Financial Times*, 7 May 1963.
[2] See Circular 1/60, paras. 5 and 8.

consultants, professional institutions, adult education centres and private entrepreneurs. The proliferation of courses is an outstanding feature of management training and education. In 1963 there were fifty-two adult education centres and professional and specialist types of organisations offering between them 237 courses. Of these bodies, eight were associated consultants' organisations. Courses on general management and those intended for senior executives were offered by fifteen centres, including the Administrative Staff College, Ashridge College, and a number of universities. There were twenty-nine centres offering courses on general management for middle executives and these again were mostly provided by Ashridge and a number of the universities. For junior managers and trainees, twenty centres offered courses on general management, many of them being colleges of commerce.[1] Finally, there are the internal staff colleges run by firms and industries. Six industries provide special management courses[2] and they are also provided by a number of large companies. As a result of this proliferation of courses there is no clear division of function either between the technical colleges (together with the CATs) and the university schools of management, or between them and the courses run by the other bodies in this field.

Proposed Developments in Management Education

After this sketch of the present pattern of management education it is essential, when conditions are changing so quickly, to examine the probable future pattern of management education before attempting to make any assessment of its effectiveness. The Diploma in Management Studies has attracted considerable interest and discussion since its introduction in 1961 but it is likely that the future pattern will be dominated more by the effect of the Robbins Report as supplemented by the Franks Report. It is possible, too, that the Crick Report will have considerable influence. The expansion of higher education called for by the Robbins Report and its acceptance by the Government involves the creation of a number of new universities and the raising of the status of the CATs to that of universities. A number of these new establishments, together with some of the existing universities, are experimenting in new approaches to undergraduate studies in business and the social sciences. In addition, much needed inter-disciplinary courses are being developed which involve a study of both technology and industrial administration. At the post-graduate level there are a number of moves visible

---

[1] *A Conspectus of Management Courses* (Pitman for the BIM), 1963.
[2] Iron and steel, iron foundry, laundry, motor, pottery and clay, and wool.

which are symptomatic of a general quickening of interest outside the university field. The most important development, however, is likely to come from the proposal made by Lord Franks and now accepted that two graduate schools of business should be established, one to be based on London University and the other on Manchester University.

These measures will help to raise the quality of a proportion of managers but the effectiveness of an education programme must be measured not only by the quality of its alumni but also by the number of students that it reaches. The lack of statistical data leads to ignorance not only of the number of students attending courses but also the number of potential students that are missed. If, for the sake of argument, the figure of 450,000 managers is accepted and again, to obtain some idea of the size of the problem, it is assumed that each manager has a working life of forty years, it means that some 11,000 students a year should receive some form of initial management training. Furthermore, because management education is a continuous process, probably as many again should be attending refresher courses. Even if such statistics were wildly inaccurate, they would throw into stark relief the inadequacy of the present approach to management education. For the Diploma, which is the only course for which statistics are readily available, 1,580 students were enrolled in the first year. This was exceptional, however, both because there was a backlog of students who had not thought the previous Diploma course worth attending, and also because the entry in the initial year included 'transitional' students who, as the title suggests, were those students already embarked on the former Diploma course, which was now closed. In the second year only 847 students were enrolled and by the third year, 1963–4, the entry had fallen to 564. The statistics are a reflection of the fact that as yet the Diploma is something of an unknown quantity. In order to survive it will have to capture the confidence of employers and students on a far larger scale than it is doing at the present time. One source of optimism is the fact that, as Table 12.1 shows, the Diploma is able to attract students of considerable academic ability but it would be optimistic to assume that it is going to reach more than a very small proportion of the potential students.

Similarly, although no statistics exist for the other available courses —and it is true that some of them, especially those administered by private bodies, are well supported—it is reasonable to assume that unless there is a dramatic and wholly unexpected reversal of employers' attitudes, these too will be unable to attract more than a small proportion of managers who should be receiving some form of training or education. Enough has been said already in this

TABLE 12.1

Qualification of Students studying for the
Diploma of Management Studies

(*Percentages*)
Degree or Dip. Tech.	35
Higher National Certificate	33
Professional qualification	11
Experience of management only	21

Source: The Department of Education and Science, based on an
extensive survey carried out in the years 1962–3 and 1963–4.

chapter to dispel any impression that the two schools suggested by
Lord Franks would meet the immediate or middle-term needs of
industry. These schools might well become centres for advanced
research, for the provision of extended management courses, such
as the Sloan programme at the Massachusetts Institute of Technology, and for the training of management teachers. In short, they
should provide a management *élite* for our leading industrial
organisations but their direct effect, in terms of quantity, would be
small.

It is clear that there will be no lack of financial and verbal
support from industry for these new schools but there must be some
doubt at this stage, despite the popularity of the Administrative
Staff College which has twelve-week courses, whether enough firms
will be willing to release the best of their middle managers for as
long as twenty weeks, as proposed by Lord Franks. This problem is,
however, small compared to that of overcoming the resistance to
management training and education which exists in that large body
of industry outside the more efficient organisations. The reasons for
the majority of firms refusing to participate in management education are worth outlining in any discussion seeking to explore the
possibilities open for its reform. On the whole, the more valuable a
manager is to his firm, the less of his time his employer wishes to
have taken up by external courses, especially if they are long and
seem of doubtful value to the firm. This attitude is clearly revealed
by the fact that many of the courses provided by consultants, for
instance, are well supported in sharp contrast to the weak attraction
of the longer courses with a higher 'educational' content that the
colleges and universities offer. The consultants' courses, and courses
offered by many other organisations, are usually short and intensive
and devoted to the study of a technique. Many firms, although these
still constitute a minute proportion, are prepared to release men for
courses which show a quick return. In many cases the prejudice
against what is regarded as an over-academic approach to business

is frequently based on the belief that a junior manager who has been on an external management course will find it difficult to fit back into his firm when he returns. In very small firms it is rare that there is even a conscious decision as to whether a manager should be sent on a course or not. Finally, the present multiplicity of courses confuses employers and makes them doubt whether any can be of particular value. As the Acton Society report, *Training Managers*,[1] pointed out, firms often do not discriminate between the various courses which are available. They send managers to courses which are not suitable to their needs or which are of a particularly low standard with the result that they are frequently disillusioned with the results.

Barriers to Effective Education

The barriers to effective management education are clearly difficult to overcome. For this reason it is important to distinguish those which can be surmounted in the fairly short term from those which constitute a longer-term problem. The shortage of management teachers, although a serious problem, is not insurmountable. The supply of teachers for the more elementary level of management education, which has already been described as suitable for induction courses for the young managers of small and medium-sized firms, is thought to be reasonably adequate and could be increased fairly easily by recruitment from industry. The problem should not be confused with that of finding suitable teachers for higher-level teaching. This type of teacher is in short supply, although recently announced training programmes and a recently observed greater readiness of managers to move out of industry into teaching may reduce the seriousness of this shortage. On the other hand, there appears to be considerable danger that the Franks schools might well take from the universities and colleges their higher-quality teaching and research staff, while the main impact of management training and education will continue to lie outside these new schools. It is commonly believed that only those who are capable of carrying out research are, on the analogy of university teachers, suitable to be teachers of management. This analogy has considerable force when applied to those who teach management subjects at the higher levels. These arguments cannot apply, however, to those teachers who are instilling an awareness of management techniques and their application to junior managers who are coming to the subject for the first time. Such teachers would not themselves need to undertake research. The major problem is to ensure, in the context of the considerable

[1] Michael Argyle and Trevor Smith, *Training Managers* (Acton Society Trust), 1962, p. 63.

resistance to management training and education by a large part of industry, that a large and increasing proportion of British managers have received at least some training and have some knowledge of modern management techniques.

An appreciation of these techniques and of the relationship between them is a major contribution towards making managers more efficient by encouraging them to examine, analyse and judge the facts as they are and are likely to be. All managers should be aware of the tools of management and also where they may obtain information designed to promote the efficiency of their firms. This involves being aware not only of work study—which is now coming to be fairly well understood half a century after its inception—but also of the principles of, for example, stock control, quality control, budgetary control and, very important, man management. Junior and middle managers in small and medium-sized firms frequently find it difficult to appreciate the concept of marketing if the whole of their firm's production is sold to one or two larger firms, yet all managers should be aware of the importance of a technique such as market research and its relationship to the other management techniques. It is an important part of a manager's skill to know the relationship between all the tools of management so that the right priority of use is established. Similarly, the benefits to be obtained from the use of organisations such as the Centre for Interfirm Comparison, productivity associations and research associations should be part of the training managers receive.

For some managers, this aim will be achieved in part by the development of first degree courses at universities, including technological universities, which cover the social sciences and quantitative techniques. There is considerable scope for applying the content of these courses to the problems of management. It is also to be expected, as has been stated, that a number of university graduates and those of a similar status will continue to seek graduate courses, similar to the Diploma or to the graduate entry course at the Franks schools. It seems likely, however, that the comparative lack of effective management development programmes will prevent the full utilisation of all the facilities which will be available. The management training and education of those who have not participated in any full-time higher education is also very important. While it is most desirable that managers should have received such education, there will continue to be for some time, despite the expansion of education envisaged in the Robbins Report, large numbers of men becoming managers who are not of graduate status.[1]

[1] See Ministry of Education, Circular 1/60 and the Franks Report.

Extending Management Education

The key question is, therefore, how can employers be persuaded to release managers for training and education. It is by no means certain precisely what system would be most effective in ensuring that a sufficient number of firms send their managers to a course on management. Three possible approaches may, however, be considered. The commonly accepted answer to this problem is that by striving for a closer relationship with industry, the colleges could have a better idea of the types of training and education which industry believes managers should have. This closer relationship should be accompanied by an improvement in the quality of the teaching so that industry will consequently have greater confidence in management training and education. Eventually, it is believed, the majority of managements will be convinced of the need for management training and education and will be prepared, as part of their normal practice, to release managers for courses. Unfortunately, this is likely to be an extremely slow process and in spite of the current quickening of interest in management training and education, it would be optimistic to expect a mass conversion of businessmen to this cause. A further question therefore arises as to whether there is any possibility of external intervention to make industry accept the idea of management training and education more quickly. One possibility is that the Government should offer a grant to firms for every member of their management who passes an approved course of management. Such a policy has in fact been adopted by the Government to cover courses for Industrial Training Officers. Unfortunately, while this might be practicable for a limited number of managers, there are probably difficulties in applying it effectively. One difficulty to contend with would be the strong temptation for firms, particularly those where the quality of management was most in need of improvement, to send to management courses not those managers who had shown that they possessed the essential personal qualities but those whose time, it was believed, could be afforded. For many firms, perhaps the majority, even the bait of a grant might not persuade employers to release managers since the work they were seen to be doing would not be considered compensated for by a mere grant.

It is, therefore, worth considering a further method of ensuring that at least junior managers receive a minimum standard of training. This is by making more attractive to firms the bait of a grant through the imposition of a special levy supervised by the industrial training boards. At the present time the Act provides for the use of a levy to help to finance such training but it appears unlikely to be extended to management training for some time, even if the Government believed it to be desirable, because the training of operatives and apprentices and perhaps foremen would have first to be put on a sound basis. Nevertheless, despite the fact that it might be some time before it can be considered in detail by the Government, it is worth a brief review of how it might be applied and what might be thought to be the major arguments for and against its application.

Because of the comparatively small number of managers involved it would be doubtful if the simple levy and grant system of industrial training described in the previous chapter would be suitable in the case of managers. In this case, a more effective alternative might be for an industrial training board to fix its levy at the level required to meet all purposes, and for it to pay out grants to firms for all branches of training as the firms reached the necessary standard in each branch. This would include management training, where the immediate basis of the grant would be that junior managers had taken part in an approved course at one of the levels specified above.

It must be conceded that, whatever the administrative arrangements, the application of the Act to management training might well be found objectionable by industry. Although there may be no difference in principle between training a craftsman and training a manager to an elementary level, businessmen tend to regard management as their particular preserve, and might therefore resent the interference of other members of the board, such as civil servants, educationalists and trade unionists. At the same time, at least the medium-sized and smaller firms would presumably recognise their inability to provide adequate facilities for management training in their own organisation, and should therefore see the justice of contributing in cash rather than in kind to the development of a cadre of trained managers.

It would not necessarily follow that the training programmes sponsored by the board would all be directly organised by the board. To some extent, management training could be common to all industries but for training at the lower levels and with the needs of smaller firms in mind, a close association with local industries would be beneficial. It is probable that the local technical colleges would play a substantial part in management training. In particular if their contribution were to include appreciation courses for senior management, this form of collaboration could do much to improve and cement the relations between industry and the colleges.

CHAPTER 13

GOVERNMENT AND SCIENCE[1]

It has already been suggested that one of the major problems facing British industry is that of being unable to take advantage of appropriate productive techniques. In particular, this problem arises in the application of scientific and technological advances, which is essential if the United Kingdom is to compete successfully with other industrialised nations in the world markets. A number of informed commentators have indicated that this is a serious problem and that the United Kingdom's performance might well be below that of other countries.[2]

Part of the explanation for this almost certainly lies in the general difficulties which have faced all investors in fixed capital in Britain during the last decade. Whatever concessions were given to expenditure on research and development (referred to again throughout this chapter as R & D), the application of these innovations to industry is, like any other capital expenditure, subject to the constraints which from time to time have been exercised by the Government on investment. Moreover, investment in a new process is always to some extent a gamble, more so even than the renewal of plant with proven machinery, but this gamble is greatly intensified if the businessman believes that future demand is likely to fluctuate considerably as the result of Government attempts to safeguard sterling.

The 'stop-go' policy followed by successive Chancellors of the Exchequer might provide a partial explanation why innovations requiring large sums to be spent in new investment have not gone forward quickly in Britain, but there has also been criticism of the rate at which less expensive innovations are adopted. Attention has frequently been called to the gap between an advance in applied research and its industrial application, especially by small and medium-sized firms, and it is beyond doubt that such firms frequently

---

[1] This chapter was written before the Ministry of Technology was established in October 1964. It is developed from a PEP broadsheet, *Government's Role in Applying Science to Industry*, Planning No. 474, 29 July 1963.

[2] See, for example, Sir Harold Roxbee Cox quoted in the *Times Review of Industry and Technology*, April 1963, p. 35.

find it difficult to assimilate technological information. It is almost certainly no coincidence that senior management in these firms does not, in general, have a scientific outlook and employs far fewer qualified scientists and engineers as a proportion of the labour force than do both large firms in the same industry in Britain[1] and their overseas competitors.[2] A similar lack of interest in scientific developments at lower levels may result from the normal system of apprenticeship, which tends to turn out people skilled in the use of older techniques rather than those who have the flexibility to apply new ones.[3]

Evidence to support this thesis is provided by the fact that such industries as machine tools and shipbuilding, which have comparatively unsatisfactory records of growth and which, among others similarly placed, were attacked for lack of design-consciousness by the Feilden Report,[4] have a noticeably smaller proportion of graduates and trained scientists and engineers in their labour force than either similar sorts of engineering industries in Britain or their direct competitors abroad.

In order to achieve the optimum application of R & D by industry, that is, to cut to the minimum the time which firms require to apply the results of scientific innovation, many changes are needed in Britain's industrial structure, not least the development of co-operation between workers and managers to speed the application of innovation. This aspect of the application of innovation will be dealt with later in Chapter 14. The present chapter will discuss how other barriers to the quick application of scientific innovations can be eliminated.

At the national level, there are barriers to growth that stem from an economically inefficient distribution of research throughout industry, which leads to a misapplication of resources as the progress of one industry or sector is delayed or made unprofitable because of deficiencies in the research effort elsewhere. The ability of the machine tool industry, for example, to market new electronically controlled machine tools has been seriously hampered by inadequate technological knowledge in either or both the machine tool industry itself and the client engineering industry. The concentration of the bulk of the United Kingdom's R & D expenditure in a handful of

---

[1] FBI, *Industrial Research in Manufacturing Industry*, 1961, p. 67, Table 3. This generalisation is true of most industries but not all. In some such as the electronics industry, many small firms are extremely progressive.

[2] See the Patton Report and the British Productivity Council, *The Chemical Industry in Western Germany*, 1961.

[3] Gertrude Williams, *Apprenticeship in Europe* (Chapman and Hall), 1963.

[4] DSIR, *Engineering Design* (HMSO), 1963.

industries raises the question, therefore, whether the Government should take steps and, if so, what steps, to improve the distribution of R & D expenditure between industries. The fact that more R & D is required in some industries is almost certainly beyond doubt. The investigations of the Economics Section of DSIR and the report of the Feilden Committee confirm this. Shipbuilding, marine engineering, machine tools and textile machinery are industries which have been the subject of unfavourable comment from one or other of these bodies.

There are thus two separate problems: first, the correcting of the imbalance in the nation's research effort and, secondly, the improving of the level of technological sophistication of most firms, especially those which are small or medium-sized. The speeding of R & D in certain sectors of the economy by the use of development contracts has been recommended strongly in recent months by a number of authorities.[1] The FBI succinctly listed several reasons why industry might not be able to undertake the exploitation of new discoveries without outside, i.e. Government, help. These were the size and cost of some of the projects; the decade or two that some of them may need to reach full commercial flower; the speculative nature of some new ideas; and, finally, 'sheer complexity in an interdisciplinary sense', a far from negligible stumbling-block that may, for example, explain the reluctance of the mechanically orientated machine tool industry to become involved with electronics and solid state physics.[2]

Civil Development Contracts

The idea of civil development contracts, and perhaps also 'earmarked' grants to research associations,[3] may be based in part on the model of defence contracts, whereby the Government encouraged private firms in the defence industries to engage in projects and sectors of production which they would otherwise have ignored[4] and which might have left serious gaps in defence production. In so far as the civil development contracts are used to overcome the uneven distribution of research in complementary industries and the resulting economic bottlenecks, they will go a long way towards solving the problem of co-ordinating industrial research. Unfortunately, the comparison with defence contracts tends to ignore certain

[1] FBI, *Civil Research Policy*, 1963, and *Committee of Enquiry into the Organisation of Civil Science* (The Trend Report) (HMSO), Cmnd. 2171, 1963.

[2] *Civil Research Policy*, p. 5.

[3] These were announced in DSIR, *Report 1962* (HMSO), Cmnd. 2027, 1963, but it is not yet clear how successful these grants will be. For a further discussion, see the PEP broadsheet *Government's Role in Applying Science to Industry*.

[4] DSIR, *Report 1962*, p. 10.

central features of civil development contracts, which make their use on a significant scale considerably more difficult for the Government. In the case of defence contracts, the Government not only sponsors research in a given field: it is also the sole, or at least the most important, customer for the final product. In civil industries this is not usually the case: the Government cannot ensure that, by sales of the final product, a firm will recoup the money it spends on R & D, and therefore such a contract is likely to require a substantially different type of negotiation and possibly more favourable terms than one for defence production. The institution of 'earmarked' grants to research associations may ease this problem slightly by encouraging the research associations to engage in basic research, for which their laboratories are especially fitted and which may appear of doubtful profitability to the businessman. This could make it easier for private firms to see the potential value to them of a proposed development contract.

In the past, joint ventures with industry in the fields of R & D and its application have been undertaken by the National Research Development Corporation (NRDC), DSIR and also by other Government departments in sectors of particular concern to them.[1] There has been a clear difference between the purpose of NRDC's joint enterprises with private industry and DSIR's civil development contracts. NRDC provides capital for developments involving technical innovation. It was designed to fill the gap caused by the reluctance of private interests to put up capital for enterprises which, of their very nature, carried a considerably higher risk than normal. NRDC has its own capital and exercises great flexibility in the conditions of partnership it negotiates for different ventures. Sometimes it gives a direct loan to a single firm to develop an idea of its own, while at other times it introduces a project to several firms, allowing each to develop away from the original blueprint in its own direction.[2] A third variation in NRDC's method of working has been to bring together a number of firms, each having a particular brand of technological knowledge, into a common venture with NRDC supplying some of the risk capital. In spite of this organisation having pioneered many successful projects,[3] there has been a basic feature in its terms of reference which has made it far less effective

---

[1] The Ministry of Public Building and Works has, since 1963, begun to encourage R & D in the construction industries far more actively than previously. See, for instance, a speech by the Minister, Mr Geoffrey Rippon, at Clacton on 11 June 1963.

[2] The Hovercraft is an example of such a development.

[3] See J. C. Duckworth, managing director of NRDC, 'NRDC—Organisation and Terms of Reference', *Statist*, 4 January 1963.

than it could have been. This has been the requirement that it should, taking one year with another, break even financially, but it seems likely that in the near future this requirement will be modified. Such a modification will enable NRDC to undertake, far more extensively, the vital task of supplying the capital to finance not only the R & D of a revolutionary product but also (and this is very important) its marketing. In many cases this latter step can cost millions of pounds and many firms are reluctant to enter into such expenditure when risk of failure is great.[1]

The DSIR development contracts are far less flexible. The Treasury has granted a specific sum of money to the Department in order to finance the development within industry of particular products selected by DSIR. The model in these cases is that of a contract with a firm or group of firms to produce an item, rather than a joint partnership between Government and industry. Few contracts, however, have been awarded by DSIR, although the scheme was first mooted in 1958[2] and a Development Committee was set up in 1959.[3] The reasons for this are not clear but it is probable that, despite hopes to the contrary, there is a shortage of projects suitable for development by the conventional DSIR approach. It would seem, therefore, that it is quite likely that this form of development contract will not play a major role in the future.

The overlapping of functions between DSIR and NRDC has been condemned by the Trend Report, which suggested that they should be merged to form a Development Division of a new authority, the Industrial Research and Development Authority. Both major political parties have in fact rejected these proposals as they stand.

The difficulties encountered in finding a market for the product of a development contract which relies for its sales on private industry have already been noted. Both the Trend Report and the FBI report, *Civil Research Policy*, suggested that the Government could play an especially important part in placing development contracts in those industries where it is a sole or important customer, but the reports ignore the fact that in only a relatively few industries (electronics is an example) can development contracts be used in this way. The FBI report, in particular, concentrates on the placing of development contracts for technologically advanced and sometimes revolutionary products (as is done by the Ministry of Defence and also by certain civilian departments such as, for example, the GPO), and says little about the system whereby a large buyer is able to ensure that the

---

[1] The proposed Hovercraft service across the Solent is an example of such enterprise.

[2] DSIR, *Report 1958* (HMSO), Cmnd. 730, 1959, p. 23.

[3] DSIR, *Report 1959* (HMSO), Cmnd. 1049, 1960, p. 22.

products bought are of a satisfactorily high quality by dictating their detailed specifications and even, on occasion, their methods of production (many larger buyers, Marks and Spencer, for example, use the latter technique with their suppliers). This latter system even when used by Government departments should not be described by the term 'development contract', but this is not to underestimate its value. Although it could not serve to advance the frontiers of science, used properly by Government departments and the nationalised industries, it would raise the level of technological competence not only of certain firms but even of industries.

This distinction serves to emphasise the limitations of development contracts as a method of materially increasing Britain's rate of economic growth. At the best they would have a tendency to shift the balance of research between industries and within industries in an economically desirable direction, but, since they are normally given to the most technologically advanced firms, they would not even touch on the problem of the large number of firms which are slow to accept any sort of scientific innovation. Thus, at best, the civil development contracts can be only one prong of the movement to deploy available scientific resources more efficiently.

Information Services

A solution to the problem of bridging the gap between successful research and its application can be achieved only by a sustained effort both to improve education, especially technological education, and also to make the business environment more competitive. In the long run the answer almost certainly lies in a better supply of technologists, and the massive increase in the British provision for technological education will in due course have its effect. It must be recognised, however, that a programme of education sufficient to provide enough qualified men to make an impact on the multitude of small and medium-sized firms would probably take a decade to get under way, and it would be longer than that before its purpose was achieved. Similarly, a fundamental change in the structure of British industry is unlikely to take place in the near future, though it is to be hoped that one function of management education, which has been discussed in Chapter 12, will be to spread an awareness of the role of technology in modern industry.

In the absence of either of these solutions a partial method of closing the gap between research and its widespread application in industry is the maintenance of an efficient network of information services. It is important, however, to distinguish between the task of these services in helping scientifically sophisticated firms and that of introducing scientific innovations to unscientific firms. DSIR is attempting to do both tasks and it is in the nature of things that it is probably having more success with the former than with the latter. Whereas a pamphlet, an article in a technical journal or an information sheet from a DSIR Research Station would be sufficient to inform a firm with a scientific outlook of an innovation, firms lacking scientists, or lacking proper channels of communication between their scientists and decision making management, are, in the main, unable to assimilate technical information passed on in this manner.[1] It has been found that the only effective method of informing such firms of relevant innovations is by direct personal visits paid by qualified men.

In order to meet the problem posed by firms without scientists in top management positions, or firms that are otherwise unreceptive to scientific and technological innovations, the DSIR Information Division has offices in Edinburgh, Cardiff and Newcastle, and, in addition, seven more regional centres have been set up by local initiative with some financial help from DSIR. All these centres do their best to keep local firms informed of scientific innovations which might help them, and they act as a liaison between Government, universities and technical colleges and industry in the scientific field. The centres are undoubtedly doing valuable work and are being called on increasingly by industry to help with its research problems. Since the amount of visiting the centres can carry out is severely limited by their financial resources, the great drawback to the scheme, as it is run at the moment, is that it requires firms not only to know of the existence of DSIR Technical Information Centres but also to be able to formulate specific scientific questions with which DSIR can help them. Only a small minority of firms are in this position and these could, in most cases, obtain help elsewhere. In order to help the less progressive firms, which are not able to identify problems to the degree of being able to ask specific questions, DSIR would have to adopt a far more active policy of going out and visiting these firms. There is little doubt that, within the confines of their limited resources, the centres are doing a worth-while task and it is difficult to criticise their achievements. The valid criticism is of the low priority given by the Government to the dissemination of scientific information.

A newer and more successful project has been initiated whereby DSIR has co-operated in the training of a senior lecturer at each of

[1] C. F. Carter and B. R. Williams, *Industry and Technical Progress* (OUP), 1957, p. 71. *Times Review of Industry and Technology*, March 1963, p. 87. T. Emmerson in FBI, *Patterns of Research in British Industry* (an account of a conference held at Eastbourne in 1962), July 1962, pp. 54–5.

four Scottish technical colleges. The function of these lecturers is to encourage local managers to understand the value of technical innovation and to make use of the advice which is available. The success of this scheme has encouraged DSIR to extend it by the projected appointment over the next three years, with a further extension planned for later on, of industrial liaison officers to thirty technical colleges in England and Wales.

The main difficulty of significantly extending these services is the cost. It has been estimated by DSIR that one visit by a qualified scientist or engineer costs £10. If this figure is multiplied, not only by the number of firms who could be expected to be able to make use of technical information of any description (assuming a satisfactory criterion could be found for separating the sheep from the goats in this way), but also by a factor representing the number of repeated visits that would undoubtedly have to be made to firms before some problems were solved, it is clear that sums of money are involved of a quite different order of magnitude from anything which DSIR has so far been able to devote to its regional information services.

The fifteen Research Stations maintained by DSIR vary greatly in the closeness of their relationship with industry. Of those which do have close contacts with industry, however, a fairly consistent pattern emerges which shows that, while their relationships with scientifically sophisticated firms are excellent, the general consensus of business opinion appears to be that the work of the DSIR Stations is often too basic in character to be of interest to the practical businessman. Since it may be assumed that these are the opinions of the more scientifically enlightened section of the business community—the less enlightened have probably scarcely heard of Research Stations at all—this scarcely augurs well for the ability of Research Stations to help firms lacking a scientific outlook or expertise to take advantage of innovations in their industries.

Many of the reasons businessmen give for their disappointment with the work of Research Stations are, in fact, not well founded. (Research Stations, for instance, frequently introduce practical innovations which are virtually ignored by industry.)[1] It would appear, therefore, in the first instance, that a systematic attempt by Research Stations to explain to industry exactly what they are doing and how they can help would do a great deal to ease the situation. At present, for example, the National Engineering Laboratory (NEL) devotes 10 per cent of its budget to the dissemination of technical information, but nearly all of this is spent in ways which can only be assimilated by firms which possess considerable scientific expertise. Few of the staff at NEL have had any industrial experience and

[1] For instance, V-bricks and hydrostatic transmission systems.

industrial contacts tend to be at a senior level with the most scientifically advanced firms.

Research Associations

Since many businessmen appear suspicious of any organisation directed from Whitehall, the final solution to this problem might lie in a move, wherever possible, away from the Research Stations and towards the co-operative research associations. Some Research Stations do not serve any particular industry, but rather industry as a whole (e.g. the Water Pollution Research Station). At the other extreme some establishments (e.g. the Building Research Station) are intimately connected with one particular industry and could easily form the nucleus of a co-operative research association except that the industries concerned do not appear willing to finance them adequately.

In many ways co-operative industrial research associations avoid the difficulties raised by other methods of disseminating information to industry. The major drawbacks to the effective use of the methods dealt with so far are:

1. The necessity to include small and medium-sized firms in any schemes to improve dissemination of technical information;
2. The advisability of having people well versed in the problems of a particular industry visiting such firms personally;
3. The suspicion felt by much of private industry of any Government dominated organisation;
4. The very large increase in Government expenditure which any significant contribution to the solution of this problem by any of the means so far mentioned would necessitate.

In theory, at least, the research association is open to none of these objections. One of the intentions behind the creation of research associations in 1917 was that they should impart the benefits of research to all firms in an industry, not merely the large ones and not merely those which had their own contribution to make to research. At the same time, if firms were to be visited by scientists and technologists employed by a particular industrial research association, then presumably these would be experts in the particular industry which employed them. Further, a research association, unlike a DSIR Research Station, is not under the control of the Government; it is governed by its Council made up largely of businessmen who are active within the industry concerned. It is true that the Government, through DSIR, makes grants to the research associations and is in some position to influence them, but this influence is not overt and it seems true that research associations arouse less hostility and create less suspicion within industry than do Research Stations. The vital role which industry believes such associations to play in the whole problem of technical development was shown quite clearly in the conference held by the FBI in 1962 at Eastbourne, which discussed the pattern of research in industry.[1] It is also significant that one of the major recommendations made by a recent study into the clothing industry was that a research association should be created in order to improve the efficiency of the industry.[2]

It has been shown in Chapter 7 that some research associations are much appreciated by their members. Eventually there is no reason why their advisory services should confine themselves to information about technological innovations. The Production Engineering Research Association (PERA) has gone some way towards widening its scope of operation by giving advice on factory architecture and methods of reducing factory costs.[3] In all such functions, co-operative effort can overcome some of the disadvantages of small size. The difficulty of persuading many businessmen to accept and put into practice ideas implementing technical innovation should not, however, be underestimated. Besides having a basic scientific or technological training, the key requirement of such research association advisers would be that they should be capable of selling ideas to businessmen.

If research associations, at the moment, play a central role in disseminating information to smaller units, the question is how effectively they perform this function. It is very difficult and probably misleading to give a general answer to any question about research associations because they vary so enormously. The largest research association (the British Iron and Steel Research Association) has a budget of over £1 million a year, while the smallest has under £10,000. Further, the industries with which they are concerned differ in the general level of technology which the average firm requires, in the size of the average firm, in the number of graduates as a proportion of the labour force, in short, in every possible determinant of the standard of technical progressiveness in an industry. Bearing this in mind, it is not surprising that almost anything that can be said about research associations will prove to have exceptions. Nevertheless, certain strong tendencies can be discerned. Below a certain level of income, useful research is virtually impossible, while economies of large scale do exist in this field. Because of the variations existing between different industries, it is probably impossible

---

[1] G. Baily in *Patterns of Research in British Industry*, p. 16.

[2] E. Belbin and R. Sergean, *Training in the Clothing Industry* (Twentieth Century Press), 1963, pp. 122-3.

[3] Council of PERA, *Annual Report for 1962*.

to lay down hard and fast rules as to the budget which research associations require in order to be efficient, although an estimate made at the FBI conference at Eastbourne was that no independent research association with a budget of under £25,000 a year can survive for long.[1]

Forty-eight of the fifty-three research associations depend for their income on voluntary subscriptions from the industries they serve while the remaining five[2] are financed by means of a statutory levy on the member firms of their industries. Additional grants are given by DSIR on the basis of a proportion of the sum raised from industry,[3] although a small fraction of DSIR expenditure in this field is allocated on other grounds. A research association serving a non-scientifically based industry, especially one largely made up of small firms, is likely to find itself in a vicious circle. The typical small firm in such an industry is more than likely to have a management which is incapable 'of understanding the concepts and terminology used in technical literature and of translating the ideas into its own surroundings'.[4] It is probable that most firms are not even aware of the existence of a research association. Even of those that are, many nevertheless feel, with practical justification, that if they pay a subscription to the association, the money so spent will yield either a very small or no return at all. Consequently, the research associations of such industries find it difficult to raise their membership and revenue.

There is thus no easy way out of the dilemma, which often produces consequences that exacerbate the initial situation. A research association which is chronically short of funds is unable to attract good enough scientists and so it is likely to be still less able to help its member firms sufficiently to justify the money they pay in subscriptions.

Further DSIR grants, special assistance grants, were given to research associations during the limited period 1959–64 to enable them to make their information techniques more effective. The basic reason for giving special assistance grants for a limited period only is in accordance with the philosophy of DSIR that the activities of the research associations and of the DSIR Information Centres should, in the long term, be paid for by industry. A shortcoming of

---

[1] C. J. Virden in *Patterns of Research in British Industry*, p. 54. See also Sir Walter Drummond, ex-Chairman of the DSIR Industrial Grants Committee, *Research for Industry 1961* (HMSO), 1962, pp. 37–8.

[2] Wool, cotton, cutlery, furniture and lace.

[3] The total income of all research associations is £9 million per annum of which the DSIR contribution is £2 million.

[4] Emmerson, loc. cit.

the scheme was the fact that additional funds had to be raised from members of the research association concerned in order to attract this DSIR grant and some associations which had a great need for an extension of their information services to enable them to break out of the vicious circle which has been described could not raise the additional income from their members to benefit from the DSIR proposals. While it is too early to attempt to evaluate their precise beneficial effects, it appears that the more energetic of the research associations, which have used the grants to employ liaison officers and now keep these officers on their staffs, are finding their resources generally strained. This state of affairs can largely be attributed to the fact that the five-year period during which the special assistance grants have been available has been too short and the amount of money deployed through this scheme too small to achieve a sufficient participation of firms to make the project self-financing. There are, therefore, strong grounds for believing that, if these grants were to fulfil their function effectively, they would not only have to be operative for a longer period but would have to be larger than has been envisaged so far.

The Similarity to Industrial Training

There are close similarities between the difficulties facing many small and medium-sized firms in the fields of industrial training and the application of science. In both cases firms are prevented by lack of knowledge from reaping the benefits of increased productivity. By the introduction of the Industrial Training Act, the Ministry of Labour has now acknowledged that only an industry-wide organisation, working in close co-operation with the relevant Government departments and financed by a compulsory levy on the industry, can hope to solve the intractable problem of training in industry.

The implementation of the Act and the welcome afforded to it by both sides of industry mean that there logically should be no objections of principle to a compulsory levy for science. This is especially necessary since, as has already been shown on page 253, many research associations are unable adequately to fulfil their obligations to their industries and some industries are not prepared to finance a research association at all.[1] However, the application of this principle is, in some respects, less of an innovation in the field of dissemination of scientific research to industry than it is in industrial training, since the research associations already exist whose function is to foster

[1] The building industry is an example. See the report of the working party headed by Mr. D. E. Parish: Ministry of Public Building and Works, *Building Research and Information Services, Report of a Working Party* (HMSO), 1964.

the application of science within industry, and the principle of the compulsory levy has already been accepted in certain industries. Nevertheless, there are certain technical difficulties in applying a compulsory levy for science which do not occur when applying the levy for training and which would have to be overcome before a workable system could be implemented. Unlike the industrial training boards, the boundaries of which will be drawn with regard to the most effective method of providing training within an industry, the efficiency of many research associations is impaired by their not serving a sufficiently wide field to deal with the basic problems affecting their industry. To meet this difficulty there has been a move by research associations to recruit members from wider spheres of industrial activity, but in some cases, especially where a research association serves only a small sector of industry, amalgamation may be a preferable alternative.

A second important respect in which the situation in the field of industrial scientific R & D and the dissemination of information would differ from that of industrial training is the fact that a firm may be awarded a rebate if the industrial training board's inspectors regard its training programme as satisfactory. Since it is impossible to inspect a firm to determine whether its application of scientific innovation is adequate, the whole system of rebates is inapplicable. It is, however, unnecessary for a reward to be given to a firm which applies scientific innovations. The creation of a more mobile skilled labour force, which is the object of the Industrial Training Act, is in the national interest and is often only in the long term to the interest of the individual firm, whereas the application of scientific innovation is of more immediate advantage to the firm which employs it.

A third difficulty would be the enormous cost of visiting all the firms in almost any industry when it is remembered (see page 250) that a single visit costs £10. This situation, however, is not as serious as it might appear. In those industries where, at present, research associations are supported by a compulsory levy, the payment of the levy does not automatically make a firm a member of the association. In order to join, firms have to submit a formal application. This may appear to be merely a technical and unimportant point but, in fact, it plays a vital part in the running of these research associations. A great many firms, even though they pay the levy, do not apply for membership, which means that the servicing costs of the research associations are cut down to manageable proportions. The membership of a research association in an industry where a compulsory levy has been declared does tend to rise quite considerably, but the greater proportionate increase in its funds makes it more capable of providing those services which its members require.

The way in which this scheme works is especially useful since it appears to go a considerable way towards solving a further problem, namely that of separating those firms which require help in order to grasp scientific innovations from those firms which are, because of a poor management, incapable of applying any technical innovation. The criterion of whether or not they care to apply for membership of the research association, though a rough and ready one, may well appear approximately to distinguish these two groups. Those firms whose managements are unable to gain any advantage from membership of a research association do not, on the whole, take up the opportunity they have of seeking a return for the money they are compelled to pay.

The fourth, and perhaps most fundamental, difficulty is that some research associations have still not adapted themselves to the idea that they should act more dynamically by disseminating to firms relevant scientific innovations as opposed to merely conducting research for their industries.[1] Furthermore, it has been suggested that this situation would be worse if the directors of research associations were not kept constantly financially dependent upon the firms in their industries. A typical argument runs as follows: 'When research associations stop having to fight for contributions from industry, their main incentive to give an industry what it requires is removed and lethargy sets in. In my opinion, a compulsory levy is the kiss of death to a research association.'[2]

However, it does not necessarily follow that a policy which keeps research associations constantly short of money is the best method of ensuring that they serve their industries well. Although more attention has been paid recently to the problem of dissemination by DSIR and research associations,[3] it would be optimistic to assume that there is no further room for improvement. The majority of firms in most industries do not have the scientific knowledge to assess how relevant a research association's programme is to them and without more money being spent on dissemination—in the main by personal visits—no improvement in the quality or type of research carried out by the association would improve the level of support from such firms. But, without greater support, the research association would not be able to reinforce its dissemination programme. The kind of argument quoted above against the compulsory levy would be valid only in an industry made up of scientifically sophisticated firms. Since few industries fall into this category, the argument cannot be

---

[1] See, for example, *Industrial Research and Manufacturing Industry*, paras. 52 and 53.

[2] Letter to the *Financial Times*, 9 August 1963.

[3] See DSIR, *Report 1961* (HMSO), Cmnd. 1734, p. 17.

generally applicable. A further objection to the argument is that under the present circumstances the directors of most research associations are forced to spend a great deal of their time raising money, an activity which provokes criticism[1] since it appreciably reduces the time a director can give to the administration of research.

It can thus be seen that to allow the healthy functioning of research associations to depend on the judgement of scientifically unsophisticated firms is to reduce the system to impotence. This, however, does not remove the need for direction of research associations by those qualified to judge in both industry and Government.

There is already some provision for this inasmuch as the council of a research association has the power to remove a director if he should prove incompetent. At the present time the chronic shortage of money which faces most research associations very often makes it difficult to determine how efficient a director is, since most shortcomings can be blamed on lack of money. If this major obstacle to efficiency were eliminated, it would make possible a more objective appraisal of the work of the research association by the council. DSIR representatives currently perform part of this function, being represented at meetings of each research association council. However, since the Industry Division of DSIR, which is responsible for the research associations, is understaffed, it is difficult for it to have a detailed enough knowledge of an industry to enable it to make a detailed appraisal of the situation. It is therefore desirable that some method be found to ensure that each research association has a balanced council composed of both laymen and technologists working within the industry.

Future Possibilities of Research Associations

So far, only the role of the research associations in disseminating scientific and technological innovations has been discussed. However, there seems to be no reason why, if the research associations are financially strong and under the control of first-class directors, they should not become centres of research able to attract the best graduates by virtue of their width of experience in industry and, at the same time, their close proximity to academic research. To achieve these two features it would probably be advantageous for a number of them to follow two lines of policy. The first has been outlined by the FBI, which suggested that: 'Bigger groupings are likelier to attract livelier brains. One way of achieving this might be to group a number of research associations on a campus so that

[1] T. A. Uthwatt in *Patterns of Research in British Industry*, p. 35. Drummond, op. cit., pp. 40–1.

I

some services and costly apparatus would be shared under a co-ordinating administration.'[1] The question of amalgamation is one that has been studied by the directors of research associations, so far without result, but there would seem to be a strong argument for the grouping of research associations in a vertical direction through an industry so that the manufacturers of raw materials, makers of machinery, the processors, and perhaps even the distributors, would be drawn together in a single powerful research institute. The major advantage of such a policy is that it would bring together supplier and user industries, thus preventing each industry from complaining that the conservatism of the other inhibits the application of changes in technology.[2]

The Government would have to decide which industries should have a compulsory levy and to determine the broad lines of policy to be followed by the new research associations, in consultation with representatives of the industries and of the research associations themselves. The co-ordination of research associations with other bodies that are concerned with factors affecting productivity in the same industries is considered in Chapter 15.

[1] *Civil Research Policy*, p. 7.
[2] The machine tool and shipbuilding industries are examples of this situation. See Chapter 7.

CHAPTER 14

INDUSTRIAL RELATIONS AND JOB SECURITY

It is clear from the interviews in Chapter 5 that some of the barriers to the introduction of more progressive techniques and methods within industry come from the side of labour. This resistance on the part of the workers points to a conflict within firms, and it is only by examining the structure of industrial relations that an attempt can be made to suggest remedies.

It appears that in general the causes of industrial conflict can be broken down into three categories, although of course any particular example of conflict could be caused by a combination of any or all of these factors, plus, perhaps, an additional element of chance. The three categories are:

1. A lack of understanding and trust between management and labour, which leads to disagreement on subjects where the material interest of both sides would be better served by agreement;
2. Wage disputes and similar conflicts of interest over hours of work, overtime payments, etc.;
3. Fear of redundancy and determination to maintain the prerogatives of an existing job.

It is worth examining each category in detail to see what role it plays in exacerbating industrial relations and whether this could be minimised in the short term.

Lack of Trust

The lack of comprehension between the two sides of industry presents a serious impediment to growth, and it is almost impossible to suggest any short-term means of bridging it; at the same time, in material terms, it is the most easily soluble of all areas of conflict. This apparent paradox is illustrated most clearly by a quotation on pages 71–2. In a machine tool factory, the installation of decent lavatories for the shop-floor workers would be a trivial piece of investment. The difficulty is to persuade management that this is a matter of importance to the men, and that such investments would have as high a yield, in purely material terms, as many measures of more apparent relevance to the productive process. It is in improving communication between the two sides of industry that joint consultative councils serve one of their most important purposes, but these councils will succeed only under circumstances where a rapport already exists between management and labour. Otherwise, even where they exist officially, they will not perform any real function but, as was shown by a number of interviews, will simply wither away through lack of use. The corollary of management's indifference towards labour is a mistrust on the part of workers of anything said or done by those who employ them. This can lead, especially in regions with a history of poor labour relations, such as Clydeside, to workers regarding suspiciously, and possibly even rejecting, many sincere advances made by management.[1]

In the long term, the only *complete* answer to this problem lies in the gradual replacement of present managers and workers' representatives by men who are fully capable of understanding the factors which matter in achieving a basic framework for good industrial relations. It is to be hoped that the expansion of the number of university places suggested by the Robbins Committee and the raising of the school-leaving age to sixteen, accepted by all parties for 1970, might eventually go some way towards meeting the first point. A management force with a much higher proportion of graduates and a work-force with a higher level of education might well be willing to take, and capable of benefiting from, management education, foreman training and courses for shop stewards. Such courses would bring home the importance of labour relations and the comparatively simple and cheap ways in which they could often be improved. All these proposals, however, are essentially part of a long-term solution. It cannot be expected that the present situation will change materially within a decade, and even then it is not certain that it will begin changing rapidly, since the basis of antagonism between management and labour runs deep in the British consciousness and there are few positive ideas as to how it can be eradicated. It is for this reason that the problem of mistrust, even in the absence of genuine grounds for conflict, is, and is likely to remain, the most intractable breeding-ground of industrial strife.

Wage Disputes

In many ways, wage disputes in industry are the opposite in character of those conflicts that are due to a breakdown in communication and understanding. The latter have little or no rational economic

[1] See p. 99.

justification, but are extremely difficult to overcome, while the former have every rational economic justification but usually, so far as the individual firm is concerned, do not present insurmountable problems. Because the economic justification for wage disputes is clear and continuous, representing a conflict between management's responsibility for keeping down costs and labour's interest in increasing wages, every firm will have evolved its own methods of dealing with it. The factors affecting the determination of any particular wage are usually a complex mixture of trade union pressures, supply of and demand for labour, and historical and local factors, but recognised procedures do exist whereby a solution can sooner or later be reached. Even when wage bargaining leads to strikes (which is far less common than the press might lead one to suppose) the amount of time lost is seldom serious and they seldom constitute long-term threats to industrial progress.

Fear of Redundancy

The role played by fear of redundancy in hindering Britain's industrial progress is frequently underrated. Perhaps the most important reason for this is that good industrial relations are often thought of in terms of eliminating strikes and their causes. Fear of redundancy is not a serious cause of strikes, since, when a firm wishes to dismiss labour, workers are in a weak bargaining position. In order to gauge the extent to which fear of redundancy poisons industrial relations, it is necessary to take into account the range of practices inimical to efficiency in industry which have grown up to safeguard the jobs and wages of the workers. As Chapters 5 and 11 have shown, these block many opportunities of increasing productivity in industry.

Restrictive practices are often described as though they were the results of mere unthinking conservatism on the part of the workers. This may be true on some occasions and in some industries, but it is a very partial explanation. It cannot be denied that, however good may be the net effects to the nation of the replacement of an inferior by a superior technique, the man who formerly had a job and now finds himself unemployed is worse off. There is thus a rational justification for men who believe that they are going to be made redundant to do everything in their power to prevent the adoption of new techniques which may have this effect, just as there is every rational justification for employers to adopt new techniques as rapidly as possible in order to raise their profits.

Sleepy managements may refuse to innovate in order to avoid possible trouble with their labour force. The temptation to adopt this policy is especially great in industries operating in a sellers' market, as was the case in much of British industry for the first post-war decade. This policy is often changed only after it has led a firm or industry into severe economic difficulties. This helps to explain the apparent paradox that it is industries which have had their existence threatened, such as cotton or coal-mining, that concentrate most on overcoming problems of opposition to modernisation, while expanding industries, which might be expected to have greater opportunities for this exercise, frequently remain passive.[1]

On the assumption that the high level of employment which Britain has enjoyed since the war will continue for the foreseeable future,[2] it is clearly worth enquiring whether it is possible to develop a positive policy for minimising labour's fear of redundancy, in order to facilitate the introduction of new industrial techniques. It will be the argument of the rest of this chapter that some advance in this field can be achieved more quickly than in most other areas of industrial conflict and that, as the speed at which industry modernises is directly involved, it is perhaps of even greater concern than most other sectors of industrial relations.

The amount of warning given to workers is of prime importance in questions affecting redundancy. It is a far greater blow for a worker to learn that he is redundant only when he receives his cards with his pay at the end of a week's work, as in the examples in Chapter 5 on pages 73 and 74, than it is if he is told that there is likely to be some redundancy in his particular craft in the course of the next three or four years. In general, the longer the time that both management and workers have to adjust to the idea of a particular technical change and its effects, the more easily it can be adopted and the less friction there is likely to be.[3] The way in which technical change affects a firm's labour requirements varies considerably according to the scale of the innovation being adopted. At one extreme is the installation of a radically new plant, which suddenly changes the quantity and quality of labour demands on a large scale. At the other end of the spectrum is the gradual improvement in tools and techniques which leads to the possibility of a reallocation of work so as to use less labour. A large-scale investment project of the sort that is likely to render a considerable number of men redundant is usually sufficiently expensive to cause a management to consider in advance the likely consequences of its adoption and sufficiently complex to

[1] But a firm in a modern, expanding, capital-intensive industry, such as oil refining, is capable of achieving, as the Fawley agreements have shown, considerable increases in productivity by negotiating with the unions large-scale changes in working practices.

[2] The plausibility of this assumption will be dealt with later in the chapter.

[3] For an instance of this point see Olive Banks, *The Attitudes of Steelworkers to Technical Change* (Liverpool University Press), 1960.

require several years of preparation between the decision to install it and the start of production.[1] Smaller projects may take less time to approve and install but they normally affect the jobs of correspondingly fewer workers. Equally a change in techniques permitting considerable increases in labour productivity can usually be forecast in advance.

Manpower Planning by the Firm

The actions which management can take in the time between the decision to install new plant and the actual replacement of existing plant vary according to the industry and the nature of the technical innovation. Certain procedures are, however, common to all situations. The immediate aim is to forecast the time available before the new technique is fully operational and the phasing of changes in the labour force required. Two basic factors have to be considered in calculating the latter: the possible effects of shifts in demand for the product, which can be estimated by the use of market research methods, and the specific effects on labour requirements of the innovation itself. It can then be seen whether the labour force required is likely to increase or decrease during the intervening period and also how the need for different types of skill is likely to be affected. Quite clearly, it is impossible to forecast with complete accuracy, but this is not generally necessary, since the object is to try to assess whether more or less people will be required in the various different categories of labour employed by the firm. Once this has been done, the aim will be to assess:

1. The natural wastage of labour (e.g. through retirement, death, change of occupation);
2. The possibilities of moving labour within the firm from a declining occupation to one which will need more people;
3. The effect on the wages and conditions of men transferred in this way.

To a large extent, the mobility of its labour force can be determined by a firm itself. In the time it has available before a new technique becomes operational it can begin, in co-operation with the Ministry of Labour and the technical colleges, a training programme designed to increase the flexibility and capacity of its workers. Such programmes should, in fact, be a normal part of all firms' training policy[2] but the imminence of technical change gives them an especial value and urgency.

---

[1] Three to five years is regarded as normal gestation period for a major project. See *Three Case Studies in Automation* (PEP), 1957, p. 40.
[2] See Chapter 11.

There is evidence that workers are not opposed to technical change as such.[1] It is often the fear of redundancy which tends to make workers more conservative than they would otherwise be. If management had frank discussions with the workers' representatives, took them fully into its confidence about investment plans and enabled them to be committed to the planning which is involved, particularly retraining and the re-allocation of jobs, it might well increase union co-operation. These measures do not, of course, guarantee workers' agreement to the plans: there may be certain areas where compromise between the positions of management and labour may be almost impossible. Given mutual trust, however, and a sufficiently long period to make adjustments to the labour force, it is to be hoped that much of the animosity which is found in certain firms and industries could be eliminated.

The use of the manpower planning techniques outlined above should make it possible to minimise the number of men who have to be laid off. This will allow firms to pay generous redundancy allowances without causing too great a drain on their finances, and the men to get new jobs more easily.

Having sketched out a version of manpower planning at the level of the individual firm, it is necessary to assess the practical difficulties of applying it at present. It must first be emphasised that it is not utopian to expect some firms to be capable of planning at this level of complexity. Many giant firms already make detailed estimates of the manpower requirements of new plant at various levels of output, and they do the best they can to estimate the future level of demand for their products. They also frequently do a great deal to give any redundant employees the greatest possible assistance in finding a new job and trying to ensure that there is as little hardship as possible among their workers. Most managements, however, do not plan their future manpower requirements because they have never considered such a possibility. Even if they were to consider it, they would require a reasonable forecast of the full effects on manpower requirements of any particular innovation or changed technique and of likely secular changes in demand conditions. There appears to be a need, therefore, for an organisation to collect, process and disseminate such information. Until such a body exists, there is little hope that many firms will be able to forecast their manpower requirements sufficiently accurately and sufficiently early.

The Need for Manpower Planning at the National Level

Manpower planning by firms would undoubtedly help to make the application of technical innovations easier, but this would only meet

[1] Banks, op. cit., p. 262, and Chapter 5.

part of the overall problem of redundancy. The manpower policy of firms is only one factor in the complex relationship between supply of and demand for labour in the economy as a whole. Many other determinants affect the employment situation, of which demographic changes and the level of economic activity are perhaps the most important. If labour unrest caused by fear of redundancy is to be lessened effectively, planning at the level of the individual firm is not sufficient. There must also be planning on a national scale to ensure that a simultaneous increase in population and in productivity does not lead to a large surplus of labour seeking jobs that do not exist, and equally that the level of economic activity should never be so high as to generate a demand for labour greater than can be met out of potential resources.

One possible reason for the lack of interest in manpower planning is a doubt whether such planning is necessary to dispel the fear of redundancy. Many would argue that all that is required to maintain full employment is that the economy should be run at a sufficiently high rate of activity. Except for two short periods, this situation has operated since the war but the question arises whether there is any reason to expect a change in the foreseeable future.

Automation and the Demand for Labour

At the present time the major ground for disquiet about future employment prospects in Britain is what is loosely described as 'the onset of automation'. In order to examine this problem, it is necessary to consider the nature of automation and whether it is, in fact, different in its effects from other technological changes. Since it came into common use in the 1950s 'automation' has become a vague and rather ambiguous term. Originally it was intended to apply to methods for controlling productive processes relying on feed-back systems but it now tends to be used indiscriminately for any major advance in machine technology, especially when this is labour-saving.[1] For the purposes of economists, this latter description is generally more useful since it is irrelevant when considering the consequences of increased productivity or decreased demand for labour whether they are caused by the introduction of a computer or by some purely mechanical device. Even in the United States, where the pressure of improving technology on employment is most apparent (as in the motor industry, or on the railways, where attempts are being made to dispense with firemen), it is more correct to attribute this to improved mechanisation rather than to automation. Thus the argument that the employment situation has reached

[1] See DSIR, *Automation* (HMSO), 1956.

a watershed, due to the recent discovery of the applications which computer systems can have in industry, cannot be accepted without reservations.

This does not mean to say, however, that it is possible to ignore the very real employment problems which exist in the United States at the present time and which might come to Britain in the course of the next few years. Since 1957 in the United States a steady and fairly high series of annual productivity increases has been associated with a steady and fairly high level of labour unemployment. This suggests that these increases are primarily due to improvement in productive techniques rather than to economies resulting from a fuller utilisation of productive capacity. It is interesting to note that it is the latter explanation which is the cause usually given for British productivity increases.

TABLE 14.1

US Productivity and Unemployment 1956–62

(Percentages)

	Increase in output per man hour over last year	Unemployment of civil labour force
1956	3·5	4·2
1957	3·0	4·3
1958	2·5	6·8
1959	3·5	5·5
1960	2·0	5·6
1961	3·0	6·7
1962	4·0	5·6

Source: Financial Times, 6 November 1963

The improvements in techniques which have been applied in American industry have led to an upgrading of the quality of labour required. This is generally the case. As technology becomes more complex, a generally higher standard of labour competence is required. The illiteracy that was prevalent among workers in the mid-nineteenth century would not be possible or tolerated in industry today. It may therefore be assumed that workers of low talent and capacity, who could formerly find jobs comparatively easily, might, in the course of time, find greater difficulty.

It is unlikely, however, that similar changes in technology in Britain would lead to as much unemployment as they have in the United States. The difficulty of integrating negroes into the labour force, the weakness of Federal government, and the large regional differences in welfare and education, all make the American position very different from the British. At the same time, it is possible that there might, during the next decade, be a comparatively sudden increase in output per man hour, allied to a greater demand for technically qualified workers and a smaller demand for the unskilled.

If this reasoning is correct, the problem facing Britain, although considerably less grave than the Jeremiahs of unemployment forecast, might still require decisive action to prevent the formation of what Gunnar Myrdal calls a 'perpetual underclass' of unemployed.[1] It is questionable whether the simple reflation of the economy on strictly Keynesian principles, which has been the traditional answer to problems of unemployment since the war, will always be practicable and effective. The question turns on the ability of an expanding economy to absorb all who seek work, irrespective of their skill, or lack of it. It might be that any attempt to stimulate economic activity would very quickly founder on a shortage of skilled labour, while there was still a pool of unemployed and unemployable labour which had no talent useful to any employer.

Regional Unemployment

There is little sign that these trends have yet become established in Britain. Whatever may be the case in the United States, it is difficult to substantiate the thesis that technological progress is the cause of a decline in the overall demand for labour. With the example of the United States in mind there was general surprise at the speed at which unemployment fell in the United Kingdom after the recession of 1962–3. Further, those areas in Britain where there are most modern industries and where technology can be expected to be advancing most rapidly are also those areas where there is least unemployment. The difficulty of finding employment in areas such as the north-east where staple industries are declining has little or nothing to do with the level of education of the unemployed, as is amply demonstrated by the fact that if they move to more prosperous areas of Britain they can be employed very quickly. This still suggests that a general increase in economic activity in the country would not solve the problem of regional unemployment. The pressure on resources in the midlands and the south-east (not merely skilled labour resources but labour as a whole) would act as a bottleneck long before the unemployment in the depressed areas had been eliminated. As Figure 14.1 shows, what are lacking are jobs in certain geographical regions, not jobs in the country as a whole.

[1] Gunnar Myrdal, *Challenge to Affluence* (Gollancz), 1963, Chapter 3.

FIGURE 14.1

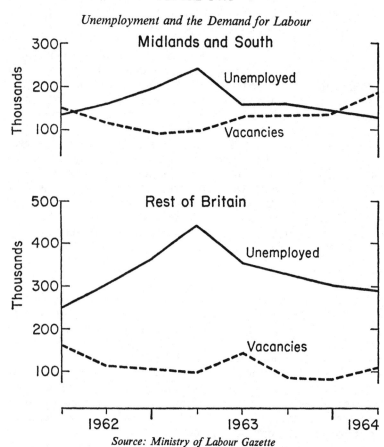

Unemployment and the Demand for Labour

Source: Ministry of Labour Gazette

The forecast that Britain is unlikely, at least for the next few years, to repeat the American pattern of large increases in output accompanied by increasing unemployment has important consequences for a discussion on redundancy policy. It means that there will usually be full employment in Britain, except for certain depressed areas, which make up a small enough proportion of the population to permit them to be treated separately. The typical industrial situation, however, will be one where the total labour demands of industry would be as great as, or greater than, the supply of labour available. The difficulty will be to ensure that the available labour is of the right quality (that is, with the sort of skills that are in demand) and in the place where it can be used.

The First Steps towards Practical Manpower Planning

Basically the provision of the right sort of labour for the future economic growth of the country requires knowledge of four sets of facts:

1. The existing stock of labour skills;
2. The present optimum structure of skills needed by industry;
3. The amount of labour of different types and degrees of skill expected to become available over the next five to ten years;
4. The expected changes in demand for labour caused by technological progress and secular changes in demand over the next five to ten years.

This need is beginning to be realised both at home and abroad.[1] In Britain, in addition to the unsuccessful attempt made by the Advisory Council on Scientific Policy in 1961[2] to forecast the demand for scientific manpower, there have been two major attempts to do something about this problem.

The first is the 'Cambridge Model' of the economy for which a computer is used in an attempt to build up on the basis of available data possible pictures of the economy in 1970. The model is still in its very early stages, and can provide little more than an intelligent amalgam of guesses as to the nature of the economy in the future. These are based on so many necessarily unknown factors that the probability of any particular prediction being justified cannot by the nature of things be very high. Of all the fields examined, that of labour utilisation is perhaps the least fully determined. This is largely due to the lack of specific description of the various jobs which people do. The category of 'craftsmen', for instance, which the model suggests will greatly increase by 1970, covers a wide range of skills—from the maintenance engineer, who can be expected to be in very great demand as automation becomes more frequent, to the man with a particular simple skill who is likely to be replaced increasingly by machines. Nevertheless, in spite of its many obvious deficiencies, the model is a step in the right direction. If the official statistical services were to obtain relevant data in greater detail, more valuable forecasts might well be made.

Secondly, the Ministry of Labour has clearly begun to appreciate the necessity for some kind of an approach to manpower planning. A manpower research unit was set up at the beginning of 1963 and is

[1] For continental reactions to this problem see Gosta Rehn, OECD Director of Manpower and Social Affairs, *OECD Observer*, 1 December 1962, p. 14, and Bertil Gardell, *Social Implications of Automation in Sweden* (The Swedish Council for Personnel Administration, Stockholm), 1963, p. 5.

[2] *Long Term Demand for Scientific Manpower* (HMSO), Cmnd. 1490, 1961.

being expanded rapidly at the present time. It is undertaking or helping to finance a mixed bag of studies on a number of important sectors of the labour market including an enquiry into the construction industry, and a study of the effect of automation on office employment. Its most ambitious project to date, but one which at the same time highlights certain basic weaknesses in its present operations, is the attempt to discover labour requirements in the engineering industry. The method employed is to send a questionnaire to 300 firms enquiring how their present labour force is made up and what categories of labour it is believed will be employed five years from the present. This is an unsatisfactory method of forecasting future manpower requirements since, as was noted earlier, comparatively few firms have any idea of the changes they might expect in the structure of their labour force in five years' time. It is doubtful if more than a few of the 400 firms questioned have carried out any sort of systematic manpower planning for themselves, thus enabling them to give worth-while answers. There is, too, the considerable danger that inarticulate managements will fail to make clear their demand for certain types of skilled manpower which they have given up hope of finding in sufficient quantities.[1] It seems quite probable, therefore, that the answers which the Ministry of Labour receives will suffer from a systematic bias, and, if their conclusions are drawn directly from these answers, they will not be of great predictive value. It must be remembered, however, that at the present there does not exist any other means of gaining the necessary information, and, if the manpower research unit can build up from its questionnaire an accurate picture of the present structure of skills required in the engineering industry, it will have helped to facilitate future attempts at manpower planning. Its present work, however, can only lay the foundations and, before these can be built on to provide an adequate national manpower budget, there will have to be a complete change in the scope of the information that is collected and in the time which is needed to process and disseminate it.

The Next Phase in Manpower Planning

Since the war there has been a revolution in the speed with which information can be processed and the complexity of the data which can be used and, as computers become more advanced, there is less excuse for data to be dealt with slowly by trial and error. There is

[1] There is a possibility that this may have been one of the factors leading to the inaccuracy of the forecast for scientific manpower made by the Advisory Council on Scientific Policy in its report, *Long Term Demand for Scientific Manpower*. See the Appointments Board of the Universities of Newcastle and Durham, *Eighteenth Annual Report, 1962-1963*, p. 7.

scope for a great expansion in the use of computers by the Government, and it may be expected that, as more detailed models of various sectors of the economy are produced with the aid of computers, forecasts will become more coherent and consistent. At the same time, a mere increase in the number of computers used by the Government cannot be expected to solve industry's manpower problem or eliminate doubts about redundancy.

In the first place, the answers given by computers are only as reliable as the information fed into them, and, although computers can deal rapidly with complex data from a large number of firms, their success would still depend on factors such as a generally agreed job analysis within an industry and between industries. It might well be that one of the more important jobs which the new industrial training boards could do would be to provide such definitions and ensure that individual firms were acquainted with them. The present work of the manpower research unit in the engineering industry would be a pilot study for such a task.

In the second place, even if the Government succeeded in building a fairly accurate model of future labour trends, it would only be of use in combating fears of redundancy if two conditions were fulfilled. First, the Government's forecasts would have to be published in a comprehensible form to, at the very least, a considerable proportion of firms in all industries, which would have to know not only what action the Government's conclusions called for but also be prepared to take it. Secondly, machinery would have to exist to ensure that workers whose skills were not required were given fresh jobs so as to prevent fears of redundancy, which have been shown to be one of the major barriers to industrial change.

Channels of Communication

In meeting the criterion of comprehensibility it is necessary to appreciate the difficulty of the task of persuading firms, especially small and medium-sized firms, to adopt a manpower planning policy. There is a dual problem here. First, it would be difficult for the Government, which is the only body having the resources for discovering and processing statistics sufficiently well to make reasonable estimates of manpower trends, to have that intimate knowledge of a particular industry which would be required if it was to give advice in a form which could be applied directly by the firms in that industry. Secondly, in many industries there is a suspicion of the Government and the 'men from Whitehall' which would make it still less likely that Government advice would be taken.

Thus, if the advice which only the Ministry of Labour can give is

to be acted on by firms, there must clearly be an intermediary body
which should be acquainted with the problems facing an individual
industry and at the same time should have the confidence of the
firms in it. Such an intermediary should have a specialised staff
capable of helping to collect and interpret revelant data from the
industry and passing it on to the central statistical services and also
capable of criticising the conclusions of a Ministry of Labour planning unit about the industry. At the present time, employers'
associations sometimes fulfil some of these conditions but they are
extremely variable in quality and are often expected only to act as a
pressure group on behalf of their industries, not as a body for
collecting information in order to promote change.

A more likely choice of organisation to fulfil this function would
be the new industrial training boards which are being set up under
the Industrial Training Act.[1] If they are to fulfil their training function
adequately, they will need to be fully apprised of forecast manpower requirements since the type of training which they will be
accepting as satisfactory should obviously reflect the pattern of
demand for labour which the industry will have in the future. The
industrial training boards will also possess a knowledge of their
industries and their particular manpower problem and, if they are
successful in their major function, that of industrial training, they
will also have the confidence of firms in their industries.

The responsibility for manpower planning would, however, require
the boards to have a larger staff than would be needed for the
industrial training function alone. As a book-keeping decision the
cost of this could perhaps be met by the Ministry of Labour. These
costs would not be large since it would be unnecessary for the
boards to undertake the specialised statistical work which would
remain the responsibility of the Government.

As mentioned above, it is not necessary that the task of disseminating information about manpower planning in a form which most
firms could assimilate should be performed by industrial training
boards, although their connection with job evaluation and training
might give them certain built-in advantages. Nevertheless, effective
'little Neddies' (Economic Development Councils), or even the sort
of research association advocated in Chapter 13, could perform this
task, particularly in industries which did not possess training
boards.

Manpower planning is closely linked with technical change.
Industrial training boards or the other organisations mentioned
would, in advising firms how to adapt their labour policy so as to
allow technical innovations to be introduced with the least possible

[1] See Chapter 11.

friction, also speed the introduction of innovations: when firms learn that their competitors may adopt certain new production techniques, they are likely to adopt similar techniques themselves.

Since the growth of the economy depends on the quick adoption of new techniques, any means by which firms can be advised of available technical possibilities and persuaded that they ought to adopt them is economically useful. As a two-way channel of communication between a central manpower planning unit and individual firms, industrial training boards would be well placed to help with this function. By explaining what technical changes had been adopted in other advanced countries, and would probably be adopted in Britain in the immediate future, they could, in liaison with the research associations mentioned in Chapter 13, accelerate the speed at which such innovations were introduced.

Retraining and Redundancy

The fact that employers and leading trade unionists have been informed of the expected changes in the pattern of employment does not mean that these changes can take place inside a firm without causing friction. Provision has to be made for those whose job is to be changed or downgraded in such a way that bitterness is avoided. This chapter has already dealt with the ways in which an enlightened firm can ease its redundancy difficulties. It is clear, however, that an effective policy cannot be left to the initiative of individual firms, many of which are not enlightened. Government intervention of some kind is required not only at the macro-economic level of maintaining full employment but also at the micro-economic level of assisting firms to smooth out problems arising from threatened redundancies. It must be stressed that general full employment is a pre-condition for any such attempt. In regions where unemployment is relatively high, little can be done to allay the anxiety of a worker who fears that he might become redundant. Even under conditions where demand for labour is high, however, the solution to problems of redundancy is more difficult to find than is usually believed.

When the role of Government in curing redundancy and providing more skilled workers is considered, a key role is frequently given to the Government training centres. The centres first established after the first world war to help ex-service men were then used between the wars mainly to help the unemployed. After the second world war the emphasis was again on ex-service men and also on disabled persons on the passing of the Disabled Persons Act. When there was no longer such a flow of ex-service men, training in Government training centres contracted until 1962-3 when an expansion of Government training centres was decided on to help to provide trained men to meet shortages of skilled labour and to retrain redundant men from declining industries. By the end of 1965 there will be thirty such centres in the United Kingdom—more than double the number existing before the expansion programme was undertaken. Those who think that Government training centres can play a key role in alleviating redundancy believe that, if men who have become unemployed can be sent to a centre and taught a skill which is in short supply, they should experience little difficulty in finding a new job. The men themselves must, of course, be capable of benefiting from retraining at a centre but, given full employment and more latitude by the craft unions to the entry of workers who have not served a proper apprenticeship, such a hope is not utopian. In fact, a similar system works admirably in Sweden.[1]

As a palliative, however, for the bad labour relations caused by fear of redundancy such a method leaves much to be desired. Its major drawback is that, at the present time, the training centres deal only with unemployed workers and therefore a man must lose his job before being admitted to one. This naturally acts as a very considerable deterrent to a more general use of the centres, since the attitude towards redundancy which is ingrained in many workers[2] ensures that they will not give up a job voluntarily unless they have another one to go to.

If Britain is to reach the position of Sweden, where retraining is accepted as a perfectly normal part of a worker's life, the system under which the Government training centres operate will have to be altered considerably. In addition, far greater co-operation will be needed between the trade unions and employers (both those with a declining demand for labour and those who need more labour) and Government and other training facilities. In general, the ideal situation would be for a worker in a declining industry to be treated as though he were still at work while he was being trained for a job with better employment prospects. One possibility would be for a subsidy to be paid by the Ministry of Labour or Industrial Training Board to encourage firms to engage and train specified adult workers in skills which are likely to be in short supply. A combination of this method with higher redundancy benefits, higher unemployment benefits, and longer periods of notice would greatly contribute to making the loss of a man's job less of a bogy than it is at present.[3] Allied to manpower planning these measures might well provide a

[1] See Gardell, op. cit., p. 3, and 'Retraining: The Swedish Approach', *Times Review of Industry and Technology*, April 1964, p. 89.

[2] See p. 226–7.

[3] The Contracts of Employment Act, 1963, is a move in this direction, but there is a long way still to go and a great deal of opposition to overcome.

means of easing the tension in industrial relations, even in the comparatively short term.

Since, in the last resort, the function of the Government or industrial training boards in this field can only be persuasive and indicative, the task of ensuring maximum employer co-operation is beyond their scope. That this is a genuine problem is shown by the interviews in Chapter 5 and it is clear that employers with conservative attitudes towards labour would be most reluctant to take part in any scheme which they saw as a partial surrender to the traditional enemy.[1] It should be considered whether persuasion would not be more effective if it were backed by the institution, by the Government, of a compulsory redundancy payment, possibly proportional to the time the worker has been with the firm, to be paid in full by the employer unless he has complied with the regulations of his industrial training board and of any organisation, such as a regional development council, designed to combat local unemployment. Such a scheme could have beneficial effects in forcing employers to begin planning their labour force, thus easing the task of manpower planning units. In the United States motor industry, where an agreement was made between the employers and the Autoworkers' Unions ensuring that every man was to receive at least six months' notice before he could be dismissed, the resulting forward planning which employers have been forced to undertake has proved of considerable economic advantage to them.

It has already been pointed out[2] that the industrial training boards will find it difficult to advise firms effectively on retraining because of the lack of adequate manpower planning facilities. By actually tying in the normal work of the Boards with the function of manpower planning, this difficulty would be alleviated. It could also be hoped that the impetus given in this way to retraining schemes in firms might do a great deal to eliminate some of the difficulties involved in retraining. The vital point to be reiterated is that only a scheme of such overall dimensions as that proposed here is sufficient to ensure that Britain's manpower resources can be used to the full without limiting the speed at which technological changes can be adopted.

[1] See pp. 73–4.
[2] See Chapter 11.

CHAPTER 15

AN ENVIRONMENT CONDUCIVE TO GROWTH

The major conclusion of Part Two of this report is that those managements which assess, formulate and execute their policies systematically and thoroughly with the assistance of a variety of modern management techniques tend to be more efficient and profitable than their competitors who work by instinct or habit. From this it may readily be deduced, then, that the best method of rapidly improving the productivity of British firms is to secure a faster increase in the category of firms employing such techniques. To achieve this objective there are three conditions that it is necessary to meet:

1. More firms should accept the need to adopt more efficient techniques;
2. Firms should know what such techniques are, and be able to judge which are relevant to their particular problems;
3. As many external aids as possible should be provided to help firms' attempts to increase their competitiveness.

These points can now be examined in turn.

Encouraging the Urge to Grow

There is now general approval of economic growth as an abstract concept, but there is less readiness to take the active, and sometimes painful, measures without which opportunities for growth will be lost. There have always been strong voices ready to point out cases where sectional self-interest conflicted with the economic interests of the nation as a whole. What has attracted far less attention is the fact that the national interest can be harmed as much by industrial apathy as by positive action on the part of any sectional interest group. Such apathy leads to firms failing to make the best use of their existing productive capacity, and ignoring opportunities to keep pace with technological developments. The interviews in Part Two and the more general examination of the industrial environment in Part Three both suggest that many firms could easily become considerably more efficient than they are at present. Further support is given by the findings of the Centre for Interfirm Comparison as to the remarkable differences in profitability between firms in the same industry (see Chapter 4). Lack of efficiency is also suggested by Britain's continually declining share of world exports, and the way in which Britain is falling behind in sectors vital for continued growth, such as the use of computers in industry.[1]

There are signs that more people are appreciating the need to make large sections of British industry more dynamic. It is significant that in intellectual circles one of the most favoured arguments for British entry into the Common Market was that it would provide precisely the shock that was needed in order to convince firms that the older ways were no longer adequate[2] and the then Prime Minister supported this thesis.[3] Now that it is clear that, for some time at least, Britain will not be joining the Common Market, British industry needs a new incentive to change its ways. Although the abolition of resale price maintenance has given a sharp jolt to several sleepy corners of British business, it only goes a comparatively short way towards arousing the country as a whole. Many other policy decisions could help to augment its effect. No Government has ever tried to mobilise the many fiscal weapons at its disposal with the consistent purpose of stimulating growth.

Within such a policy attempts to stimulate competition could play a very salutary part. However, these should be applied selectively rather than merely as a general attempt to deflate the economy. For instance, bilateral or multilateral tariff cuts could do a considerable amount to increase the market for the products of efficient firms and industries while frequently forcing the less efficient to re-examine their position. It is also generally agreed that the present tax system could be more directly geared to the need to stimulate growth, although there are often doubts as to how efficacious any particular change in the structure of taxation would prove for this purpose. In general, a shift from taxes on earned incomes and company profits to taxes on capital might go some way towards achieving the desired result, if only to make people use their capital profitably in order to prevent its diminishing.[4] In addition to providing incentives towards greater economic activity, taxation could be further used

---

[1] See Michael Shanks, 'Britain's Slow Move towards Automation', *Financial Times*, 30 December 1963, and also Chapters 13 and 14.

[2] See C. A. R. Crosland, *The Conservative Enemy* (Jonathan Cape), 1962.

[3] See Harold Macmillan, *Britain, the Commonwealth and Europe* (Conservative and Unionist Central Office), [1962], p. 8.

[4] See NEDC, *Conditions Favourable to Faster Growth*, para. 170, for a discussion of this point.

to favour particular business practices. Firms, for instance, could be encouraged to try new labour-saving machinery by giving more selective depreciation allowances, possibly making special grants for the purchase of certain specified types of machinery, such as computers, while the introduction of labour-saving machinery could possibly be encouraged in regions with over-full employment by means of a regional pay-roll tax. It might even be possible to devise some general means of taxing the inputs of firms, so that the efficient use of all inputs is suitably rewarded.[1] But these are only a few instances of the ways in which taxation might be used to increase productivity. It seems difficult to believe that with the vast resources of incentives and penalties which the Government has at its disposal, it cannot do more to encourage firms to adopt thrusting practices.

The Use of Techniques

Given that more firms became imbued with a desire to improve their economic performance, there would still remain barriers making it difficult to put this intention into practice. It is certainly true that the desire to increase productivity is a necessary condition determining a businessman's economic activity and effectiveness, but, as has been shown in earlier chapters, he will usually also need the help of a number of techniques and the provision of relevant information.

The methods required include work study; operational research; budgetary control; market research at home and abroad; a positive attitude towards the application of science and machinery replacement; plans for meeting expected labour requirements; and good training methods and promotion opportunities at all levels from non-apprentice to top management. Although, in theory, a firm can simply decide to begin applying these techniques as a means to greater efficiency, in practice it requires some sophistication to recognise their relevance in specific instances and to understand how to set about bringing them into a firm. No doubt the long-term answer to the problem of how businessmen can acquire such sophistication is through management training, but at present only a small proportion of Britain's managers have received any form of training (see Chapter 12) and it will not be possible to alter this position materially within the next decade. Management consultants could bridge this gap to some extent if firms with untrained managers could be persuaded to make sufficient use of them. Many managers, however, seem unwilling to go to the very considerable expense of

[1] See Edward Nevin, 'Taxation for Growth—A Factor Tax', *Westminster Bank Review*, November 1963, pp. 13–25.

bringing in consultants to advise them on all aspects of their firms' activities, although they may ask for help on specific points—if they have sufficient information to know which specific points are relevant.

The barrier to a better appraisal by firms of their own and their competitors' relative efficiency is not merely lack of interest in making such assessments. At the moment the acquisition of relevant information is extremely difficult. Before a manager can try to determine whether he is more or less efficient than a competitor he needs, at the very least, to be in a position to compare such basic data as capital assets, the number of workers employed and the amount of goods produced. For any kind of detailed comparison, he needs a great deal more. In practice, even the most basic statistics cannot be determined accurately. The Centre for Interfirm Comparison demands from firms statistics which are largely different from those which the firms publish and which are far more detailed. The difficulties which even full-time researchers find in attempting to make such comparisons without the individual co-operation of firms have already been mentioned in Chapter 10. It can be seen, therefore, that one of the most important tests of efficiency is not readily available for use by most firms.

External Aids to Efficiency

It follows from the last paragraph that an immediate and simple means by which the Government could permit firms to become more efficient would be to reform company law so that the publication of more accurate and economically useful statistics became mandatory. This would give the triple benefit of providing more information and protection for shareholders, of forcing firms to collect relevant statistics about themselves, and of allowing other firms to have a worth-while standard against which to measure their own performance. A modest move in this direction was advocated by the Jenkins Report on Company Finance,[1] which suggested that companies ought to publish their turnover figures, but this has not been implemented by the Government.[2] Even if the recommendations of the Jenkins Report had been accepted in full, the standard of disclosure would lag behind that accepted in the United States as early as 1934.[3] In fact, a far more radical change than this would have to

[1] Board of Trade, *Report of the Company Law Committee* (HMSO), Cmnd. 1749, 1962.
[2] This was written before the proposals of the Stock Exchange Council, published in August 1964.
[3] Harold Rose, *Disclosure in Company Accounts* (Institute of Economic Affairs), 1963, p. 31.

be made if such publicity were to play a significant role in improving Britain's economic effectiveness.

More detailed and accurate company accounts can, however, by themselves achieve only limited results in the task of making the average firm more growth-orientated since only those firms which were already growth-conscious would be likely to take the trouble to engage in such comparisons. To make some impression on the far greater number of firms which have the potential to increase their efficiency but not yet the knowledge of how to go about it, more direct methods are called for.

In Part Three of this book various key sectors of a firm's activities which Part Two had shown frequently to be managed inefficiently were examined in order to determine the best means of improving the methods used by the average firm. A general conclusion reached was that, wherever possible, attempts have to be made to introduce managers to more efficient business practices. The major function of the industrial training boards will be to help to inculcate improved training methods for workers (see Chapter 11), and it is possible that this service can be extended to increase the number of managers being educated (see Chapter 12). It has been suggested (see Chapter 13) that similar methods could be effective in increasing business-men's awareness of relevant scientific developments and that this work could best be done by industrial research associations financed, like the training boards, by a compulsory levy on their industries. Finally, it was suggested that outside help was also required by firms if manpower planning was to be used sufficiently widely in industry to allow technological innovations to be adopted without arousing too much opposition from labour (see Chapter 14).

In addition to the services considered in Chapters 11–14, it is desirable that each industry should be provided with the fullest statistical and other information relevant to its affairs. Industries, like firms, benefit from keeping a constant check on their environ-ment. In periods of rapid change, the whole competitive position of an industry can alter within a comparatively few years, and, if adjustments need to be made in the productive methods of indi-vidual firms, it is advisable that they should be planned for at an early stage rather than at the last moment.

Longer-term trends can often best be observed by the study of foreign experience. If an industry in the United States or Sweden, for example, is making use of new techniques which greatly alter the quantity of labour or capital needed to produce a given output, it is of major importance that British firms in this industry should have some idea what adaptations are involved, how they will affect the individual firm and what steps could best be taken to prepare for them. At the moment, such work is sometimes done by very large firms and independent research workers and by the trade associations in some industries, but a great part of industry has no contact with either of these sources.

The problem of examining the performance of foreign industries, extrapolating the economic trends they manifest, applying them to the British situation, and ensuring that firms here appreciate their relevance and know what action to take, presents many difficulties. Nevertheless, valuable results could be produced. Among the most useful of the criteria by which a home industry's performance could be compared with that of an overseas industry are:

1. The export-import trends of the goods produced by an industry;
2. The share of world exports which an industry maintains;
3. The growth of an industry's capital;
4. The growth of an industry's productivity;
5. The number of research and development personnel as a proportion of an industry's labour force;
6. The training procedures in an industry.

Not all of the above criteria are equally valuable, as the ability of different countries to provide useful statistics varies considerably. Nevertheless, a considerable amount of information could be found on most of these indicators and a general picture of an industry's comparative success could be built up. Further, the fact that investigations are being undertaken and possibly criticisms of the industry made should be a help in making British firms more 'competition minded' and more ready to adopt new ideas. The Patton Report on shipbuilding and the Mitchell Report on the machine tool industry are now accepted by managers in those industries as being useful documents containing many worth-while prescriptions, but it would surely have been better if they had come while conditions were more propitious, since it is always easier to make reforms when the economic situation is comparatively good than in times of relative depression[1]—if only businessmen can be brought to appreciate the need for them. In fact, both reports only came as a result of much publicised external criticism. When these industries had made greater profits neither had shown any inclination to conduct a searching self-examination. Had such studies been conducted earlier, they might well have been able to prevent or minimise the difficulties in which these industries later found themselves.

Such information and studies can be fully efficacious only if they are disseminated to firms in ways that managers who possess little

[1] See Chapter 14.

formal training in technology or economics can comprehend. Means to this end have been discussed in earlier chapters, and it is clear that some combination of frequent, lucid and obviously useful written communications, assisted by occasional personal visits, would be needed. Even if such a system were instituted, however, the value of the information disseminated would clearly depend on the availability of the more important data. This is a relatively straightforward matter, in so far as it concerns information such as the sort of new machinery and advances in productive techniques being used in the more advanced firms in the industries. However, for a broader view of the industrial future, and fuller statistical treatment of data, it would be necessary for various defects in the Government's statistical services to be overcome.

The chief of these defects is that the information published is too broad and too late. Many statistics are given for such wide industrial classifications (e.g. 'engineering' and 'electrical goods') that little of value can be deduced from them and, even when the categories are narrower (e.g. 'shipbuilding and marine engineering' or 'contractors' plant and quarrying machines'), they frequently cover two or more industries with different features and prospects. Further confusion is caused by different Government statistical source-books classifying the same industry under different headings. These difficulties relate to the most basic industrial statistics, such as the value of output, the total labour force or the number of establishments. When slightly more sophisticated data are required, such as the breakdown of the age structure of the labour force of an industry, the number of its workers who are members of a trade union, the average age of its machinery, etc., the picture is even more confused, and any estimate has to be based largely on more or less intelligent guesswork. As regards the time element in collecting data, the basic National Income and Expenditure tables are published quarterly in summary form, and annually in greater, though still not sufficient, detail. This means that even Government policy is often at fault due to a lack of up-to-date statistics[1] and individual industries or firms are even less able to glean much information before it is too stale for use.

These faults are by no means irremediable. As computer techniques continue to improve it will become easier to detect significant changes in important economic determinants at a national, regional or industrial level. If business enterprises made more frequent and detailed returns and these were fed into suitably programmed computers, which were kept available for this purpose, preliminary returns could be given within a matter of weeks and the information,

[1] For instance, the budget of 1962 was designed to modify a great increase in demand that had never taken place.

together with analysis of its implications, sent back either to firms directly or to the industrial boards which would pass on the material in a form which could most easily be assimilated by firms. At the same time the Government could sponsor its own research in fields directly affecting the most important areas of economic policy. A hesitant beginning has been made in one or two fields, such as the effect of automation on manpower requirements (see Chapter 14), but far more could be done to systematise such work and to ensure that the results are disseminated to firms—again a process in which industrial councils could have an important role to play.

The Institutional Framework

It is clear that, while some of the more progressive trade associations deal effectively with some of the tasks outlined above, there are other functions which are less appropriate for them or which, in the case of less powerful associations, are beyond their scope. There are, however, precedents for bodies to fulfil such functions both abroad and in Britain. In France such bodies have existed for some time. Their function is to work closely with the Planning Commission in order to help to integrate industries into the structure of the plan, and at the same time act as a channel for statistics to pass up to the planning authorities and down from the authorities to the individual firms. It is generally accepted that these bodies have greatly improved communications between industry and the Government and made it easier for France to pursue a consistent industrial policy. The French industrial planning bodies appear, however, less interested in assisting firms to improve their productivity than in explaining the policy of the Planning Commission. Largely for this reason, there have been complaints that they do not pay sufficient attention to small and medium-sized firms whose individual output and investment would have little effect on the national aggregates in which the central planning authorities are interested.[1] Thus the French system fulfils only some of the functions outlined above.

The growing interest shown in Britain in French planning has helped to lead to proposals that similar bodies should be set up. The establishment of 'little Neddies' (Economic Development Councils) is a result. Their tasks are to include an examination of the economic performance, prospects and plans of the industry and an assessment of the industry's progress in relation to the national growth objectives; the provision of information and forecasts to the NEDC on these matters; and the formulation of reports and

[1] See Malcolm MacLennan, *French Planning: Some Lessons for Britain*, PEP *Planning* No. 475, 9 September 1963, p. 341.

recommendations on ways of improving the industry's efficiency and economic performance. In many ways, this range of activity appears similar to that of the French bodies, in that it does not directly help firms to increase their efficiency. Such a limitation is reasonable, since, in part at least, the organisations to provide a complementary service to help individual firms already exist or are in process of establishment (e.g. the research associations and industrial training boards) and it would be wasteful for the 'little Neddies' to try to duplicate their functions. It is, however, clearly desirable to ensure that the various activities designed to increase productivity in an industry are co-ordinated with the nation's economic planning.

In those industries where little Neddies have been established, they are the channel that relates the industry to the national economic plan, and they are also engaged in securing improvements in the industry's statistical and other information and in making assessments of performance. The bodies concerned directly with productivity are in general evolving liaison with them, and it is clearly desirable that this should be as close as possible. Indeed, if both sides of industry develop enough confidence in the working of the little Neddies and a sufficient sense of participation in their direction, it would seem logical that they should assume responsibility for collecting the compulsory levies by which research associations and training boards are financed, together with an additional amount for other activities such as the promotion of exports (cf. p. 28 where the wool industry's levy is considered). The little Neddies would, in this case, assume the character of industrial councils, such as the Cotton Board, with additional functions in relation to the economic planning process.

It may be found, however, that the functions of the little Neddies in relation to the plan are not easily reconciled with their assuming any direct responsibility for matters such as industrial training, industrial research or export promotion. In this event, it might be advantageous in some industries for separate industrial councils to be established, to collect and administer the compulsory levies by which these activities are financed. This is clearly also true of those industries for which little Neddies are not established.

It is not possible at present, with both the little Neddies and the industrial training boards only recently established, to make precise recommendations about the form of organisation required. It is, indeed, wrong to envisage that each industry will adopt the same pattern: their diverse circumstances are likely to call for diverse solutions. Certain principles should, however, be observed in each industry: joint activities are desirable in certain fields relating to the growth of productivity (see Chapters 11–14); such activities should be financed by means of a compulsory levy (see pp. 28, 229, 254–5); they should be co-ordinated and should have a satisfactory relationship with the national planning process; and they should be directed by a body or bodies that have the full confidence of both sides of industry.

Whenever a new departure is advocated, there is always a considerable danger that critics will dismiss the suggested course of action on the ground that it is impracticable. For this reason, it is especially useful that, in the Cotton Board, Britain has at the moment a good example of an organisation which fulfils many of the requirements of the kind of industrial council advocated in this chapter. The Cotton Board has developed over several decades as a result of the British cotton industry's attempts to meet and deal with a serious threat to its existence from low-cost producers abroad. However, it owes its present form largely to the Industrial Organisation and Development Act. The Board is financed by a compulsory levy on the cotton industry, which in the year ending March 1964 amounted to £400,000, part of which goes to support the Shirley Institute, the research association for the cotton and rayon industries. The Board consists of ten members (four each from the employers and trade unions, and two from outside the industry) and an independent full-time chairman. The Board keeps in contact with its industry by means of a standing consultative committee, where Board members can meet representatives from all sorts of interests within the industry, and a series of more specialised sub-committees. As a service to its industry, the Cotton Board supports various departments whose task is to increase the efficiency and competitiveness of the average cotton mill. These include a statistics department, a productivity centre, an overseas trade department and a market research department. Of course, the Board has not been a panacea for the industry, but it can hardly be denied that it has done a valuable job.

The Cotton Board is not only useful for disseminating statistics and the use of techniques to its industry. It can also intervene more directly to help the industry overcome a difficult economic situation with a minimum of friction. Its value was demonstrated in the reorganisation of the cotton industry which began in 1959. It had become clear that the British cotton industry could only survive on a much smaller scale than formerly and as a producer of more specialised fabrics. This required the closing of some mills and the re-equipment of others with more labour-saving machinery, thus leading to the redundancy of many operatives. Although this process was aided by a large Government grant, it was expected that it would be very difficult to manage without a great deal of trouble, both from management and labour. In fact, the contraction of the industry has taken place quickly and smoothly. This seems to have been due in large part to the propaganda work of the Cotton Board and its ability to advise firms on their particular problems on the basis of an intimate knowledge of the industry. Further, the participation of the trade unions in the work of the Board meant that there was a greater readiness on the part of labour to accept a redundancy agreement, rather than engage in a blind fight against all redundancy of the sort which is notable particularly among unions in the engineering industry.

There are obviously factors which made it easier to create an industrial council for the cotton industry than it would be for most others. The industry is highly concentrated geographically, is comparatively easy to define and was aware that it faced a very hard struggle if it was not to be rendered totally uncompetitive. Nevertheless, the success of the Cotton Board in a declining industry with comparatively little money to support it suggests that, if the climate of opinion within the industry is favourable, a similar service could be performed for many other industries—possibly even the most complex and scattered ones. The technical difficulties to be overcome in establishing industrial councils over a wide front, although great, do not in principle seem any greater than those which have already been overcome by the Ministry of Labour in setting up industrial training boards for the engineering and construction industries.[1] As in the case of the training boards it would be desirable to prepare the ground thoroughly before setting up the industrial councils so as to give them the best prospect of success.

The setting up of the councils with the co-operation of both sides of industry could help to improve industrial relations, as appears to have happened to some extent on NEDC itself. Chapters 5 and 14 pointed out that one of the greatest and most intractable causes of industrial conflict was the lack of communication and understanding between the two sides of industry. By discussing subjects, such as the best means by which an industry can fulfil its growth target, on which there is at least agreement as to ends between management and labour, the areas of rational disagreement become more clearly defined and it becomes less likely that a conflict will develop over an issue of no material advantage to either side. The councils would also gain by the participation of the trade unions, because the viewpoint they presented to the Government and the central planning authority would be that of the industry as a whole. At present,

[1] See Chapter 11.

this function is usually carried out by trade associations, or similar bodies, but these are often identified only with the employers in their industries, not the workers.

It is true that, until recently, the climate of opinion in Britain was not ripe for councils with the aims and powers here suggested. Today there is evidence to suggest that the climate has changed and that the necessary co-operation may be forthcoming. The conversion of politicians to the gospel of planning for growth seems to mirror a similar change in the country as a whole. This assumption is supported by the general welcome given by industry to the Industrial Training Act of 1964 (see Chapter 11). Many people in industry are worried about the performance of the British economy, and such people might well be prepared to co-operate in an effort to improve their own and their country's efficiency. It is the contention of this book that such an effort must be made if Britain is to prosper.

CONCLUSIONS

The conclusions of the book may be conveniently summarised under three heads:

(1) *Firms*

    (*a*) The most important determinant of a firm's potential for growth and improved efficiency is the ability of its management to learn about its environment and systematically adapt their policies to take advantage of it. A list is given in Chapter 10, pages 189–95, marking out the policies and practices which are characteristic of the more able and progressive firms. The financial analysis in Chapter 10 also suggests that firms which adopt such techniques are on the whole more profitable than those which do not.

    (*b*) The implementation of such policies depends on management: the ability of a firm is determined by its managers. At the same time, the task of capable managers can be made easier by the right sort of external services and assistance.

    (*c*) Management consultants are an important source of outside advice which can help to modernise firms in the comparatively short term. In the long run, management education is the essential basis for the development of thoroughly efficient and progressive managers. Meanwhile, industrial boards as proposed below could be of substantial help in encouraging and assisting firms to modernise.

(2) *Industrial Councils*

    (*a*) Industrial boards with enough resources to visit individual firms can be of considerable value in disseminating the relevant information and advice about modern techniques. Various areas in which such boards could help firms have been discussed in detail in Part Three.

    (*b*) The Industrial Training Boards already give assistance in the field of industrial training (see Chapter 11) and have gained the co-operation of both sides of industry.

    (*c*) Other sectors in which such work could be most valuable are: management education (see Chapter 12), the dissemination of scientific information (Chapter 13), manpower planning (Chapter 14). The idea could also be extended to other areas such as exports.

(d) The activities in these various sectors should be co-ordinated and should be undertaken in close liaison with the national planning authorities and with the relevant ministries.

(e) The functions outlined above approximate in certain ways to those of the EDCs (Little Neddies). Provided both sides of industry develop enough confidence in the activities of the EDCs, and a sufficient sense of participation in their direction, there would be a clear advantage in the EDCs being responsible for the co-ordination. The EDCs would, in this case, assume the character of industrial councils, such as the Cotton Board, with additional functions in relation to the planning process.

(f) If, however, it is found that the planning functions of the EDCs are not easily reconciled with direct responsibility for matters such as industrial training or research, it might be advisable to establish separate industrial councils. This is also the case in industries for which EDCs are not established.

(g) A compulsory levy on all firms in each industry, such as is raised in the cotton, wool and certain other industries, would be the best way of financing the industrial councils The adoption of modern practices by firms could be encouraged by grants paid for out of the levy (see Chapter 11).

(3) *The Government*

(a) The councils, in close co-operation with the Government statistical services, would facilitate both the dissemination and the collection of statistics and forecasts.

(b) As a help towards greater industrial efficiency, the Government statistical services should be improved so as to publish more detailed and accurate figures about the economy far more quickly than is done at present.

(c) Firms should be helped to appreciate their true economic position and compare their efficiency with those of their potential competitors at home and abroad. A useful move in this direction would be to reform the company law so that much fuller company accounts have to be published and a better and less variable basis for comparison can be reached.

(d) In its role as a major purchaser, the Government should act so as to encourage new and efficient techniques and products. This could be especially useful in new industries such as electronics (see especially Chapters 7 and 13).

K

(e) The Government should apply the criterion of the effect on industrial efficiency and growth to all relevant legislation, particularly in respect of taxation.

(f) The Government should help industry to establish industrial councils by imposing the compulsory levy to finance their working.

INDEX

Printed in the United States
by Baker & Taylor Publisher Services